Fundamentalism or Tradition

ORTHODOX CHRISTIANITY AND CONTEMPORARY THOUGHT

SERIES EDITORS
Aristotle Papanikolaou and Ashley M. Purpura

This series consists of books that seek to bring Orthodox Christianity into an engagement with contemporary forms of thought. Its goal is to promote historical studies in Orthodox Christianity that are interdisciplinary, employ a variety of methods, and speak to contemporary issues; and constructive theological arguments in conversation with patristic sources and that focus on contemporary questions ranging from the traditional theological and philosophical themes of God and human identity to cultural, political, economic, and ethical concerns. The books in the series explore both the relevancy of Orthodox Christianity to contemporary challenges and the impact of contemporary modes of thought on Orthodox self-understandings.

FUNDAMENTALISM OR TRADITION

Christianity after Secularism

ARISTOTLE PAPANIKOLAOU AND
GEORGE E. DEMACOPOULOS
EDITORS

FORDHAM UNIVERSITY PRESS
New York • 2020

Fordham University Press has no responsibility for the persistence or accuracy of URLs for external or third-party Internet websites referred to in this publication and does not guarantee that any content on such websites is, or will remain, accurate or appropriate.

Fordham University Press also publishes its books in a variety of electronic formats. Some content that appears in print may not be available in electronic books.

Visit us online at www.fordhampress.com.

Library of Congress Control Number:2019945311

Printed in the United States of America

22 21 20   5 4 3 2 1

First edition

CONTENTS

v

FUNDAMENTALISM

FUNDAMENTALISM OR TRADITION

INTRODUCTION: BEING AS TRADITION

Aristotle Papanikolaou and George E. Demacopoulos

In January 2015, George Demacopoulos published a short op-ed entitled "Orthodox Fundamentalism" for the *Faith Matters* blog, which is hosted by the Greek Orthodox Archdiocese of America.[1] Intended to provoke a conversation, the op-ed spurred an unanticipated amount of attention, both positive and negative.[2] Indeed, the scale of the reaction inspired us to devote the fourth *Patterson Triennial Conference on Orthodox-Catholic Relations* (2016) to a more academic investigation of the intersection of tradition, secularization, and fundamentalism, which resulted in this volume. In some ways, that short blog and the response it generated reflects a wider interdisciplinary debate, but also one that is emerging as one of the most hotly contested within the Orthodox Church—namely, whether "Orthodox fundamentalism" truly exists. One need look no further than the historic gathering of Orthodox bishops in Crete in June 2016 for the Holy and Great Council to see that some of the most prominent hierarchs in the Orthodox world view fundamentalism as one of the greatest challenges facing the Orthodox Church in the twenty-first century.[3]

Tradition, secularization, and fundamentalism—this is the web we find ourselves in today, and not just in the West, which has globalized this web. All three categories are contested, yet in their contestation, they shape our sensibilities and are mutually implicated. The discussion around the mutually implicated meanings of the "secular" and "fundamentalism" brings to the foreground more than ever, and in a way unprecedented in the premodern context, the question of what it means to think and live as tradition. The Orthodox theologians of the twentieth century, in particular, have always emphasized tradition not as a dead letter but as a living presence of the Holy Spirit.[4] But how can we discern when tradition as living discernment is not fundamentalism? And what does it mean to think as a tradition and live in tradition when surrounded by the "secular"?

Not too long ago most Western academics believed that religion would disappear, or, at the very least, be marginalized. The thesis was simple: as society increasingly modernizes, religion would decreasingly lose both its influence and visibility.[5] According to this understanding of the secular, various spheres—economy, science, education, government, law—constitute society, and the secular emerges when these spheres assume an independence from religious meanings, symbols, and, most importantly, institutional authority. Charles Taylor attributes, in part, this belief in the slow erosion of religion to the "subtraction thesis," according to which scientific progress naturally results in the subtraction of religion from the various spheres of society.[6] As Sigmund Freud stated ninety years ago in *The Future of an Illusion*, since science has already discredited many religious beliefs, better to act *as if* religion is a delusion, which means that it would eventually be proven false.[7] The belief in the subtraction thesis has produced many of the binaries that have structured the modern and, some might argue, even the postmodern imaginary, such as religion/science, religion/state, and religion/secular.

Recently, the pendulum has swung in the opposite direction, and very few now predict religion's demise. The once emblematic advocate of the secular-as-religious-decline thesis, Peter Berger, only recently proclaimed that we live in a postsecular world.[8] Academic fields, such as political science and international relations, are retooling after operating under the assumption that religion was irrelevant to modern politics or "that its influence can be neatly encapsulated in anthropological studies of a particular religious tradition and its external influence on politics."[9] This rethinking of the secular has led some to speak about a "resurgence" of religion, which begs the question: Was religion ever really absent from modern politics or the public square? If very few now operate on the assumption that religion will decline or be eliminated, then what is the secular?

In one of the most widely commented books on secularization, José Casanova divides the theory of secularization into three parts. The differentiation thesis constitutes the main thesis and refers to the process by which the various spheres of society—economy, science, education, government, law—are differentiated from religion as the "all-encompassing reality."[10] The differentiation thesis does not make the normative claim that the various spheres of society *should* be differentiated from religion; instead it provides an explanatory framework for understanding the re-positioning of religion—institutions, meanings, symbols—in relation to various spheres of society. Jeffrey Stout offers a variation on the differen-tiation thesis when he defines the secular as the absence of a "common theological perspective."[11] One could extend the differentiation thesis to the self with Charles Taylor's insight that the secular points not simply to the relations among various spheres or institutions constitutive of society but to the relation of the self with the self, as well as the slow consciousness of "unbelief" as an option that appears to the self.[12] Although there are those who would prefer to drop the word *secular* altogether, its use continues to be pervasive, even if contested.

What exactly is being contested? Most would not dispute the falsity of the decline-of-religion thesis, which was attached to the theory of secular-ization more as a prediction that masqueraded as an explanatory paradigm. The prediction betrayed the biases of those who—mostly Western or Western-trained academics—operated with the assumption that religion would disappear with the advancement of scientifically based forms of knowledge. There also existed a normative feature of the theory of secu-larization that expected religion to be privatized or marginalized from pub-lic forms of discourse, including public universities and the public political space. Although most accept the secular as (a) a negotiated repositioning of religion in relation to the various spheres constitutive of society and even to the self, (b) the absence of a common theological perspective, and (c) not entailing the decline of religion, it is this privatization thesis that is the most contested aspect of Casanova's three-part understanding of the theory of secularization.

In the Western world, the privatization thesis was usually advanced as a normative claim for the sake of securing and maintaining liberal democ-racy. John Rawls remains the most iconic figure who defended the priva-tization thesis, but who also later changed his mind on the role of religion in the public political space.[13] In the realm of political philosophy, the privatization thesis has been defeated in the sense that it is no longer con-sidered a given that liberal democracy necessarily entails the marginaliza-tion of religion, and this defeat has even influenced the assumptions of those in other academic disciplines, such as political science and interna-tional relations.[14] Casanova has also demonstrated the empirical falsity of the privatization thesis through a sociological analysis of the United States, Spain, Poland, and Brazil, where public religion has not simply coincided but also supported democratic institutions.

Beyond simply being philosophically indefensible and empirically false, the privatization thesis masks the reality that rather than being a theory that attempts to demonstrate a particular positioning of religion in society for the sake of universal values common to or shared by all human beings, the secular understood as the necessary privatization or marginalization of religion constitutes a particular Western construct that is sustained through practices, habits, and sensibilities that themselves support and are reinforced by particular types of institutional structures and legal arrangements. In short, the secular is not a neutral space attempting to promote freedom of religion or religious beliefs, but projects a particular understanding of religion, and, as Talal Asad has argued, the emergence of the secular in the West only makes sense in relation to the construction of the category of religion, whose modern meaning ultimately betrays certain Protestant Christian understandings of faith and belief.[15] This secular-religion binary has shaped not only the way in which religion is understood and legally structured within Western countries but also the foreign policy approaches of European and North American countries in relation to hot spots around the world where the political situation is affected by religious actors.[16] Whereas the secular-religious binary once fostered the assumption that religion does not play a major role in politics, now it shapes a "two-faiths" approach, where religion is categorized as either good or evil depending on its potential contribution to democratic structures.[17] Such a Western projection of the secular-religious binary does not leave room for more particularistic approaches to the challenges of pluralism and for negotiating the positioning of religion in relation to society that allows for a "variety of secularisms" or "multiple modernities."

With the acceptance of the public role of religion, the form of secularism known as *laïcité*—in which religion is expected to remain outside the border of public life to the extent that the state regulates religious forms of clothing or even, in the Kemalist Turkish version, the content taught and preached by religions, specifically Islam—is only considered one manifestation of the secular and not necessarily the norm. In fact, whereas at one time *laïcité* as a "high wall of separation between church and state" was theoretically presumed to be a necessary condition for liberal democracy, the on-the-ground reality was always much more complex both within

Europe and in North America. Casanova has labeled this type of secularism as *"secularist secularity*, that is, the phenomenological experience not only of being passively free but also actually of having been liberated from 're-ligion' as a condition for human autonomy and human flourishing."[18] More recently, some scholars, including Jeffrey Stout and Charles Taylor,[19] have argued that this type of secularization is undemocratic and borders on the ideological.

Casanova identifies two other forms of secularization: "(a) *mere secular-ity*, that is the phenomenological experience of living in a secular world and in a secular age, where being religious may be a normal viable option; [and] (b) that of *self-sufficient and exclusive secularity*, that is, the phenom-enological experience of living without religion as a normal, quasi-natural, taken-for-granted condition."[20] Although he doesn't give specific examples, one can imagine that *secularist secularity* looks something like France, *mere secularity* describes the United States, and *self-sufficient and exclusive secu-larity* reminds one of the Netherlands and Canada. Even if one can iden-tify a variety of secularisms *within* the Western and North American context, the "religion" that is imagined within the public square has a "Judeo-Christian" face to it. Islam, in much of the Western political dis-course, has now been "othered" as that kind of religion whose "publicity" would pose a threat to democratic principles. But the othering of Islam over-and-against the varieties of secularization in the West only reveals that the criteria for judging a religion's potential for "publicity" is still within the terms of the secular categories of religious freedom, human rights, and freedom of conscience. The regulating function of such categories forces the secular state to define and assess different religions in ways that are contradictory to the very norms it seeks to protect.

The fall of communism in the early 1990s has complicated matters fur-ther. The Orthodox churches found themselves in countries in which Or-thodox Christianity has deep historical roots and has played a constitutive role in shaping the cultural landscape. These countries were dominated by an extreme form of secularization that was to a greater or lesser degree ag-gressively hostile to the institutional Orthodox churches and religion in general. In the 1990s, no one could have predicted how the Orthodox churches and Orthodox Christianity in general would be reintegrated into a postcommunist context. One might expect it to look different depending on the country, but there are resemblances because of the shared Ortho-dox history and tradition of church-state relations. In addition to simply reasserting themselves as actors within the changing cultural and political landscape of Russia, Georgia, and the Eastern European countries, the Orthodox churches have begun to leverage the language of "postsecular," which they define in the narrowest sense in terms of the rejection of the decline-of-religion and the privatization thesis. Not a single Orthodox church has rejected democracy, per se, and outside of a few minority voices, there has not been a movement for reinstating imperial structures in these countries.[21]

However, there has been support for a "postsecular" reimagining of the Byzantine model of *symphonia*, in which Orthodox Christianity enjoys a privileging in these countries in the form of state support and plays a formative role in relation to culture, politics, and national identity. In Russia, this privileging has intensified since 2011, when a noticeable shift becomes evident in Vladimir Putin's rhetoric such that references to the spiritual foundations and history of Russia become more explicit. Putin has drawn on Russia's Orthodox history in order to project a Russia that is not antidemocratic but one that allows for a public role of religion and, in that sense, exists in opposition to the godless, liberal, religion-marginalizing kind of democracy that he claims represents the West.[22] Both political and religious actors in Russia have formed alliances with certain American evangelical representatives over a shared concern of the erosion of "traditional values." In fact, Russia looks a lot like what American evangelicals hope for in the United States—a legally supported moral framework that centers around sexual ethics, including laws against "gay propaganda" and proposed laws that could restrict abortion as well as freedom of religious assembly (which, ironically, affect American evangelicals).[23] In a sense, Putin has globalized the American culture wars, and one could argue that the new geopolitical East-West divide has been drawn on the basis of debates about what constitutes the secular.

The situation in Russia brings into relief the concept of fundamentalism, which is equally as contested as that of the secular. Is what is emerging in Russia a manifestation of fundamentalism or is it a particular, historically situated response to the challenge of pluralism that could also be seen as a variation of the secular? But is it really secular if, in fact, a morality based on "traditional values" is emerging as the moral horizon of Russia with legal support? In Russia, are we witnessing the evaporation of what Charles Taylor has called the "immanent frame," or has such an "immanent frame" been effectively globalized by the West that the resurgence of religion within Russia can only be a negotiation within this "immanent frame"?[24]

Even though the word was coined in the 1920s in the United States, *fundamentalism* as an explanatory category has been prominent since the late 1970s, especially since the Iranian Revolution. The Fundamentalism Project, supervised by Martin Marty and Scott Appleby, was the most comprehensive scholarly attempt to establish criteria for identifying fundamentalisms across the religious spectrum. These criteria are summarized in terms of organizational and ideological traits, and fundamentalism is identified as manifesting a kind of intersection of these particular traits.[25] More generally, fundamentalism has been interpreted as a "modern anti-modern" form of being religious,[26] meaning that it reacts against the perceived antireligious impulse of modern thought even while appropriating many of its achievements, especially the technological advancements; but that view does not enjoy a consensus. Scott Appleby has argued that to see fundamentalism as simply a negative reaction against the secular is to fail to notice how those forms of being religious that meet the criteria of the Fundamentalism Project are themselves attempting to negotiate the secular within the "immanent frame."[27] Appleby is suggesting something similar to the secular critiques that are attempting to politicize and historically situate the secular and, in so doing, he defends the category of fundamentalism as identifying a religious form of negotiation within the secular, not over against it. Whether the category illuminates or obfuscates, *fundamentalism* names a context with which religions must contend and to which they must respond—the secular.

Although both the category of fundamentalism and the applicability of it to Orthodox Christianity remain contested, it is clear that no one within the Orthodox communion wants to have the term applied to them.[28] Even the most rigorist and sectarian among the Orthodox communion decry the term, preferring to self-define as guardians of an unchanging holy tradition, which to their eyes is the lone acceptable version of Christian life. So, once again, we return to the questions, what is tradition? Who are its rightful defenders? But recent developments in the Orthodox world prompt a further question—what is the difference between Orthodox tradition and traditional Orthodoxy?

One of the most fascinating developments in modern Orthodox identity construction is the emergence of traditional Orthodoxy as category of self-designation. Naturally, such a formulation was developed in response to and is advanced against the broader Orthodox community, which is perceived to be insufficiently traditional. But the very formulation of something called traditional Orthodoxy is a decidedly modern phenomenon that only emerged as recently as the 1980s and from within a tiny, Old Calendarist, sectarian community. In its earliest formulation, *traditional Orthodoxy* was designed to separate the authentic Orthodox from the vast majority of others who had succumbed (whether deliberately or not) to the "heresy" of ecumenism.[29] More recently, it has been coopted by a much broader set of Orthodox communicants who wish to set themselves apart from those who fail to see the danger of secularism, Westernism, and modernism.

Indeed, *traditional Orthodoxy* is now a common marker of self-identity among a wide group of Orthodox Christians. Even the most cursory of internet searches will yield dozens of bloggers, Facebook groups, parishes, and cross-jurisdictional Orthodox affiliations that employ *traditional/ist Orthodox* and *traditional/ist Orthodoxy* as a self-designated label of religious identification, which sets them apart—implicitly or explicitly—from other Orthodox Christians.[30] Whereas that distinction initially coincided with sacramental isolation, it no longer does. Indeed, one of the most fascinating evolutions that has occurred as the slogan has become more popular is that even though its adherents often assert aggressive anti-ecumenical, anti-Western, and antimodern positions, they typically do not reject sacramental unity with those Orthodox Christians they perceive as having capitulated to those forces.[31]

The convocation of the Holy and Great Synod in June 2016 provided the traditional Orthodox across the world with a galvanizing moment. While some heralded the council as the most significant gathering of Orthodox bishops in more than a thousand years,[32] for many self-described traditional Orthodox, the council represented a new level of institutional betrayal of the Orthodox Church's tradition. The most radical among the traditionalists asserted that the council marked the coming of the Antichrist.[33] Few went that far, but many of the more measured traditionalists objected to the council's document "Relations of the Orthodox Church with the Rest of the World" because it not only affirmed the church's participation in the ecumenical movement but also officially proscribed ecumenical obstructionism.[34] Indeed, hundreds of self-professed traditionalists—which now include canonical bishops as well as priests, monks, and laity—undertook a loosely coordinated propaganda campaign to thwart all or part of the council.[35] One of the most fascinating aspects of the transnational dissemination of traditionalist rhetoric was the role played by bilingual converts to Orthodoxy, who, for American audiences, appeared in the vanguard of the condemnation of the council on the basis of its supposed capitulation to ecumenism, modernism, and general Westernism.[36]

What all of the modern advocates of traditional Orthodoxy fail to understand is that the shift from Orthodox tradition to traditional Orthodoxy has genuine theological significance. Whereas the noun tradition (stemming from the Latin *traditio*) has been understood within Christianity to mean the continuous act of handing over from one generation to the next the faith of the apostles, as an adjective, the word functions as a modifier for Orthodoxy—thus implying that there are multiple forms of Orthodoxy, only one of them traditional. The great irony is that the very supposition that there could be multiple forms of Orthodoxy lies in contradistinction to the confession of a singular faith that the traditional Orthodox claim to profess. In effect, traditional Orthodoxy not only implies a certain redundancy, it also contains an inherent self-contradiction.

In Christianity, it is not the first time that the issue of "tradition" has risen to the surface, especially after Luther's proclamation of *sola scriptura*. It is fair to argue that part, if not most, of the rhetoric constitutive of the modern period entails diametrically opposing tradition to reason. In the Protestant/Catholic polemics of the early-modern era, tradition was associated with irrationality, affectivity, backwardness, being subject, while reason was that which elicited universal, objective truths. Latent within this distinction was the religion-secular binary, with which we are still contending.

In the postmodern era, and especially since the work of Alasdair MacIntyre, the ground of objectivity has been pulled from the modern confidence in reason producing objective truths, and we have recognized that all is tradition, including science, democracy, secularism, reason, and, of course, religion. But such a sensibility does not mean a return to premodern inhabitations of religion, because Charles Taylor's portrayal of the difference between now and then remains convincing: something like an immanent frame constitutes our current globalized horizon, and "unbelief" as an option of the self to the self exists in a way that is unprecedented. If religions are to continue living as tradition, then it is in a context in which the supernatural is no longer taken for granted. And although there seems no end in sight in the debate over the meanings of *secular* and *fundamentalism*, the debate in and of itself reaffirms that there is no traditionless existence, and also reminds us that existing as tradition in the present is not and can never be a return to the premodern past.

The essays in this book continue both the interrogation of the categories of the secular and fundamentalism, all the while either implicitly or explicitly exploring ways of thinking about tradition in relation to these interrogations. Although the contributors were not asked to address any particular theme in relation to the trifecta of tradition, secularization, and fundamentalism, each essay affirms in its own distinctive way that tradition or something like it is not the same as fundamentalism as it negotiates something like the secular. All of the essays offer a way of understanding tradition through critical engagement with meanings either of the secular or of fundamentalism.

Regarding the secular, Graham Ward argues that it would be better simply to dispense with the word *secular* and its variations as it obfuscates more than it clarifies and perpetuates the myth of linear inevitability of the secular as immanent frame or buffered self or decline of religion. For Ward, there is no resurgence of religion since religion never went away. The forms of collectivities named as religion have been reshaped in light of modern forms of thought, but in particularistic and historically contextualized settings resulting in multiple modernities. In a study based on empirical research, Slavica Jakelić also argues that the religion-secular binary simply reinforces both the biases of theorists of nationalism and critics of secularism, both of whom see the relationship between modernity and religion as one of conflict and religion as simply modernity's other. Jakelić's discussion of collectivistic Catholicisms in both Croatia and Poland reveal a much more complicated picture: although there are collectivistic forms of Catholicism that define themselves against the imagined secular and are closely aligned with nationalistic ideologies, Jakelić also demonstrates that there are collectivistic Catholicisms in which social cohesion and collective identity constitute themselves through a more expansive and generous approach to the pluralism to which these communities relate. These particular forms of collectivistic Catholicisms reveal that pluralism need not be a threat against which religious communities define themselves; it exists in ways that defy the simple reduction to nationalism or the religion-secular binary.

Brenna Moore further advances the claim that the religion-secular binary does more harm than good by illustrating how one of the most important trajectories of thought within modern Catholicism—personalism—was coopted by recent Catholic theology, most notably that of Pope John Paul II, and sexualized on the basis of the religion-secular binary. Moore offers yet another example supporting recent feminist claims of the gendered inflection of the religion-secular binary. Moore also argues that the sexualization of Catholic personalism betrays a deep irony insofar as the two people most associated with Catholic personalism, Jacques Maritain, together with his wife, Raissa, facilitated a spiritual environment that was nonsexualized and based on friendship and the multiple forms of relationality and intimacy that are possible within friendship. The appropriation of the religion-secular binary by recent Catholic "personalists" obscures the forms of Catholic spirituality based on friendship that nurtured the nonsexualized personalism of Jacques and Raissa Maritain.

Vigen Guroian rejects any of the fine distinctions between the secular, secularization, or secularity. For Guroian, it is not enough to indicate that religion is not in decline, since for Orthodox Christians, the understanding of *theosis* encompasses the whole of life. Whatever shape the secular may take, even if it includes religion rather than being defined against it, it still is too restrictive for an Orthodox sacramental sensibility, which extends to all of creation. Paul Griffiths similarly sees the secular in its political form, however much it may affirm religious pluralism, as prescinding from any explicit reference to the God of Abraham. Griffiths affirms the Augustinian axiom that there are political goods, and that Catholic theology affirms that political pluralism is conducive to the common good. A secular state is one among many political forms; however, according to Catholic theology, common political goods are better served by a state that makes explicit reference to the god of Abraham. Although not all such states do necessarily contribute to the realization of political goods, the example of ISIS does not invalidate the claim that political goods are best realized through a state that makes explicit reference to the god of Abraham, since by comparison, the atrocities committed by ISIS are similar in degree to those committed by Western secular states.

Finally, Brandon Gallaher constructs an Orthodox theological response to the secular that also troubles the religion-secular binary. He draws on the traditional theological foci of Christology and Trinitarian theology to suggest that the secular be seen as a form of kenosis of the presence of Christ that allows for a free movement toward the light of Christ. The secular is the withdrawal of Christ's presence so as to allow the secular to move toward Christ on its own accord.

Regarding fundamentalism, Edith Humphrey argues that the word *fundamentalism* has itself been wielded as a weapon that fails to capture the concern of those who wish to identify fundamentals that are core to the lived experience of a tradition. Although she recognizes maximialist tendencies within Protestantism, Catholicism, and Orthodoxy that may overly proscribe what constitutes the center, she argues that the understanding of tradition as living, which itself is central to Orthodoxy, may allow for a hermeneutics of generosity both within the tradition and in relation to social trends, without losing sight of the center. Fr. Dellas Oliver Herbel also wants to recognize a difference between restorationist trajectories and those that he identifies with tradition as movement and integration. Fr. Herbel points to moments in recent history of converts to Orthodoxy that exhibit more a desire for a restoration of purity rather than a faithfulness to a living tradition, and he argues that tradition itself is encompassing in such a way that it can integrate and correct the restorationist impulses for purity.

Scott Appleby defends the category of fundamentalism, which can be identified according to organizational and ideological traits. In addition to these traits, however, Appleby argues that fundamentalism itself is invested and sustains the religion-secular binary, insofar as it is a modern form of being religious that reacts against the perceived marginalization of religion. In this light, fundamentalism cannot be seen as a mode of being religious versus being secular but is itself a critical engagement with the secular. Appleby raises the question of whether fundamentalism is discernible within Orthodoxy, and he argues that what Vasilios Makrides identifies as "rigorists" is not fundamentalism, because the rigorists do not manifest a modern mode of religiosity that characterizes fundamentalism. He also points to theological resources on tradition, by Vladimir Lossky and Georges Florovsky, that resist fundamentalist approaches to tradition. Like the other contributors, Appleby is attempting to foreground an understanding of tradition as complex, organic, nonlinear, and living that is defined in contrast to the impatience of fundamentalists with such understandings of tradition. Nikolaos Asproulis uses Appleby's criteria in the Fundamentalist Project to argue that fundamentalism of both the Abrahamic and Syncretic kinds exist in Orthodox Christianity. Asproulis amplifies that the fundamentalistic attitude within Orthodoxy is inflected with nationalism, and it is not a reaction to the absence of religion, since the Orthodox Churches have a strong public presence; rather, it is a reaction to the fear of losing this already existing public presence. Asproulis offers a theological response in the form of a world dogmatics that would allow for a critically open and generous engagement of the church to the world.

Nadieszda Kizenko is the only essay that address the postcommunist situation in traditional Orthodox countries in Eastern Europe, with a specific focus on the sacrament of confession within the Russian Orthodox Church. In the prerevolutionary period, the sacrament of confession was required by the Russian Orthodox Church, and Kizenko raises the interesting question of what it means for this specific practice to be revived within the church. Is it fundamentalism if it becomes a requirement for communion, especially since such a condition for communion existed in the prerevolutionary Russia? Kizenko also points to voices in postcommunist Russia that argue against the link between confession and communion. Does the existence of diverse voices in the postcommunist Orthodox countries point to a fundamentalist-progressive polarization, or simply a pluralism that is itself constitutive of a living tradition? Kizenko challenges us to think about these questions through the specific, lived practice of confession.

Darlene Fozard Weaver's essay is also unique insofar as it addresses specifically the question of moral fundamentalism, which is often assumed in the broader discussions of fundamentalism, especially in terms of moral Manichaeism; but rarely, if at all, does one see the question of moral fundamentalism analyzed within the contours and terms of moral theology and philosophy. Weaver asks the question of how a faith community's commitment to moral objectivity and moral realism in a secularized world can avoid moral fundamentalism. Weaver draws on the Catholic moral reflection on conscience to show a way forward of engagement with the complexity, ambiguity, and pluralism of the modern world without sliding either to moral relativism or moral fundamentalism. She analyzes two Catholic public responses to the 2016 shooting at a gay nightclub in Orlando, Florida, to illustrate the difference between a moral response shaped by conscience and one that manifests a moral fundamentalism.

Finally, Wendy Mayer brackets the debate surrounding the meaning of fundamentalism, and claims that such questions are pointless if seen through the eyes of neuroscientific research and moral psychology. Whatever secularization may mean, it has provoked a fear in relation to the loss of the sacred, and the response being labeled fundamentalist is, from a social-functionalist perspective, perfectly moral, justifiable, and natural. The science of moral cognition helps us to understand how groups emphasizing different values—progressive versus conservative—each have difficulty understanding the internal logic of the other. Mayer suggests that scientific research may help each side understand the other and avoid the real obstacle to prosocial behavior—self-righteousness—to which both progressives and conservatives fall prey.

The contributors to this book do not resolve the questions surrounding the meaning of secularism and fundamentalism. In fact, they continue the interrogation of those categories from diverse perspectives. In this interrogation, however, one witnesses a consensus that whatever the secular or fundamentalism may mean, it is not tradition, which is historical, particularistic, in motion, ambiguous, and pluralistic, but never relativistic. If the wider debates about the secular and fundamentalism seem interminable and often frustrating, perhaps the real contribution of these discussions is to provide a clearer sense of what it means to live and think like—to be as—tradition.

Notes

1. George E. Demacopoulos, "Orthodox Fundamentalism," blogs.goarch.org, January 29, 2015, https://blogs.goarch.org/blog/-/blogs/orthodox-fundamentalism.

2. The blog post has been translated into at least a dozen languages, including, Greek, Romanian, Russian, Serbian, and Ukrainian.

3. In his formal address at the Holy and Great Council, Archbishop Chrysostomos of Cyprus suggested that fundamentalism and ethnophyletism were the two greatest challenges to the modern Orthodox world. The same concerns were acknowledged by the closing document of the council. See https://www.holycouncil.org/-/message.

4. For a concise summary of an Orthodox understanding of tradition, see Marcus Plested, "Between Rigorism and Relativism: The Givenness of Tradition," *Public Orthodoxy*, accessed March 28, 2019, https://publicorthodoxy.org/2017/05/25/between-rigorism-and-relativism/. See also Aristotle Papanikolaou, "Tradition as Reason and Practice: Amplifying Contemporary Orthodox Theology in Conversation with Alasdair MacIntyre," *St. Vladimir's Theological Quarterly* 59, no. 1 (2015): 91–104, and more recently, "I am a

traditionalist; therefore I am," *Public Orthodoxy*, accessed March 28, 2019,
https://publicorthodoxy.org/2019/02/19/i-am-a-traditionalist-therefore-i-am/.

5. See Peter Berger, *The Sacred Canopy: Elements of a Sociological Theory of Religion* (New York: Anchor Books, 1990).

6. Charles Taylor, *A Secular Age* (Cambridge, MA: Belknap Press, 2007).

7. Sigmund Freud, *The Future of an Illusion* (New York: W. W. Norton and Company, 1989).

8. Peter Berger, "The Desecularization of the World: A Global Overview," in *The Desecularization of the World: Resurgent Religion and World Politics*, ed. Peter Berger (Grand Rapids, MI: Eerdmans, 1999). Even the Ecumenical Patriarch's address at the *Muslim Council of Elders' Global Peace Conference* in Cairo, Egypt, argued that we were living in the postsecular age and this reality should offer opportunity to multireligious cohabitation. For an English translation, see https://publicorthodoxy.org/2017/04/30/religions-and -peace/.

9. Elizabeth Shakman Hurd, "A Suspension of (Dis)Belief: The Secular-Religious Binary and the Study of International Relations," in *Rethinking Secularism*, ed. Craig Calhoun, Mark Juergensmeyer, and Jonathan van Antwerpen (Oxford: Oxford University Press, 2011), 167.

10. José Casanova, *Public Religions in the Modern World* (Chicago: University of Chicago Press, 1994).

11. Jeffrey Stout, *Democracy and Tradition* (Princeton, NJ: Princeton University Press, 2004).

12. Taylor, *Secular Age*.

13. John Rawls, *Theory of Justice*, 2nd ed. (Cambridge, MA: Belknap Press, 1999) and *Political Liberalism*, exp. ed. (New York: Columbia University Press, 2005). See also Jürgen Habermas, "Religion in the Public Sphere," *European Journal of Philosophy* 14, no. 1 (2006): 1–25.

14. See Elizabeth Shakman Hurd, *Beyond Religious Freedom: The New Global Politics of Religion* (Princeton, NJ: Princeton University Press, 2015), 26.

15. Talal Asad, *The Formations of the Secular: Christianity, Islam, Modernity* (Stanford, CA: Stanford University Press, 2003).

16. Saba Mahmood, *Religious Difference in a Secular Age: A Minority Report* (Princeton, NJ: Princeton University Press, 2015).

17. Hurd, *Beyond Religious Freedom*, 26.

18. José Casanova, "The Secular, Secularizations, Secularisms," in *Rethinking Secularism*, 60.

19. Jeffrey Stout, *Democracy and Tradition*. See also, "2007 Presidential Address: The Folly of Secularism," *Journal of the American Academy of Religion* 76, no. 3 (2008): 1–12. Charles Taylor, "Religion Is Not the Problem: Secularism and Democracy," *Commonweal*, February 25, 2011, 17–21.

20. Casanova, "The Secular, Secularizations, Secularism," 60.

21. "Religious Belief and National Belonging in Central and Eastern Europe," Pew Research Center, May 10, 2017, accessed March 28, 2019, http://www.pewforum.org/2017/05/10/religious-belief-and-national-belonging -in-central-and-eastern-europe/.

22. Putin sent a clear if veiled signal in his 2013 state of the nation speech, when he said: "Today, many nations are revising their moral values and ethical norms, eroding ethnic traditions and differences between peoples and cultures. Society is now required not only to recognise everyone's right to the freedom of consciousness, political views and privacy, but also to accept without question the equality of good and evil, strange as it seems, concepts that are opposite in meaning. This destruction of traditional values from above not only leads to negative consequences for society, but is also essentially anti-democratic, since it is carried out on the basis of abstract, speculative ideas, contrary to the will of the majority, which does not accept the changes occurring or the proposed revision of values" (http://en.kremlin.ru/events/president/news/19825). In theological language, what we have is a political apophaticism—defining Russian against what it is not, which is, of course, the West in all its decadence.

23. For recent developments, see Christoph Stroop, "After the Yarovaya Laws," Public Orthodoxy, accessed March 28, 2019, https://publicorthodoxy .org/2016/10/25/yarovaya-conservatives-traditional-values/#more-1641.

24. Taylor, *Secular Age.*

25. Gabriel A. Almond, Scott Appleby, and Emmanuel Sivan, *Strong Religion* (Chicago: University of Chicago Press, 2003). It is very telling that the Fundamentalism Project did not consider Orthodox Christianity. This is a serious gap, as it assumes that Orthodox Christianity is either similar to Protestant fundamentalisms or not prone to fundamentalistic manifestations, as is argued for Roman Catholicism. Both claims are addressed in this book.

26. Casanova, *Public Religions in the Modern World.*

27. R. Scott Appleby, "Rethinking Fundamentalism in a Secular Age," in *Rethinking Secularism*, 225–47.

28. For an excellent example of why the term *fundamentalism* remains problematic, see Edith Humphrey's essay in this volume.

29. For a genealogy and analysis of the emergence of the category "traditional Orthodoxy," see George Demacopoulos, "'Traditional Orthodoxy' as a Postcolonial Movement," *Journal of Religion* 97, no. 4 (2017): 475–99. Several of the observations in subsequent paragraphs of this section of this essay were previously articulated in the *Journal of Religion* article.

30. For example, as of December 9, 2016, the Facebook group "Traditional Orthodoxy (Canonical)" had more than thirteen thousand members, including the president of the largest Orthodox seminary in the United States.

31. Perhaps this is because they have essentially elided "traditional Orthodoxy" with notions of political and cultural conservatism rather than religious isolationism. For an impressive study of the significant overlap between theological groups within the Russian Orthodox Church and their political ideologies, see Irina Papkova, *The Orthodox Church and Russian Politics* (New York: Oxford University Press, 2011). Papkova identifies three camps—liberals, traditionalists, and fundamentalists—and compellingly shows how these religious communities reflect distinctive approaches to contemporary Russian politics, particularly as they pertain to Western engagement.

32. The complete text of the six documents confirmed by the council is available at the official website at http://www.holycouncil.org. For a thorough overview of the challenges and opportunities provided by the council, see John Chryssavgis, *Toward the Holy and Great Council: Retrieving a Culture of Conciliarity and Communion* (New York: Department of Inter-Orthodox, Ecumenical and Interfaith Relations, 2016).

33. In Russia, fear-mongering by some activists reached such a state that Metropolitan Hilarion Alfiev, head of the Department of External Church relations, had to issue an official statement saying that there was no reason to view the coming Synod as a precursor to the Antichrist. "Russian Church Calms down the Believers Who Consider Pan-Orthodox Council 'Anti-Christ,'" pravoslavie.ru, accessed May 22, 2017, http://www.pravoslavie.ru /english/90349.htm.

34. "Relations of the Orthodox Church with the Rest of the Christian World," Holy and Great Council, Pentecost 2016, accessed May 22, 2017, https://www.holycouncil.org/-/rest-of-christian-world.

35. An extreme and largely uninformed example of episcopal neotraditionalism would be that of Metropolitan Seraphim of Pireaus. See George Demacopoulos, "Innovation in the Guise of Tradition," Public Orthodoxy, accessed May 22, 2017, https://publicorthodoxy.org/2016/03/22 /innovation-in-the-guise-of-tradition-anti-ecumenist-efforts-to-derail-the-great -and-holy-council/.

36. The most comprehensive study of the phenomenon of Protestant conversions to Orthodoxy in the United States is Oliver Herbel, *Turning to Tradition: Converts and the Making of an American Orthodox Church* (Oxford: Oxford University Press, 2013).

Secularization

SECULARISM: THE GOLDEN LIE

Graham Ward

My aim here is to loosen the associations between secularism, modernity, and atheism and open a space for future refashionings of religious traditions and their continuing impact. There is no warrant for the association between secularism, modernity, and atheism in fact. The power of this set of associations lies in its role in public rhetorics and cultural narratives, which have constructed certain linear and historical accounts of modernity that bind us (for example, Charles Taylor's understanding of the formation of the "immanent frame" and the move from an enchanted to a disenchanted ethos). We can get caught up with juggling the concepts that actually stitch secularism into a public disavowal of the transcendent, the divine, or broadly "God." The linear trajectory of such narratives of modernity (mirroring modernity's own obsession with "progress" and conceptions of time) make secularism a fate waiting to happen an inevitability. My own sense is that this set of associations in being contested today is being considerably weakened. It is being weakened by an awareness of multiple modernities and the recognition of a single and monolithic modernity as Western and colonial.[1] Nonlinear understandings of the modern emerge in which the transcendent God is not "decapitated."[2] Under the gravity of the overall weakening of modernity, there is pressure to either get rid of the word *secular* as no longer a term with any explanatory and analytical power or rethink *secular* in a way that severely limits its current employment. As far as I can see, its current use is mainly by reactive and threatened religious groups and national governments.

My essay is structured according to three topoi. I begin by plotting, rapidly, a semantic shift in secularism taking place in France at the moment
as a cameo for both our current situation and the traditions of thinking
that have brought us to this situation. Next, I address the question of modernity and the secular, drawing in part upon the work of Bruno Latour,
and in the process problematize the relationship between secularism, modernity, and atheism. I then present a second cameo, a cultural rather than
a social one, that puts some flesh on the idea that the divine is still in play
in what might be termed the secular imagination. Finally, I return to some
of those concepts forged in our linear narratives of modernity that bind us
and, hopefully, demonstrate that secularism, like the founding myth of
Plato's *Republic*, is a golden lie—convenient for some, repressive for others,
and a conjuror's mist obfuscating any more truthful account of what it is
to be human and what it is to live collectively.

The Semantic Shift

Historians, philologists, and linguists have recognized for a long time that
words undergo a semantic shift. Usually, they are able to trace a slow,
century-long process as cultures adapt and morph under the pressures of
contingent circumstance from wars to weather. The word remains the same,
but its content takes on different colorings from the way it is used and back-
lit across changing contexts. But this drift has been much more rapid in
one particular instance—with the French use of *laïcité*.

Brief background: following 9/11 Chirac commissioned a report in the
summer of 2003 from a think tank headed by Bernard Stasi on *laïcité* in
France—given that the word is enshrined in the First Article of the French
Constitution. The report was hastily done. It was delivered by Christmas
of the same year. But it wasn't an audit of social and cultural conditions
and the role of religion with respect to them; it actually made specific recommendations for legal prescriptions. In March 2004 Chirac was already
signing a bill for passing a French law on secularity and the conspicuous
display of religious symbols in schools. Despite controversy over the quality of the research done and the vociferous resistance among many who
saw this as asserting a state-sponsored ideology, encoding an infringement
of civil liberties, and constituting a political break with the importance of
government neutrality, in spring 2011, the law on *laïcité* was both reinforced
and amplified with new legislation extending to the ban on religious sym-

bols in all public spaces throughout France. What became clear is that *laïcité* was now understood as intrinsically antireligious—which was, in fact, the way the word was being used by the anti-Catholic state of the Third Republic which first enacted the law in 1903. This antireligious note is still sounding among Muslims, such as Naser Ghobadzadeh, who are developing what he terms "religious secularity"—in part because neither *secular* nor *laïcité* have any equivalents in Arabic, Turkish, or Persian.[3]

Now there are a plethora of issues here that are beyond the scope of this essay concerning terrorist threats to national governments, the perceived failure, if not complicity, of multicultural projects with respect to those threats, recourse to an older, right-wing political strategy toward assimilationist policies,[4] and a fear of rising Islamophobia in a nation state with the largest Muslim population in Europe, a population producing far more offspring than the indigenous French. I need to leave all this aside and jump to my point about semantic drift—for the terrorist attacks on Paris in January and then November 2015 have affected a change with respect to, and something of a crisis concerning, *laïcité*.

First, the publicity that accrued to such events made evident to the world that France was not a secular state, let alone the most advanced secular state, in the way that people had been led to believe following the headscarf debates. Here was a Jewish supermarket under fire, a supermarket that served the needs of a large Jewish community in the heart of Paris. Here also was a Muslim quarter served by mosques and devout people going about integrating their worship and beliefs into their very ordinary occupations—bar owners, taxi drivers, even gendarmes. The Place de la Concorde, that site of royal and then revolutionary power, became a shrine for those killed, with prayers said, candles lit, and flowers laid in a great public act of mourning. The religious outpouring was not in the control of any church, mosque, synagogue, or temple and that raises other questions about institutional affiliation. Nevertheless, the religious sentiment was evidently there.

Second, the current French education minister, Najat Vallaud-Belkacem, herself born in Morocco and a self-described "nonpracticing Muslim," started to make a series of public statements about the need to overhaul the teaching of secularism and civic values in France. Interestingly she spoke of the need "to reappropriate the concept of *laïcité* so that we can explain to our young pupils that whatever their faith, they belong to this idea and they're not excluded. . . . If a large number of young pupils felt secularism was an attack on them, it was because the term had been misused and deformed in the public for years. . . . The term had often been misused to point out that Muslims were different [from] others, and that is clearly problematic. . . . So, we really wanted to work on that concept of secularism."[5] There are lots of ambivalences here: the language of "reappropriation" is not going to rescind any legislative acts or invoke constitutional reform, and she speaks in the past tense as if the change is already at such a point it can be described as current. But the decoupling of secularism from being antireligious, from itself endorsing a cultural atheism that masks as something just technical and procedural, is a beginning. And the move toward secularism—as actually meaning neutrality or, more positively, the pursuit of equality (before the law and with respect to education and opportunities for human flourishing) or (even better) inclusivity—means the semantic drift is underway in a direction that should be welcomed and encouraged. However, we cannot underestimate the effects of recent waves of new migrations into Europe bringing new levels of xenophobia and right-wing sympathies. The way ahead is not going to be easy. There's a lot of work to be done on what the "neutrality" of governance actually means in practice. And perhaps the largest obstacle is that very modern (and Western) idea of the nation state itself. Despite the increasingly evident global mix of peoples and traditions and despite the enormous integration of economic markets, who is going to start problematizing that notion?

Multiple Modernities

Enter Bruno Latour. What is surfacing in this semantic shift and the cultural changes that lie behind it are notions made prominent by linear narratives of modernity: such as the exclusion of religion from the public sphere, the desire that citizens throughout the world belong to and are assimilated into discrete national blocks, obedience to the civil laws and the traditions of those national blocks, and the acceptance that such national blocks are sovereignties requiring fundamental allegiance. The historical development of such notions, related to the formation of the public sphere, are all key to the way we have constructed our cultural narratives of Western modernity. A variety of scholars of different disciplines have been characterizing modernity throughout the twentieth century, beginning with Max Weber. They have been defining discrete historical periods such as early, classical, and late modernity, fostering a vocabulary for distinguishing differences between what came before or, if you accept post-modernity as an independent cultural era, what followed. Terms such as disenchantment, demythologization, detraditionalization, individualism, instrumentalism, naturalism, and rationalization, for example, constructed a conceptual map for analyzing cultural change according to a logic of cause and effect. Because of the largely negative association of this vocabulary with respect to religion, secularism was viewed as a corollary of such change. And thus we get, with Charles Taylor's monumental book *A Secular Age*,[6] a host of terms defining both modernity and secularism in terms of the "buffered self," the "immanent frame," the "great disembedding," and "exclusive humanism." Debates about secularism and secularization and its effects have been defined by and conducted in accordance with these two-dimensional conceptual maps of Western modernity. More recently, postsecularism radically questions the categories (such as naturalism and rationalization) and re-enchants the world—but again, it only does so because of already familiar ideas.

Beginning with his early anthropological work at the Salk Institute for Biological Studies in La Jolla, California, Latour has questioned modernity or our constructions of it.[7] He was also a close friend and advisor to French President Hollande and has turned his attention to thinking and writing about "political theology." Again, there are any number of aspects of Latour's presence as an advisor to the French government and his recent work following the terror attacks in France of 2015. For brevity—and the sake of pushing an argument—I cut to the chase. What was discerned in the practices of scientists that he observed was that they worked with an implicit metaphysics that created the space for their empirical work with its scientific rationality. This space issued from the concept of nature as something external, unified, universal, independently stable, and indisputable. The implicit metaphysics with which they worked meant that "a fact only becomes such when it loses all temporal qualifications and becomes incorporated into a large body of knowledge drawn upon by others. Consequently, there is an essential difficulty associated with writing the history of a fact: it has, by definition, lost all historical reference."[8] He thus concludes, and this is the basis of his *We Have Never Been Modern*, that the rationality espoused by modernity (that disenchanting, instrumentalism that Weber spoke of) contradicts the way it is actually constructed and deployed by the moderns. In other words, by extracting the objectivity and universal validity of the "fact" from the material and historical practices that make it possible, they believe they are establishing it more securely, ridding it of all the determinations of time, place, and production. He calls this "freeze-framing." Truth is established only by this extraction from the mediating chains and series from which it emerges and upon which it depends. Such truth is linear and in accordance with a conception of time challenged since at least Einstein.

In *We Have Never Been Modern*, and this brings me back to the association of modernity with secularism, Latour examines the contradictions both in terms of scientific and political practices and concludes that the stable universalisms that are forged all rest upon a fundamental premise— that God is "crossed out."[9] The original French phrase is important: *le Dieu debarré, hors jeu*—literally, God is ruled "offside," as in a game of football. God is conceived as outside, exterior, extrinsic, and wholly other. But note, as Latour does, this *Dieu debarré* is exactly what scientific rationality maintains in order to establish the objectivity and truth-value of a "fact." However much modernity's constructions rule God as "offside," what has been traditionally been understood as "God" haunts those self-same constructions albeit shorn of any explicitly religious dressing.

The Secular Imagination

Let me illustrate what I think Latour is pointing to here by exploring an example of what we might call the secular imagination. The Marina Sands Hotel, designed by the secular Jewish architect Moshe Safdie, is the focal point of downtown Singapore: a magnificent, award-winning building standing on an edge of land reclaimed from the sea. It is one of the most extravagant and imaginative examples of contemporary architecture I have ever seen. Surrounded by much smaller structures, the iconic luxury resort consists of three towers that rise fifty-five stories high against the backdrop of the Indian Ocean. The sloping geometry of the towers resembles an Egyptian Ankh or a freeze frame of a deck of playing cards in the process of being shuffled. Bridging the tops of the towers is the expansive, ship-shaped SkyPark, which sits almost seven hundred feet above the city and features its own jogging paths and a vast infinity pool lined with palm trees and sunbeds. The spectacular complex houses multiple bars, restaurants, a museum, two theaters, a conference center, a hotel with more than twenty-five hundred rooms, and a casino. At night the mythological resonance of the architecture sings across the city: three gargantuan pillars upon which a ship sails through the vast constellations of the universe framed by the dark stretches of the Indian Ocean and the cosmos. Of course, the ship goes nowhere, but among the passing clouds or the shifting moon and stars it *appears* to be sailing through time and space—indifferent to both.

Its technological ingenuity (that uses gravity to offset the effects of high winds and seismic effects) is built on money (over $5 billion). It's built to generate more money, and it's locked into Singapore's tourist economy— not least because the huge and controversial casino it lodges has certain tax exemptions on winnings. It is an icon of modernity's progressivism. But what is most evident in the whole of its form and activities is a yearning to transcend the labors and belittlements of ordinary, lack-luster existence. It's a yearning for escape into more enchanted realities; escape war, famine, migrant crises, economic depressions, homelessness, sickness, and mental frailties. The harbor below it, for example, is full of ships lying idle because the glut in the oil and manufacturing industries of southeast Asia has taken a bite out of the trade economy. At night, with a vodka martini costing you an eye-watering amount of Singaporean dollars, you can sit atop the city, enjoy a balmy breeze coming off an ocean warmed by an equatorial sun and fanned by tropical trade winds, and stare out across the infinities of space as the earth turns slowly and the planets circle the sun. The more vodka martinis you drink, the deeper the experience of transcendence such that one might *imagine* a new religion being born— imagine, that is, until you get your next credit card statement, because all this imagining comes at a very high price. But it's not the price that interests me, or the fact that such experiences are reserved for a tiny portion of the world's population. In a sense, just by this place being there, even if you can't afford it, you might nevertheless dream of experiencing it: *If* I win the lottery or that game show or that radio competition. *If* I come into an inheritance. *If* my book gets the global attention it deserves and is translated into thirty languages. The secular imagination doesn't need money; even the destitute can dream. Below it are public parks and spaces for public meetings. People can look up and transcend the materialities of the diurnal "getting by" through aspiring and dreaming.

The use of the word *transcendence* for the experience at the top of SkyPark or for those looking up might seem overly religious, but we might describe it as pop transcendence: a secular form of being othered or being expanded beyond one's individualist horizons that doesn't necessarily involve God or an experience of the divine. The "new religion" that might be born is an aesthetic one. It has none of the theological weight that accumulates from a spiritual discipline and belonging to a tradition of faith. But SkyPark is akin to Latour's transcendent God, the X factor ruled offside in order to create the conditions of Western modernity's universalist metaphysics. It is a space that is beyond space (utopia), it is a timeless exteriority that is only made possible through the material practices that give rise to it, serve it, and produce it. There is nothing explicitly religious about it—other than the mythic resonances in the architecture itself that, as I said, could just be a luxury cruiser standing on three pairs of playing cards. It provides an imaginative and material image of what it is that people with or without religious allegiances dream of, hope for, and aspire to: a paradise of rest beyond unceasing restlessness. The mythic resonances of the building are related to the local. Singapore is a city where Western and Eastern religions meet and overlap. The building situates its paradise above and beyond the terrestrial and outside time. It offers release from the burdens and vagaries of history—a transcendence of the human lot by the consummation of desires recorded in its ancient texts. If this recalls the innocence of origins in the monotheistic faiths, it also recalls the Hindu and Buddhist ideals of escaping from the cyclic time of birth, death, and rebirth. The architecture gives expression to an observation made about myth and secularism by Mircea Eliade in 1957: "in the great majority of individuals who do not participate in any authentic religious experience, the mythical attitude can be discerned in their distractions [or ways of being entertained], as well as in their unconscious psychic activity (dreams, fantasies, nostalgias, etc.)."[10]

As I mentioned, a secular Jewish architect from Israel conceived of and designed the resort. I take this self-designation to mean something close to what France's Minister of Education Najat Vallaud-Belkacem called being a nonpracticing Moroccan Muslim. What does this account of being secular or nonpracticing mean? For no one is divorced from a tradition of thinking, evaluation, and cultural practices. That's why traditions cannot be "detraditionalized"; they can only undergo a continuous "retraditionalization." We are born into and raised within certain nonlinear matrixes that give us a language, shape the meaning of the world we live in, and require us, in turn, to use and adapt that language and reshape the meaning of the world we inherit. So here we have Moshe Safdie, Najat Vallaud-Belkacem, or my son, David, each of whom was raised within traditions of piety that they no longer practice—Jewish, Muslim, Christian. My question is, even if they self-identify as secular, what does secular designate?

Just because you don't practice a faith doesn't mean that you are indifferent to those beliefs or beyond their impacts. They have affected you just as much as modernity is affected by the God it rules to be offside. They have formed something of the habitus out of which and from within which you dwell and work. No one can erase the ways of thinking that have scored neural connections within the brain and lay down memory tracks that subsequent experiences reactivate—in present encounters, in dreams, in the work of the creative imagination. As nonpracticing, they want to opt out of the organization and institutionalization of their tradition, they may also want to opt out of believing its doctrinal tenets—and there may be many reasons they don't feel "it's for them," why they don't wish to belong and be counted among those who are practicing. But a tradition is lived in complex nonlinear ways; it is not reducible to a set of propositions that summarizes its *credo* and circumscribes its adherents. Furthermore, neuroscience has made it clear that we don't have access to dispositional beliefs that inform our behaviors and escape our conscious control. That inheritance, beyond its institutions and doctrines, cannot be sponged away as if it were no more than pen marks on a whiteboard. And every reminder, public reminder, of a synagogue, a mosque, a church; every reference to the symbolics of that piety; every encounter with those who continue to practice will reactivate not just memories but feelings (good or bad) laid down by that tradition—a continuing tradition.

We see this all the time with creative artists. The Catholic imaginary is still the operational base from which avowed atheists such as Jean-Paul Sartre undertake their imaginative work. His fiction cannot escape its deeply implicit Catholic worldview. The pointed question here is: where is life lived? It is not lived at the level of ideas or institutions. It is not lived in linear ways despite our clocks and calendars. It is lived in and through affects and conscious, preconscious, and unconscious memories. It is lived across various overlapping practices and jurisdictions that render complex any flattened and uniform time. In the same way, we can look beyond the individual to the social. Where is the social lived? Again, not simply with what society is told is the case, but with its dreams, aspirations, hopes, and desires. In short, the cultural imaginary. And the religious is written deep into the cultural imaginary and fills and shapes all those dreams, aspirations, hopes, and desires with a felt content and a pertinent sensibility. To say that the nonpracticing Jew, Muslim, or Christian is secular is a very reductive form of labeling that misconstrues and misrepresents the complexity of persons and their embeddedness in time. It is an ascription that has already accepted notions of individualism and rational choice theory—in short, the "buffered self." The label "freeze-frames" in Latour's language abstracts the person from the hybrid and rhizomatic contingencies, processes, and practices of lived experience.

A Nonlinear Account of Modernity

Given what I said, let me return to just three of those characterizations of modernity that seemingly ushered in a secular age for Charles Taylor. First, the "immanent frame." Based on Latour's analysis, the very possibility for the conception of the immanent is a metaphysical view from nowhere, a God's-eye view. For within the dynamic complexities of interassociation, how can we arrive at a judgment that frames a domain labeled immanent? There can only be what is, which is a pluralist ontology shot through with difference and otherness because otherwise there can be no movement and no relations. Movement and relations are multidirectional; as loosely governed by the logic of cause and effect as emotions, moods, and all subconscious activity. And where there is difference and otherness then there is exteriority and transcendence. How, in any account of unfolding of pluriverses and gravity waves, can we determine the limits and logics of immanence, never mind frame immanence as such? I am not a tree. The recognition that I am not a tree is the recognition of otherness and transcendence, which is written into alterity—so who can delineate where immanence begins and transcendence ends? Immanence is the spatializing of linearity and uniformity. Any notion of a purely immanent state is a metaphysical and theological claim—a claim from a divine perspective that has been ruled offside [*debarré, hors jeu*].

Second, the "buffered self." Everything from cell biology to neuroscience informs us that nothing exists in a monadic state; all things are interdependent. The single cell has no existence outside of the molecular structure that makes it possible and the organization of other cells into an electro-chemical exchange that is the basis for sentience and life itself. Consciousness is not an abstract property. It is only possible in and through relation to the world and sensory-motor processing in the brain. Any notion we have of self or ego arises from our radical dependencies, emerging from socio-bio-psycho enactments. That is not to say we cannot create philosophies and ideologies describing states of social atomism and value systems around the cult of the individual and the personality. But we cannot read off such philosophies and ideologies in their construction and dissemination as if they are or were incontestable truths that govern life from then on. Descartes's famous elaboration of the *cogito* was not how Descartes lived or could live, and as Marion, among others, has shown, it is internally inconsistent, and Descartes knew it, as his last work on the passions indicates.[11] Kant's transcendental ego is a fabrication Kant himself recognized, and the deduction that gets us to the unity of apperception is riddled with difficulties, as Paul Franks has shown.[12] As Foucault concluded at the end of *The Order of Things*, "man cannot posit himself in the immediate and sovereign transparency of a *cogito*."[13] Furthermore, the establishment of the analytical abstraction of "buffered selves" occludes the great eighteenth-century explorations into sympathy, empathy, and fellow feeling that became the basis for the advocacy of a new social sensibility to govern both ethics and action. Hobbes may have championed the ubiquity of self-interest, but Shaftesbury was the first in a long line of critics to challenge it.

Whatever the claims, there never were and there never can be "buffered selves." *We* have created the concept and generated its history, just as *we* have created the history of the immanent frame, and *we* have similarly created the notion of disenchantment. Mechanical and instrumental reason may have reached its apogee in Newton, but so did the researches of alchemy, the enquiries into the organic processes not only in the world but in the relations between human beings and the world, and the creativity of the imagination sensed by Thomas Addison and extolled by Edmund Burke and Adam Smith. Whereas human beings have the capacity to imagine and the curiosity to quest there will never be a disenchanted world— or a world without wonder. The creative surge of scientific enquiry joined the creative surge of artistic endeavor. By the mid-eighteenth century both enterprises were being viewed as exercises of the imagination, of longing, and of belief-formation.[14]

As for exclusive humanism: there are as many humanisms as there are anthropologies and worldviews. Atheistic humanism, agnostic humanism, and Catholic, Protestant, Orthodox, Buddhist, and Hindu humanism as well as the humanism are enshrined in the United Nation's Universal Declaration of Human Rights. Exclusive humanism is an intellectual abstraction that reifies and freeze-frames something as shape-shifting as human nature itself.

Now let me be clear here. This is not an attack upon Charles Taylor. In fact, as Taylor moves toward his own lengthy constructive position in the closing sections of *A Secular Age*, I am very much in agreement, and he is critical of the reductive, abstracting social and cultural positions articulated by a secular age. My argument is an attempt to counter the way we have produced secularism and its profound association with Western modernity and atheism. My argument is that this intellectual construction gets passed as "the way things were," what Roland Barthes would call a myth.[15] There is nothing historical, natural, or inevitable about the processes we name secularism, modernity, or atheism. The naming describes reductively nonlinear sociohistorical processes that are as complex as they are contingent. As Talal Asad has pointed out, descriptions of these processes as secular come from schools of thought deeply indebted to Christian narratives, however retraditionalized, such as Enlightenment progress.[16] Taylor is one more proponent of such linear narratives.

Conclusion

We have created the cultural narratives that have shaped modernity and its association with secularism and atheism through our reductive histories and our selective cultural analyses. It is a story (for the most part Christian) we tell about where we have come from and where we are that *we* have fabricated and promulgated and in which secularism is viewed as both an inevitable destiny and a *de facto* condition. The story creates a neutral space and a new temporal start (*ab novo circa* 1500) that is a purely metaphysical and theological construction, an ideology—that is, a space that is nowhere (utopian) and timeless (anachronistic). We have never been modern in the way the categories have defined being modern, and we have never been secular in that way either. I agree with Latour. Now, under the pressure from a proliferation of modernities and the genealogies that question the stability and universalism of the cultural givens we have inherited; under the pressure also of a global phenomena in which the religious cannot be erased or God "ruled offside"; and with the increasing inadequacy of describing as secular the bureaucratic ideal of impartiality—then we have to face the complexities of the way things emerge in the way things are lived. That does not prove the existence of God—as if the existence or nonexistence of God could ever submit itself to human demonstrations— but it enables us to recognize traditions of pieties exist and, as far as we know from the remnants of Neanderthal burial sites, they have always existed in one form or another since probably *Homo erectus*, and always will.

With this, we can finally return to the title of this essay: secularism—the golden lie. It's a reference, of course, to Plato's *Republic* and the foundation of a polity upon a lie necessary for its establishment: a founding universal myth. Modernity is the founding myth here. The myth of the new start created in all the images of light that separated us from the dark superstitions that reigned before then. This is the golden lie that we have constructed and inherited. The secular as God being ruled as offside was the necessary condition for that foundation, as Latour has pointed out. Georges Sorel taught us more than a century ago: myths cannot be dissolved through processes of rationalization or demythologization.[17] And it is not the case that the myth of the modern is without good effects. It has, to return to Plato, founded a republic of sorts with enormous benefits, even if what the secular in Western Europe now identifies and consolidates is not necessarily the democratic, but the bureaucratic state. But it has to be recognized that the golden lie is not itself the way things are. It is not the true case of what is. It is a story of what is, riddled with the fractures of its mythic foundations. It is like the crack in Henry James's golden bowl (in his novel with that title): it requires that we reconsider its value. In the re-evaluation, things can be lived differently as we move as a human race toward a greater holism in, through, and with our religious proclivities. If we do not undertake this reevaluation, then we will continue wrangling with and even waging war against conceptual ghosts, fears, risks, and threats that do not actually exist.

There is something profoundly ironic about the myth of modernity and what, in *Unbelievable*, I called the "myth of secularism"—because modernity did not believe in myths and attempted to expunge them at every opportunity in its commitment to scientific reason. Mythic thinking was, accurately, associated with all the mystique and obscurantism of religion. Nietzsche rightly saw that the trajectory toward "extreme secularism" was accompanied by the loss of myth and the advance of culture based on baseless illusions that he despised.[18] A people so enthralled to "a resolute process of secularization . . . breaks with the unconscious metaphysics of its former existence,"[19] and this does not bode well. The unconscious does not go away; nor does the power of the mythic. They bide their nonlinear time—and then the repressed return, not necessarily with healing in their wings.

Notes

1. On multiple modernities, see the introduction to Nicholas Adams, George
Pattison, and Graham Ward, *The Oxford Handbook of Theology and Modern
European Thought* (Oxford: Oxford University Press, 2013), 1–17. On Western
and colonial modernity, see, among many other voices from Frantz Fanon
onward, Dipesh Chakrabarty, *Provincializing Europe: Postcolonial Thought and
Historical Difference* (Princeton, NJ: Princeton University Press, 2000).

2. See Eric Voegelin, *Die politischen Religionen*, translated as *Political
Religions* in *Modernity Without Restraint*, vol. 5 of *The Collected Works*, ed.
Manfred Henningsen (Columbia: University of Missouri Press, 1999).

3. Naser Ghobadzadeh, *Religious Secularity: A Theological Challenge to the
Islamic State* (Oxford: Oxford University Press, 2015).

4. For an in-depth study of these issues, see Yolande Jansen, *Secularism,
Assimilation and the Crisis of Multiculturalism: French Modernist Legacies*
(Amsterdam: University of Amsterdam Press, 2013). For more details
surrounding *laïcité*, see my *Unbelievable: Why We Believe and Why We Don't*
(London: Taurus, 2014).

5. *Guardian*, January 21, 2016, 15.

6. Charles Taylor, *A Secular Age* (Cambridge, MA: Belknap Press, 2007).

7. See Bruno Latour and Steve Woolgar, *Laboratory Life: The Construction of
Scientific Facts* (Princeton, NJ: Princeton University Press, 1979).

8. Latour and Woolgar, 106.

9. Bruno Latour, *We Have Never Been Modern*, trans. Catherine Porter
(Hemel Hempstead: Harvester Wheatsheaf, 1993), 32–35, 127–28, 138–38.

10. Mircea Eliade, *Myths, Dreams and Mysteries: The Encounter between
Contemporary Faiths and Archaic Reality*, trans. Philip Mairet (London: Fontana
Library, 1968), 37.

11. See Jean-Luc Marion, *On Descartes' Metaphysical Prism: The Constitution
and the Limits of Onto-theo-logy in Cartesian Thought*, trans. Jeffery L. Kosky
(Chicago: University of Chicago Press, 1999); *Cartesian Questions: Method and
Metaphysics* (Chicago: University of Chicago Press, 1999); and *Sur la théologie
blanche de Descartes* (Paris: Presses Universitaires de France, 2009).

12. See Paul Franks, *All or Nothing: Systematicity, Transcendental Arguments,
and Skepticism in German Idealism* (Cambridge, MA: Harvard University Press,
2005).

13. Michel Foucault, *The Order of Things: An Archaeology of the Human
Sciences* (London: Tavistock Publications, 1970), 322.

14. For a detailed account of the role of the imagination from Hobbes and
throughout the eighteenth century, see James Engell, *The Creative Imagination:
Enlightenment to Romanticism* (Cambridge, MA: Harvard University Press,

1981). For a revisionist account of the history of early science that debunks its association with atheism, see Allan Chapman, *Stargazers: Copernicus, Galileo, the Telescope and the Church* (Oxford: Lion, 2014).

15. Roland Barthes, *Mythologies*, trans. Annette Lavers (London: Vintage, 2000): "the very principle of myth: it transforms history into nature" (129).

16. Talal Asad, *Formations of the Secular: Christianity, Islam, Modernity* (Stanford, CA: Stanford University Press, 2003).

17. Georges Sorel, *Reflections on Violence*, trans. and ed. Jeremy Jennings (Cambridge: Cambridge University Press, 1999).

18. Friedrich Nietzsche, *The Birth of Tragedy*, trans. Shaun Whiteside (London: Penguin, 1993), 99.

19. Nietzsche, 111.

Collectivistic Christianities and Pluralism: An Inquiry into Agency and Responsibility

Slavica Jakelić

T his essay addresses the relationship between religious traditions, secularisms, and fundamentalisms by looking at collectivistic Catholicisms in communist and postcommunist Croatia and Poland. My analysis is organized around one question: how do Catholic actors who affirm the close links of Catholicism and a particular group identity relate to their religious and nonreligious others? Catholicism can constitute narratives about collective identity in more than one way. This multiplicity of collectivistic meanings of Catholicism is important for analytic and normative reasons. Analytically, it indicates that Catholicism as a lived collectivistic tradition is internally plural even within the same social contexts. Normatively, the multiplicity of collectivistic Catholicisms provides insights into the spaces of agency that religious actors have in their engagement with modernity and pluralism.

Between Religious Nationalism and Religious Fundamentalism

I propose that one ought not to approach collectivistic Catholicisms merely as upshots of modernity's secularizing drive or as forces inherently opposed to pluralism. The variety of collectivistic Catholicisms that I trace challenges the narrow readings of the links among religion, nationalism, and secularism; it especially calls into question the consensus about the nature of those links, which we can identify in the works of the canonical theorists of nationalism and contemporary critics of secularism. There are important disciplinary and normative differences between scholars of nationalism (such as Ernest Gellner, Benedict Anderson, and Anthony Smith[1]) and the critics of secularism (such as Talal Asad, Saba Mahmood, Elizabeth Shakman Hurd, Markus Dressler, or William Cavanaugh[2]). Gellner, Anderson, and Smith think that religion yields to the secular ordering of social life as a consequence of modern historical developments.[3] By contrast, the critics of secularism seek to *unmask* the secular as a central component of the homogenizing and hegemonic drive of the (Western) modern project, focusing on the ways in which the nationalist ideologues and secular nation-states co-opt religious symbols, narratives, and powers. The described differences between theorists of nationalism and critics of secularism notwithstanding, what they have in common is a twofold theory of modernity and of religion: of modernity as secular and secularizing, and of religion as the modernity's other.

Such views of modernity and religion are framed within two analytic and normative frameworks—a modernist reading of collective identity and the discourse of power. Both have problematic outcomes for the study of religion, group identification, and pluralism. As I elaborate in my *Collectivistic Religions: Religion, Choice, and Identity in Late Modernity*, in considering religion as a source of collective identity, scholars largely see it as linked to nationalisms and as secularized by virtue of those links. This understanding results from an ahistorical understanding of collective identity, which presents the history of collective identities as a march of nationalisms at the expense of all other sources of group identities—regional, linguistic, tribal, and religious. The normative implications of such theorizing are significant: the modernist view of collective identity in effect takes away the agency from religious actors and institutions and precludes the explorations of the role that religious actors *continue* to have in the construction and reconstruction of narratives of collective belonging.

In response to these historical, conceptual, and normative concerns, I proposed the notion of *collectivistic religion* to refer to religions that are public in manifestation, historically embedded, and constitutive of specific group identities—*next to* linguistic, territorial, cultural, *or* national identities—and defined in part by the presence of religious (or nonreligious) others. When considered within the framework of collectivistic religiosity, the relationship between religious and national identities does not serve as an a priori indication of a secularized or weakened religion but is always examined empirically. Put differently, although the concept of collectivistic religions sustains the exploration of religion-nationalism links, it approaches them as only one possible manifestation of collectivistic religiosity.

Furthermore, the notion of collectivistic religions gestures toward the need for a more complex understanding of the late modern forms of religious belonging. Instead of envisioning such experiences as necessarily and progressively moving toward the varieties of religious voluntarism, this notion asserts a complicated relationship between traditional and modern forms of religious identification. As a result, (collectivistic) religiosity that is often experienced as ascribed rather than as chosen, as a constitutive rather than as attributive aspect of one's identity, emerges not as a carryover from the past that will eventually disappear but as a significant element of contemporary religious pluralism.

The assertion that religious actors and institutions do not have much space for agency—because they are trapped by the archaeology of secular modernity and co-opted by (purportedly) secular nation states—carries a twofold difficulty. The first one lies in the focus on secularism as a political phenomenon and the emphasis on its place in relation to the modern state and the realm of law. This perspective leaves out the possibility to retrieve the secular as it shapes the spaces of the ethical which inform secular subjectivities as well as the manner in which these can be enacted in the public arena.[4]

The second problem with the assumption that religion is constrained within and appropriated by modernity and its secular constellations is the reiteration of the view that religious-secular encounters always happen as conflict and power struggle. I proposed elsewhere that this view, so central to narratives of modernity that long dominated social sciences, ends up being reaffirmed by the least predictable suspects—the critics of secularism for whom the uncompromising critique of modernity is one of their key tasks.[5] It is possible to see this development as ironic or as a result of a flattened understanding of modernity.[6] Yet, it is also plausible to argue that the reiteration of the modernist view of religious-secular encounters as contestations—*within* the critique of modernity and modernist assumptions—is unavoidable because the framework of analysis that dominates much of the study of religious-secular phenomena is dictated by the discourse of power.[7] The latter creates serious obstacles for our discussion of collectivistic religions and how they relate to religious and nonreligious others because of how it can limit our vision of pluralism. Concretely, when the scholars working within the discourse of power attempt to move outside the narrative of conflict, they can offer only one possibility—the understanding of the religious and secular identities as fluid, evasive, or hybrid.[8] Although this move can open new analytic possibilities for the study of the religious and the secular,[9] the sole focus on their fluid and hybrid character is problematic because it confines and thus impoverishes theorizing of religious pluralism as well as of religious-secular pluralism.

In the following sections, I will build on my critique of the discourse of power and the modernist conceptualizations of collective identity as well as on the idea that religions continue to be actively constitutive rather than passively reflective of group identities.[10] First, I probe the various expressions of collectivistic Catholicisms in relation to pluralism. My goal is to expose what, following Charles Taylor, we can identify as yet another subtraction story about religion and modernity—to problematize the commonly accepted notion that, when religion is in the domain of nationalism, it loses agency because, intentionally or unintentionally, it has to give in to the powers of the modern secular. Second, and even more central to the constructive thrust of this essay, I explore two types of collectivistic Catholicisms in Croatia and Poland. On the one hand, I consider the collectivistic Catholicisms that reject the cultural and moral pluralism of modernity but, in the process, end up espousing one of modernity's aspects—its homogenizing impulse. This is the same impulse that Charles Taylor sees as an expression of the modernity's rage for order.[11] On the other hand, I trace two instances in which collectivistic Catholicisms in Croatia and Poland affirm the links between Catholicism and national identities but remain open to their Muslim and secular others respectively. In other words, I uncover the types of collectivistic Catholicisms that are particularist, even exclusivist in character, associated with national identities, but also open to pluralism.

Through a juxtaposition of the two types of collectivistic Catholicisms— one that advocates homogeneity, the other more open to differences—I argue that what is at stake in the conversations about religious tradition, secularization, and fundamentalism is the question of pluralism. My proposal does not lie simply in the idea that the more open collectivistic religions are toward the other, the more conducive for contemporary public life they are. Although I do think this is the case, I see these collectivistic traditions as even more instructive in two other ways. First, they show that religious actors possess the agency and thus the ethical responsibility to articulate the narratives of collective identity.[12] Second, the more open forms

of collectivistic religious traditions uncover a particular ideal of pluralism—
the one in which the encounters with different others do not diminish the
deep differences but rather sustain them.

Croatian and Polish Collectivistic Catholicisms in Communist and Postcommunist Contexts

A comparison of the Croatian and Polish cases provides a fruitful framework for understanding the variety of collectivistic Catholicisms. Both
Croatia and Poland are postcommunist societies, with the histories of
communist oppression of Catholicism. In both instances, the Catholic
Church played a central role in the preservation of the Croatian and Polish national identity during communist rule, standing as the main institutional opposition to communist regimes which earned the church the
respect of believers and nonbelievers alike.[13] Today, the Catholic Church
is the most privileged religious institution in both Croatia and Poland, with
almost 90 percent of the population identifying as Catholic. Perhaps the
most significant difference between the Croatian and Polish cases lay in
the earliest years of their democratic transition. In Croatia, this was the
time of a bloody conflict; in Poland, the 1990s were a period of peaceful
political transformation. The differences in the early democratization processes are directly pertinent to our discussion because of the impact they
had on religious developments.

Rejecting Pluralism, Succumbing to Modernity

One of the unintended consequences of the communist attempts to priva-
tize and marginalize religious and national identities in the former Yugoslavia was the cementing of the collectivistic meaning of Croatian
Catholicism, which then came to the forefront of political life during the
war for Croatian independence in the 1990s.[14] The war had multiple
causes,[15] but it quickly turned into a struggle for the sovereignty of the
newly established Croatian state against the Serbian claims to parts of the
Croatian territory. In this context, the Croatian collectivistic Catholicism
became posited first and foremost against the Serbian Orthodox Christians.
The result was an even greater proximity of Catholic and Croatian national
identity. In the war against the Yugoslav army and the Serbian parami-
tary forces, Croatian soldiers wore rosaries around their necks and marked

their weapons with the images of the Virgin Mary. During the years of conflict, the representatives of the Croatian Catholic Church did not shy away from linking their religious messages to the anti-Serbian rhetoric. While some individual members of the church hierarchy advocated peace,[16] the majority of Catholic clergymen did not see problems with "the cross of Christ stand[ing] next to the Croatian flag" or the Croatian bishops standing "next to Croatian minister of state."[17] According to one Catholic commentator, the Croatian Catholics and those in the Catholic Church leadership felt an overwhelming satisfaction that the Croatian people could be free "'from the twofold' slavery: Serbian and Communist."[18]

The war helped promote the Catholic Church into the most privileged religious institution in the Croatian society but significantly delayed the broadening of the church's agenda beyond its narrow focus on the Croatian political and national sovereignty. The war also postponed the more active public involvement of the Catholic lay activists, which became more organized and more vocal very gradually. It was thus only recently, on May 21, 2016, that these Catholic lay groups were able to organize the Walk for Life. Thousands of people participated in this protest, which was supported by various Catholic groups and individuals,[19] including the wife of the (then) Croatian prime minister and figures such as the indicted war criminal Dario Kordić.[20] The protest highlighted a novel development in Croatian Catholicism. Its central argument against the intrusion of the secular modern values into the public and private lives was hardly new—it is a claim traceable in the cases of Catholic activists from the United States to Australia. One feature, however, made the Croatian context different: Catholic activists saw secularity as a legacy from communist times, something preserved due to the atheist political elites who (purportedly) still controlled Croatian public life. The activists, moreover, revealed their antisecular, anticommunist stance as inseparable from their concern for the moral and national, demographic well-being of Croatia. The connection that the Catholic activists established among the antimodern, antisecular, and nationalistic orientations was reflected very clearly in the name of the chief organizer of the Walk for Life, the organization "For life, family, and Croatia" (which recently morphed from a civil society organization into a political party). But one crucial impetus for this new form of collectivistic religion—the antisecular, antimodern, and anticommunist nationalist Catholicism—came from the sphere of politics. An example of a poster that the Christian-democratic coalition selected for elections several years ago helps illustrate my point. According to Jadranka Rebeka Anić, Catholic feminist theologian and a Franciscan nun, the poster showed two hands: a male one—which is "dirty and bloody," holding "a star, sickle and hammer in its palm"—and a female, more gentle and clean hand next to it, holding "a cross in its palm."[21] The poster displayed one message: "A Simple Choice for a Secure Future." Those who commissioned the poster argued that the poster's "intention [was] to convey to citizens" that theirs was a choice between the past and the future, between values of the Communist Party and the freedom represented in the Catholic Church.[22] But by showing a clean woman's hand gently holding the cross, the poster also intimated that the central role in the perpetuation of Catholic faith and tradition belonged to women. One political advertisement thus brought together Croatian nationalism, Catholicism as a source for traditional family values, and antimodernism and antipluralism as the rejection of communism. In 2013, these themes and concerns reached an entirely new level, with the heated debates about health education (and most specifically, sexual education) in public schools and the status of homosexual marriage. These questions divided the Croatian society by pitting the Catholic lay organizations, Catholic Church, and small but vocal portions of Catholic parents against the left-leaning government and large portions of society (which, although predominantly Catholic, seemed to have been in favor of educational changes as well as modifications of the family law).[23]

The methods of the Catholic activists and the divisive implications of the moral questions that help constitute a form of the Croatian collectivistic Catholicism are all too familiar for any observer of American culture war. Some analysts of the Croatian situation suggest that the similarities in question are not an accident because the Croatian Catholic lay activists had been receiving financial help and education from their counterparts in the United States.[24] Moreover, some of the most prominent Catholic lay figures at the forefront of the new Croatian Catholic activism have been the Croatian immigrants from the countries where the culture wars have been playing out for a while. The similarities between the Croatian and North American culture war activists notwithstanding, Anić is correct to highlight one distinguishing feature of the Croatian situation—its historical experience of communism.[25] When the Croatian activists reject secular modern values, they do not reject modern pluralism in general; they reject *communist* secular legacies as secularizing and pluralizing elements of social life. This is especially obvious in the activists' and church's responses to what they see as "gender ideology." Just like their many counterparts in the United States or Europe, the Croatian Catholic actors reject the conversation about gender within the church.[26] Unlike culture warriors in other contexts, the Croatian Catholic actors link their condemnation of gender-discourse to the denunciation of feminist organizations that preserved their "anti-church and anti-national" agenda from the communist period (when these organizations were first established).[27] Such narratives serve as a tool to homogenize Croatian Catholics around one single story of what it means to be a Croatian Catholic. Those who provide a different account of Catholic experience can expect to be criticized as well as institutionally marginalized. Such was the case with Anić: her book *How to Understand Gender?* critically assesses the apocalyptic tones of the Catholic culture war approach to gender, discusses the intellectual and theological trajectories that are at the foundation of this approach in Croatia, and shows the already existing paths that can lead toward a more open conversation about gender within the Catholic Church.[28] Because of this book, the Catholic Church and the Catholic activists and bloggers publicly attacked Anić and, whenever possible, excluded her from Croatian theological conversations.[29]

If the Croatian Catholic activists brought their struggle against secularism and pluralism to the Croatian public only recently, the Catholic Church in Poland and a segment of the Polish Catholic believers began to battle the pluralization of Polish society already in the 1990s. This was the time when the Poles started to talk about their cultural and political integration into Western Europe. While the Polish Pope John Paul II was a fervent supporter of Poland in the European Union, a large number of Polish Catholic clergy and laity perceived Western Europe as a source of cultural and moral pluralization and a threat to the Polish cultural and religious identity. The earliest and most forceful spokesperson for these views was Fr. Tadeusz Rydzyk. His Catholic radio station, Radio Maryja, focused on various religious programs and regularly condemned Europeanization and globalization.[30]

Rydzyk's radio and media empire was only one facet of what the Polish commentator Slawomir Sierakowski two decades later identified as a "raging . . . culture war" that (as he saw it) the Catholic Church and activists introduced to Polish society.[31] The concerns about the foreign influence, the fears that Poland would lose its Catholic character within secular Europe, the insistence on the Catholic traditional values as guiding principles for the public and legal life of the whole Polish postcommunist society—all these orientations helped bring the Catholic doctrinal traditions and moral teachings under the umbrella of the nationalistic and anticommunist agenda of the leading figures of Polish postcommunist Catholicism. A good illustration for these developments has been the church's struggle against the legality of abortion which dates back to the 1990s. In arguing against the law that, since the communist times, permitted abortion, the Polish bishops invoked the Fifth Commandment, the "inviolability of human life,"[32] and the right to life of unborn children.[33] But they also stated that the legality of abortion was "contrary to 'the moral and biological well-being of the nation, . . . [will place] the 'state's functioning in peril,'" and was a matter of responsibility for the "the motherland" and "the well-being of Poland."[34] The bishops' advocacy of the anti-abortion law thus linked the matters of doctrine to demographic and national survival, and (just as that was recently the case in Croatia) to the rejection of communism—the "tragic legacy of intolerance and cruelty toward those completely defenseless,"[35] a legacy that had to be left behind as part of the "rebirth" of Polish society with the "new legal, moral, and political system."[36] In other words, while their Croatian counterparts first marched for life in 2016, the Polish Catholic activists have been doing it since the early 1990s, prominently and jointly displaying the pro-life slogans, crosses, and the Polish national flags.

Such images, it is important to note, were hardly new: in 1979, when Poles of all ages enthusiastically welcomed John Paul II during his first visit to his homeland, the symbols of Polish nationhood also stood next to crosses. But the meanings of the religio-national character of Polish Catholicism in the 1990s and in 1979 could not be more different. The particularist content of Catholicism during the papal visit stood against the communist secular state and Russian control; in the postcommunist period, it was a stance against democratization that would allow and institutionalize pluralism through the preservation of communist legacy. Moreover, although the Catholic Church clergy and activists hardly addressed gender questions in the 1990s, twenty years later (just like their Croatian counterparts) they saw feminism, abortion, birth control, and LG-BTQ rights as constituting "an ideology 'worse than Nazism and Communism combined.'"[37] The Polish case emerges as part of the larger phenomenon in which the universal Catholic doctrines acquire particularist, "culturally salient" meanings.[38] What differentiates the Polish postcommunist story about pluralism, Catholicism, and secularism, what defines the specific content of the Catholic antimodern and antisecular platforms in Poland is, like in the Croatian case, this society's communist past.

According to the Polish secular intellectual Adam Michnik, Polish Catholicism is currently undergoing an internal struggle between integralism and progressivism. The former brings together the nationalist discourse with the conservative approach to theology and rejection of any criticism or dialogue; the latter carries the spirit of the Second Vatican Council in the engagement with the contemporary issues of Polish society.[39] Michnik's evaluations ought to be taken seriously: he has long been a thoughtful and important observer of Polish Catholicism, and defended the Catholic Church against communist totalitarianism in which he sees a courageous advocate of human rights and freedom of conscience.[40] There are, however, other possible interpretive approaches to contemporary Polish Catholicism. Following José Casanova's work on public religions, one could identify the exclusivistic, antipluralistic Polish collectivistic Catholicism as a possible challenge to the global capitalist economy.[41] Or, adopting Chris Hann's challenge to Casanova, one could focus on the power of the Catholic Church in postcommunist Poland,[42] showing that this church is not simply one actor in Polish civil society but the most powerful religious institution that, with the help of Catholic activist organizations, attempts to control all domains of social life.[43]

Michnik's, Casanova's, and Haan's proposals are all valuable for a nuanced, multilayered understanding of the antimodern, antipluralist, antisecular character of the nationalist collectivistic Catholicisms in postcommunist Poland and Croatia. For our discussion, their observations are especially helpful as they highlight that the Catholic Church and lay Catholic actors have a very broad space of action in both the Croatian and Polish stories. The religious actors, clergy, and lay representatives of Catholicism *are* the ones attempting to define the dominant narrative about the "right" meanings and expressions of collectivistic Catholicisms: they are the ones articulating the close connections between theological traditionalism and national exclusivism, putting them forward as a framework for morally and culturally homogenous societies; they are the ones not shying away from the marginalization or rejection of others, the perpetuation of prejudices and sometimes, as is the case in Croatia, from assisting the justification of violent conflicts. Should we see collectivistic Catholicisms emerge from these processes as a result of secularization in which nationalism wins over (as nationalism studies scholars suggest)? Or, do these instances demonstrate the powers of secular modernity in which secular states govern religious symbolism to shape their citizens' subjectivities and intersubjectivities (as the critics of secularism might propose)? In my reading, the drive toward homogeneity that I traced in the postcommunist Croatian and Polish collectivistic Catholicisms is neither an accident of history nor merely an outcome of the homogenizing powers of the secular. It is the result of the Catholic actors' own vision of what Catholic identity is when defined by a particular identity. In both Croatian and Polish cases, the church elites and the Catholic civil society actors emerge as critical for articulating the narratives of belonging; in both cases, they emerge as having both agency and responsibility in their approach to others, within and outside of their own tradition.

Affirming Particularities, Transforming Modernity

Some of the strongest, most recent expressions of Croatian collectivistic Catholicism have been defined against religious or nonreligious others—those who held power in the name of the communist atheist values and the Orthodox Christian Serbs who made claims on the Croatian territory. These recent manifestations of collectivistic Catholicism, however, came together with its much more tolerant facet, the one developed in the approach toward local Muslims. On the institutional level, we see this open approach legally, in the exceptionally well-regulated status of the Muslim minority in Croatia. As the Croatian sociologist Siniša Zrinščak points out, the Muslim community in Croatia has "the right to organize confessional education in public schools, the right to establish their own schools, educations, cultural and social institutions which the state recognizes and co-funds, . . . [and the right to] official recognition of religious marriage, the inclusion of Muslim chaplaincy in military and police forces."[44]

Moreover, the legal status of Muslims in Croatia, Zrinščak suggests, is often better than the status of the Croatian Protestant minorities. To interpret these developments, Zrinščak uses the notion of collectivistic religion and argues for the validity of my proposition that collectivistic religions do the boundary-work in multiple directions, excluding as well as including various groups. In that sense, the established religious rights of the Muslim community that Zrinščak describes are important institutional indicators of the ways in which the collectivistic Croatian Catholicism delineates the nature of pluralism in this society. But to uncover the narratives that help shape the more open and more tolerant form of Croatian collectivistic Catholicism it is necessary to move beyond the legal sphere of life—to take a look at a broad social acceptance of Islam as a distinctive, public, and communal identity that is part of the cultural makeup of Croatian society.

The recent opening of the new mosque in Croatia helps illustrate this point. In many European nations, one can trace a palpable uneasiness about the presence of Islam and sometimes outright Islamophobia,[45] both of which increased with recent attacks in France but have long been inextricably linked to the European colonial past and the unresolved ethical and legal questions surrounding the status of immigrants in Western Europe. Thus, long before the recent Swiss ban on mosque minarets,[46] European Muslims have faced obstacles in attempts to build mosques as centers of their communal and religious life. In contrast, the Muslim community in Croatia, whose sixty thousand members constitute about 1.5 percent of the total population in the country,[47] just opened its third mosque and the new Islamic center in one of the biggest Croatian cities, Rijeka. Designed by one of the most famous sculptors in the region, the mosque is celebrated as a major monument of the contemporary sacred architecture. A long period of planning and fund-raising, as well as negotiations about the minaret's size, preceded the building of the mosque.[48] But its place (with the view of the Adriatic in the background), its architectural style, and the ceremony of the mosque's opening, all suggest that Muslims are not only accepted but also welcomed in the postcommunist Croatian context. This was the case even during the 1990s wars in Bosnia and Croatia, when many Bosnian Muslim refugees found shelter in Croatia at the same time as the Bosnian Croats and Bosniak Muslims fought each other. With this in mind, it is not surprising that the leader of the Islamic Community in Croatia, Aziz ef. Hasanović, recently said that the Croatian approach to its Muslim minority can serve as a model for all Europeans.[49]

How to account for the openness of the Croatian collectivistic Catholics toward Muslims in a society that recently underwent a violent conflict and whose religious identity—especially when positioned against the Serbian Orthodox minority—has hardly been the model of openness to religious or national differences? To Muslims in Croatia, their good status is not a result of the governmental or Croatian citizens' acceptance of their presence;

it stems as well from their own active contribution to the creation and building of the new Croatian democratic society.

There are other reasons for the good status of Muslims in Croatia, one of which is the fact that Muslims in Croatia are not a new religious community. There is a long history of Catholic-Muslim encounters in the region—rich narratives, historical and fictional, about both coexistence and conflicts between Catholics and Muslims. They also have a shared linguistic and cultural background. The overlapping histories of Muslims and Catholics in Croatia necessarily involve the Catholics and Muslims in the Bosnian-Herzegovinian context. The modern Croatian national ideologues, just like their Serbian counterparts, wanted to acquire the majority in the Bosnian context and thus tried to win over the Bosnian Muslims.[50] The latter group most often saw the Croatian and Serbian ideologies as paternalistic, especially in light of the emerging distinctive Bosniak national identity, and as equally threatening to the unity of the Muslim community. But as historian Ivo Banac writes, there were also striking differences in the nature of the Serbian and Croatian claims.

The Serbian national ideologues showed a pronounced "antagonism toward Islam and 'Turks' and the expectation that the Muslims would 'return to Orthodoxy.'"[51] Croatian national ideologues also often desired to convert Muslims but most "flattered the Muslims" and some even advocated the idea that the Bosnian Muslims were "the best Croats."[52] Although Muslims see such arguments as paternalistic and even offensive, the cultural and political positions of many Croatian national ideologues also contributed greatly to the marginalization of the long-standing narratives of the Croatian lands as the bulwark of Western Christianity—the *antemuralis Christianitatis*—against Islam.

All narratives of collective belonging related to and constitutive of the Muslim-Catholic encounters—especially the *competing* narratives of conflicts and collaborations—require additional studies. Yet, if one is concerned with the character and possibilities of contemporary pluralism, it is particularly valuable to trace the roots and trajectories of the narratives that opened rather than closed Catholicism's view of its religious others. Much work remains to be done to understand the features of the Croatian collectivistic Catholicism that is tolerant of Muslims. First and foremost, how did the narratives of Catholic-Muslim collaborations outweigh the narratives of their conflicts? Second, why and how was this possible in the case of Catholic-Muslim encounters and not in the case of Catholic-Orthodox

Christian relations? Is the latter group perceived as threat because the Orthodox Christians living in and next to Croatia have more demographic and political weight than the Muslims?[53] Or, are the reasons for such differences historically, culturally, and sociologically more complex? Most importantly, what has been the role—the agency and responsibility of religious actors and religious institutions—in articulating the narratives of collective belonging that exclude others or open the door to encounters with them? It is plausible to suggest that, in various historical periods, it was precisely the Catholic actors who had the imagination and power to use the cultural resources needed to affirm the religious distinctiveness of both Catholicism and Islam within the pluralistic framework.[54] They were the ones able to articulate and perpetuate the narratives that opened collectivistic Catholicism toward Islam and, even if just implicitly, gave the possibility of Catholic-Muslim collaborations in today's Croatian society.

Put differently, unlike the antipluralistic collectivistic Catholicisms that greatly resemble similar phenomena around the globe, the tolerant type of collectivistic Catholicism in the Croatian context is embedded in a specific cultural and historical location. Rather than defined by narrow confines of politics or the matters of morality, this is a public religious tradition shaped by the *particular* narratives of belonging. And, while remaining nationally specific, this is a Catholicism open to religious pluralism—it accepts Muslims as religious (and most often as national) others constitutive of the Croatian public life.

If the Croatian collectivistic Catholicism open to Islam leaves us with many questions, the Polish case provides us with a fuller account of the actors and sources involved. I am referring here to a type of Catholicism that was most publicly expressed in Poland in the late 1970s and early 1980s, and which became embodied in Solidarity.[55]

Solidarity was the first independent trade union in the Soviet bloc that quickly became a powerful social movement of millions of Polish citizens— including workers, engineers, secular intelligentsia, and clergy. The central inspiration for the movement came from the first visit of John Paul II to Poland in 1979. On this occasion, hundreds of thousands of Poles welcomed the first Polish pope of the Catholic Church and listened to his many homilies. John Paul II's words were filled with references to the dignity and freedom of each human person, but they were also appealing to the central place that Catholicism had played in Polish history.[56] One significant narrative in this history—and yet another example of the

striking similarities between the Polish and Croatian cases—has been
the narrative about Polish Catholicism as the *antemuralis Christianitatis*
and about Poland as the defender of true faith in the face of various religious
and nonreligious threats. Many commentators emphasized the central
place that Catholicism had in the ethos, rise, and successes of Solidarity.
But as one of its advisers, Józef Tischner—a priest, personalist theologian
and philosopher, and John Paul II's close friend—wrote, what characterized the spirit of Solidarity was the emphasis that both believers and nonbelievers put on being truly who they were—faithful to their consciences.
This was, Tischner explained, "not only a social or economic event, but,
above all an ethical one."[57]

Solidarity's orientation toward the realm of the ethical was possible
not only because of the Polish church leaders but also because of the Polish secular thinkers and activists. The latter group, with an especially
outspoken and influential representative in Adam Michnik,[58] helped define Solidarity in two important ways. First, their focus on the dignity of
all Poles, whether religious or nonreligious, enabled the movement to be
an alliance of religious and secular forces against the Polish communist
regime. Second, in the very act of linking Polish Catholicism to the universal Catholic and secular articulations of human dignity and freedom,
figures from John Paul II to Tischner to Michnik provided a platform for
a different, more capacious kind of Polish Catholicism.[59] In the context
of Solidarity, we see the kind of collectivistic Catholicism that is cen-
trally constitutive of Polishness but, although political and particular in
relation to the concrete Polish historical moment and the communist regime in power, this Catholicism was only secondarily a matter of
politics.

Adam Michnik, one of the advisers to Solidarity and a central figure in
the rapprochement of the religious and secular Poles, wrote in the early
years of Polish transition that Solidarity was defined by the "spirit of dialogue, the climate of openness to others' arguments, and conviction that
one who thinks differently is not necessarily an enemy."[60] This openness
of Polish Catholicism toward the secular others, however, cannot be con-
flated with the idea of consensus. The representatives of the Catholic
Church, the Catholic and secular Solidarity leaders, helped articulate ideas
that led toward the religious-secular dialogue, but none of them understood
their common work as a path toward a compromise. What they offered
instead was a distinctly Polish form of dialogue. For Michnik, to open

oneself to dialogue with others who are different is to find a point of meeting with the "the tension of contradiction,"[61] and with "the rigor of brotherhood."[62] For Father Józef Tischner, Michnik's conversation partner and one of his most thoughtful critics, dialogue did not entail losing one's particularity but the ability to look "at myself . . . with the eyes of others, as from the outside."[63] In the case of Solidarity and collectivistic Catholicism it helped engender, pluralism was envisioned and practiced as the encounter with different others in which one is not moving toward harmony or shared identity. Rather, dialogue and common action as its outcome led first and foremost toward one's capacity for reflexivity.

Conclusion: Affirming and Sustaining Differences

It is not surprising that Croatia and Poland have instances in which religious nationalisms merged with the rejection of modernity and rejection of pluralism in the name of traditional religious values. This particular development, as scholars of comparative fundamentalism and of religious revivals suggest, happened in other places.[64] What merits more discussion in the Croatian and Polish cases are two other developments. The first is specific to Croatia and Poland as postcommunist contexts; it concerns the ways in which Catholic actors engage communist legacies and use them as interpretive frameworks for what modernity and secularity are. At least two questions arise in this regard: first, what does secularism mean in relation to the historical experiences and historical legacies of communism? Second, how does the communist-enforced secularization map onto other histories of secularization, especially those that occurred within the framework of liberal democracies?

   The second moment that needs more exploration has to do with the dynamics involved in the Croatian and Polish antimodern collectivistic Catholicisms as they strive to establish the single dominant narrative of belonging—as they link the exclusivist nationalism with the rejection of modernity and the absolute authority of the church's moral doctrines. Although observers sometimes see these phenomena as instances of fundamentalist or conservative Catholicism, I refrained from such categorizations because they indicate not only what the contents of the modern are but also what they should be.[65] Rather than undertaking the work of classification, therefore, I attempted to highlight how collectivistic Catholicisms positioned against the cultural and moral pluralism of modernity end up espousing a homogenizing impulse that they, paradoxically, share with modernity, they so strongly critique.

Charles Taylor speaks of the drive to reform as the democratizing force of Western modernity—as inaugurating a vision of human agency that is capable of transforming the world.[66] But Taylor also states that this drive to reform that brought about a more humanistic perspective to the world also contained another, interventionist drive to make the world more ordered and thus more uniform. Similarly, social theorist Adam Seligman understands the return of group identities in our time as a response to the Western modern impetus to take "difference . . . as either a failure to achieve sameness" or as something that is "most often denied by aestheticizing the category" as "a matter of taste."[67] Scholar of religion Robert Orsi also writes that modernity "likes similarity and in the pursuit of that similarity denies the 'other.'"[68] What is needed, Orsi therefore argues, is that we decenter this view of modernity.[69]

In stating this, Orsi gestures toward the sociological idea that there are many modernitites, not just one—vernacular, contending, *multiple* modernities.[70] Some of the main sources of this sociological insight are religious traditions and the ways in which they particularize patterns of modernization—ways in which those representing religious traditions interpret, critique, reappropriate, and redefine modernity. Collectivistic Christianities, I have argued elsewhere, have done that kind of normative work as well but with various results.[71] As discussed with reference to the Croatian and Polish cases, collectivistic Catholicisms that affirm the religio-national homogeneity as the ideal of social life aim to critique modernity but, in the movement toward the sameness, reinforce and succumb to an aspect of the modern project, especially as they yield to hegemonic discourse of nationalism. With this in mind, it is not surprising that the agendas and methods of Croatian and Polish Catholic Church and Catholic activists look very similar to other antimodern religious movements around the globe.[72]

However, in the cases in which collectivistic Catholicisms asserted their particularity, including religio-national identities, by broadening the discourse toward the particular cultural or ethical horizons, Catholicism was more open to differences and pluralism. In the process, these types of collectivistic Catholicisms helped undermine the exclusivist nationalistic agendas, and, as lived and particularized religious traditions, offered both a normative critique of modernity and a possibility to reconstitute it. Put succinctly, the juxtaposition of different types of collectivistic Catholicisms in Croatia and Poland highlighted two themes central to the constructive proposal of this chapter. First, collectivistic religions are lived and changing traditions, and those who articulate and embody them do not develop their agency only through the withdrawal from or rejection of modernity. They do so also in an active and critical contribution to the meanings and institutions of modern social life, showing that Catholicism constitutive of collective identities can widen the ethical and political spaces of agency for religious actors. Second, collectivistic Catholicisms open to others push us to rework normatively how we think of pluralism, its ideals and practices. In the Croatian case, collectivistic Catholicism open to Islam allows for the distinctiveness of both. In the case of the Polish Solidarity movement, those who inhabited religious and secular orientations worked together to define the sense of Polishness, while maintaining the differences between religious and secular identities. In both instances, collectivistic Catholicisms helped shape the norms and practices of pluralism that does not diminish or marginalize but rather affirms and sustains the deep differences.

This model of pluralism is challenging. It proposes that the objective in the encounters with different others is not a transformation and a movement toward some universal notion of humanity but the upholding and understanding of what separates us. Although the latter might not look like a positive account of pluralism, it is an account that underscores that pluralism can be pluralism only if it is constituted by deep differences—only if it turns our encounters with others into an opportunity for reflexivity.[73] In the world defined by culture wars, this understanding of pluralism might not solve all of our problems, but it might offer a chance to fruitfully address at least one type of fundamentalism of which, according to Michnik, most of us, progressives and conservatives alike, are guilty. It is a fundamentalism that blurs "the distinction between the moral norm and the principle of political struggle" and, in the act of moralizing, attributes irreparable flaws only to the other side.[74]

Notes

This essay, first presented at the conference at Fordham University in June of 2016, was made possible through the generous support of the Kroc Institute for International Peace Studies at the University of Notre Dame's Keough School of Global Affairs and the 2016 Luce Visiting Professorship.

1. See Ernest Gellner, *Thought and Change* (London: Weidenfeld and Nicholson, 1964); *Nationalism* (New York: New York University Press, 1997); and *Nation and Nationalism* (Ithaca, NY: Cornell University Press, 1983); Benedict Anderson, *Imagined Communities* (London: Verso, [1983] 1991); and Anthony Smith, *Nationalism and Modernism: A Critical Survey of Recent Theories of Nations and Nationalism* (London, New York: Routledge, 1998); *Nationalism: Theory, Ideology, History* (Cambridge: Polity Press, 2001); and *Chosen Peoples* (Oxford: Oxford University Press, 2003).

2. See Talal Asad, *Formations of the Secular: Christianity, Islam, Modernity* (Stanford, CA: Stanford University Press, 2003); Saba Mahmood, *Politics of Piety: The Islamic Revival and the Feminist Subject* (Princeton, NJ: Princeton University Press, 2005); Elizabeth Shakman Hurd, *The Politics of Secularism in International Relations* (Princeton, NJ: Princeton University Press, 2008); and Markus Dressler, "Public-Private Distinctions, the Alevi Questions, and the Headscarf: Turkish secularism Revisited," in *Comparative Secularisms in a Global Age*, ed. Linell E. Cady and Elizabeth Shakman Hurd (New York: Palgrave-Macmillan, 2010), 121–41. See also Dressler, "Making Religion through Secularist Legal Discourse," in *Secularism and Religion-Making*, ed. Markus Dressler and Arvind-Pal S. Mandair (Oxford: Oxford University Press, 2011), 187–208; and William Cavanaugh, *Migrations of the Holy: God, State, and the Political Meaning of the Church* (Grand Rapids, MI: Eerdmans, 2011).

3. On the differences among scholars of nationalism, see Slavica Jakelić, *Collectivistic Religions: Religion, Choice, and Identity in Late Modernity* (Farnham, MA: Ashgate, 2010), esp. chap. 1.

4. See Slavica Jakelić, "From Law to Solidarity," in *Law, Religion, and Love: Seeking Ecumenical Justice for the Other*, ed. Paul Babie and Vanja-Ivan Savić (New York: Routledge, 2018).

5. For this line of argument, see Slavica Jakelić, "Secular-Religious Encounters as Peacebuilding," in *Religion, Conflict, and Peacebuilding*, ed. Atalia Omer, Scott Appleby, and David Little (Oxford: Oxford University Press, 2015).

6. On the irony inherent in critiques of modernity, see Atalia Omer's "Modernists Despite Themselves: The Phenomenology of the Secular and the Limits of Critique as an Instrument of Change," *Journal of the American Academy of Religion* 83, no. 1 (2015): 27–71. For the argument about the reductionist way in which the critics of secularism view modernity, see Jakelić, "Secular-Religious Encounters as Peacebuilding."

7. See the responses to my lecture "Sustaining Religious-Secular Pluralism: Beyond the Discourse of Power" on the *Contending Modernities* blog, April 2016, accessed on June 15, 2016: Kyle Lambelet, "Secular, Religious Engagements beyond Power?," http://blogs.nd.edu/contendingmodernities/2016

/04/18/secular-religious-engagement-beyond-power/; Cecelia Lynch, "Recongifuring the Discourse of Power," https://blogs.nd.edu /contendingmodernities/2016/04/18/reconfiguring-the-discourse-of-power/; and Heather Dubois, "St. Hedwig's or St. Casimir's and why the difference matters," http://blogs.nd.edu/contendingmodernities/2016/04/18/st-hedwigs-or -st-casimirs-and-why-the-difference-matters/.

8. For the critical take on these approaches to religious-secular plurality, see Slavica Jakelić, "From Power to the Spaces of the Ethical," *Contending Modernities*, May 2016, accessed June 16, 2016, http://blogs.nd.edu /contendingmodernities/2016/05/06/from-power-to-the-spaces-of-the-ethical/.

9. Janet Jakobsen and Ann Pellegrini, "Introduction: Times like These," in *Secularisms*, ed. Janet Jakobsen and Ann Pellegrini (Durham, NC: Duke University Press, 2008), 1–35.

10. I am grateful to Grace Davie for this point about my *Collectivistic Religions*; see Davie, "A Response to Slavica Jakelić's *When Religion Is Not a Choice*," accessed August 20, 2016, https://divinity.uchicago.edu/sites/default /files/imce/pdfs/webforum/112010/Davie%20Response%20to%20Jakelic.pdf.

11. Charles Taylor, *A Secular Age* (Cambridge, MA: Belknap Press), 2007.

12. For one of the earliest and most influential conceptualizations of the agency of religion, see R. Scott Appleby, *The Ambivalence of the Sacred: Religion, Violence, and Reconciliation* (Lanham, MD: Rowman and Littlefield, 2000).

13. Jakelić, *Collectivistic Religions*.

14. See Petrovich in Vjekoslav Perica, *Balkan Idols* (Oxford: Oxford University Press, 2002), 5.

15. Among the causes were the collapse of communism in Yugoslavia and the breakdown of the Yugoslav federation. For a detailed analysis of the causes of war in Croatia, see Ozren Žunec, "Rat u Hrvatskoj 1991–1995. 1. Dio: Uzroci rata i operacije do sarajevskog primirja," *Polemos* 1, no. 1 (January–June 1998): 74.

16. For the example of the Bishop of Šibenik, Srećko Badurina, see his interview in *Vjesnik*, August 14–15, 1995, 6–7; for the example of priests Stjepan Kožul and Josip Ćorić, see Perica, *Balkan Idols*, 193.

17. See Josip Beljan, writer for the popular Croatian Catholic magazine *Veritas*, as quoted in Mitja Velikonja, *Religious Separation and Political Intolerance in Bosnia-Herzegovina* (College Station: Texas A&M University Press, 2003), 269–70.

18. Velikonja.

19. See the announcement for the Walk for Life on the website of one of the supporting Catholic lay organizations, accessed August 25, 2016, http://vigilare .org/en/vijest/hod-za-zivot-2016/.

20. Ana Brakus, "Hodom za život Željka Markić izašla je iz ormara," *Faktograf*, January 22, 2016, accessed August 21, 2016, http://faktograf.hr/2016 /06/10/zeljka-markic-zabrana-pobacaj/Faktograf.

21. Jadranka Rebeka Anić, "Gender, Gender 'Ideology' and Cultural War: Local Consequences of a Global Idea—Croatian Example," *Feminist Theology* 24, no. 1 (2015): 7–8.

22. Anić.

23. "Crkva pobijedila državu: Ustavni sud ukinuo zdravstveni odgoj!," tportal.hr, May 22, 2013, accessed September 15, 2016, http://www.tportal.hr /vijesti/hrvatska/263280/Ustavni-sud-ukinuo-zdravstveni-odgoj.html.

24. Brakus, "Hodom za život Željka Markić izašla je iz ormara."

25. Anić, "Gender, Gender 'Ideology,' and Culutral War," 11.

26. See Anić, *Kako razumjeti rod? Povijest rasprave i različita razumijevanja u Crkvi* (Zagreb: Institut društvenih znanosti Ivo Pilar, Biblioteka Centra za religijske studije Knjiga 2, 2011).

27. Anić, 13.

28. Anić, 13.

29. See Josip Markotić, "Komu smeta kritika rodne ideologije?," Bitno.net, accessed September 15, 2016, https://www.bitno.net/vjera/formacija/komu -smeta-kritika-rodne-ideologije/; and "Osvrt fra Roščića na novu knjigu Gabriele Kuby," Laudato.hr, accessed September 15, 2016, http://www.laudato .hr/Novosti/Kultura/Osvrt-fra-Roscica-na-novu-knjigu-Gabriele-Kuby.aspx.

30. See Stanisław Burdziej, "Voice of the Disinherited? Religious Media after the 2005 Presidential and Parliamentary Elections," *East European Quarterly* 40, no. 2 (June 2008): 208.

31. Slawomir Sierakowski, "Poland's Culture War Rages On," *New York Times*, July 3, 2014, accessed September 2, 2016, http://www.nytimes.com/2014 /07/04/opinion/slawomir-sierakowski-polands-culture-war-rages-on.html. Rydzyk's media network included the daily *Nasz Dziennik* ("Our Daily") and an association of the station's listeners, Rodzina Radia Maryja (The Family of Radio Marya). See Burdziej, "Voice of the Disinherited?" 208.

32. Michele Dillon, "Cultural Differences in the Abortion Discourse of the Catholic Church: Evidence from Four Countries," special issue, *Sociology of Religion* 57, no. 1 (Spring 1996): 29.

33. Dillon, 30–31.

34. Dillon, 32.

35. Dillon, 32.

36. Bishops quoted in Dillon, 32.

37. Sierakowski, "Poland's Culture War Rages On."

38. Dillon, 25–36.

39. On Adam Michnik's lecture "After the Election of Pope Francis: What Paths for the Catholic Church?," held in 2013 at the New School, see Helen Chmielewska-Szlajfer, "Adam Michnik on the Church: The Opening of a Polish Dialogue," Deliberately Considered, May 6, 2013, accessed August 20, 2016, http://www.deliberatelyconsidered.com/2013/05/adam-michnik-on-the -church-the-opening-of-a-polish-dialogue/.

40. More than 70 percent of Poles disapproved of the manner in which the church threw itself into the political life of democratic Poland. See Wanda Nowicka, "Roman Catholic Fundamentalism Against Women's Reproductive Rights in Poland," *Reproductive Health Matters* 4, no. 8 (November 1996): 22.

41. José Casanova, *Public Religions in the Modern World* (Chicago: University of Chicago Press, 1994). In my *Collectivistic Religions*, I use some of Casanova's observations to interpret the developments within the European collectivistic Christianities.

42. Chris Hann, "Problems with the (De)privatization of Religion," *Anthropology Today* 16, no. 6 (December 2000): 16.

43. The Catholic Church as well as Catholic activists also join forces in the attempts to control the domain of arts and culture they perceive as anti-Christian. See Sierakowski, "Poland's Culture War Rages On."

44. Siniša Zrinščak, "Re-Thinking Religious Diversity: Diversities and Governance of Diversities in 'Post-Societies,'" in *Religious Pluralism: Framing Religious Diversity in the Contemporary World*, ed. Giuseppe Giordan and Enzo Pace (Cham: Springer, 2014), 12.

45. "Islamophobia Threatens Democracy in Europe, Report Says," *Washington Post*, April 13, 2016, accessed June 12, 2016, https://www.washingtonpost.com /news/worldviews/wp/2016/04/13/islamophobia-threatens-democracy-in-europe -report-says/.

46. "Swiss Ban Building of Minarets on Mosques," *New York Times*, November 30, 2009, accessed June 12, 2016, http://www.nytimes.com/2009/11 /30/world/europe/30swiss.html.

47. In Croatia, there are 30,000 Muslim Bosniaks, 10,000 Muslim Croats, 10,000 Muslim Albanians, 6,700 Muslims by nationality, 5,000 Muslim Roma, as well as some Turkish, Macedonian, and Montenegrin Muslims.

48. "U Rijeci otvorena najljepša džamija u Europi," Jutarnji, accessed January 15, 2016, http://www.jutarnji.hr/vijesti/hrvatska/foto-u-rijeci-otvorena -najljepsa-dzamija-u-europi-na-svecanost-doslo-20-tisuca-vjernika/1143017/; "N Islamski centar u Rijeci ponosna je cijela Hrvatska," Novilist, accessed January 15, 2016, http://www.novilist.hr/Vijesti/Hrvatska/dr.-Aziz-ef. -Hasanovic-Na-Islamski-centar-u-Rijeci-ponosna-je-cijela-Hrvatska.

49. See, for example, Aziz ef. Hasanović's 2016 interview, "Zagrebački muftija Aziz ef. Hasanović: Muslimani žele biti dio rješenja, a ne dio problema," Faktor, accessed June 12, 2016, http://www.faktor.ba/vijest/zagrebacki-muftija -aziz-ef-hasanovic-muslimani-zele-biti-dio-rjesenja-a-ne-dio-problema-203900.

50. Ivo Banac, *The National Question in Yugoslavia: Origins, History, Politics* (Ithaca, NY: Cornell University Press, 1984), 361.

51. Banac, 362.

52. On this idea of one the greatest Croatian national ideologues, Starčević, see Banac, 363–64.

53. I am grateful to George Demacopolous for this question.

54. On the historical and contemporary role of the Bosnian Franciscan community "Silver Bosnia" in articulating this vision of pluralism, see my *Collectivistic Religions*, especially chaps. 2 and 3.

55. For the account of the meaning Polak-Katolik in the context of Solidarity, I draw on my earlier work, especially "Catholicism and Belonging, in this World," in *Beyond the Borders of Baptism: Catholicity, Allegiances, and Lived Identities*, ed. Michael Budde (Eugene, OR: Cascade, 2016).

56. Jane Barnes and Helen Whitney, "John Paul II and the Fall of Communism," Frontline, accessed February 17, 2019, http://www.pbs.org/wgbh /pages/frontline/shows/pope/communism/.

57. Józef Tischner, "The Ethics of Solidarity," *Thinking in Values*, no. 1 (2007): 38.

58. Adam Michnik, *The Church and the Left* (Chicago: University of Chicago Press, 1993). Michnik's book gave an important impetus for the opening of the Polish secular Left toward the Catholic Church.

59. Which is why in 1980s Poland, nobody found it surprising that Cardinal Wyszyński could receive a delegation of pious Catholics and Jewish socialists and hand out to all of them a copy of the signed Bible. See Timothy Garton Ash, *The Polish Revolution: Solidarity* (New Haven, CT: Yale University Press, 2002), 89.

60. Adam Michnik, "Market, Religion, and Nationalism: Fundamentalism in the New European Order," *International Journal of Politics, Culture, and Society* 8, no. 4 (Summer 1995): 532.

61. Tadeusz Mazowiecki quoted in Michnik, *Church and the Left*, 183.

62. Adam Michnik, foreword to Józef Tischner, *Marxism and Christianity: The Quarrel and Dialogue in Poland* (Washington, DC: Georgetown University Press, 1987), ix.

63. Tischner, 152.

64. Martin Riesebrodt, "Fundamentalism and the Resurgence of Religion," *Numen* 47, no. 3 (2000): 269–70.

65. Robert Orsi, "The Disciplinary Vocabulary of Modernity," *International Journal* 59, no. 4 (Autumn 2004): 879–85.

66. Taylor, *Secular Age.*

67. Adam Seligman, "Particularist Universalism: A Response to Abdullahi Ahmed An-Na'im," *Common Knowledge* 11, no. 1 (Winter 2005): 81–88.

68. Orsi, "Disciplinary Vocabulary of Modernity," 883.

69. Orsi, 883.

70. S. N. Eisenstadt, "Multiple Modernities," *Daedalus* 129, no. 1 (2000): 1–30; Dominic Sachsenmaier, Jens Riedel, and Shmuel N. Eisenstadt, *Reflections on Multiple Modernities: European, Chinese, and Other Interpretations* (Leiden: Brill, 2002).

71. See my *Collectivistic Religions.*

72. Gabriel A. Almond, R. Scott Appleby, Emmanuel Sivan, *Strong Religion: The Rise of Fundamentalisms Around the World* (Chicago: University of Chicago Press, 2003).

73. I draw here on William Connolly's discussion on deep pluralism, in his *Pluralism* (Durham, NC: Duke University Press, 2005).

74. Michnik, "Market, Religion, and Nationalism," 539.

What Difference Do Women Make? Retelling the Story of Catholic Responses to Secularism

Brenna Moore

In the Western European context, the plotline involving the Catholic Church's response to secularism unfolds, more or less, along these lines: for most of the modern period, the church promoted a kind of aggressive counter-revolution in which it cast itself as the besieged victim of secular modernity.[1] A bit of a caricature, to be sure, but examples from the infamous nineteenth-century pope Pius IX abound, and Rome's hostility continued well into the next century.[2] Things began to change, the story continues, in the 1930s, 1940s, and 1950s, when a network of Catholic intellectuals working in Germany, Belgium, and France inspired a renaissance that initiated a movement for renewal and made a decisive contribution to the reforms of the Second Vatican Council.[3] These thinkers engaged the challenges of secular modernity by drawing on language that was more universal in tone, steering the conversation in another direction, and casting aside the countercultural defensiveness. Philosophers such as Jacques Maritain (1882–1973) and Emmanuel Mounier (1905–1950), for instance, adopted the language of the human person made in the image of God to ground human dignity and eventually assert the universalism of human rights. Their model of the human person was not only eventually embraced among Catholics, but as historians have recently argued, it also became ultimately responsible for elevating the prominence of human rights in Western liberal democracy.[4]

Today, however, most would agree that this renaissance of deeply influential Catholic engagement with secular modernity is now thoroughly behind us. In the European context, scholars have described Catholicism

60

as almost "disappearing" if not at least entirely "irrelevant" since the 1960s.[5] Describing the widespread "declining identification with the institution of the Church,"[6] scholars cite statistics from places such as France, once the epicenter of Catholic renewal, where today less than 5 percent of the population attends mass.[7] Although Pope Francis is revitalizing somewhat the more open-minded spirit of the early Vatican II pioneers, at least in Europe, it may be too little too late, and the possibility of a politically and culturally relevant Catholicism seems remote, and if it continues to exist it would perhaps be in the southern hemisphere.[8]

What happens, though, if we introduce women as thinkers and protagonists into the story of the Catholic responses to secularism in Europe? How does the story change? What happens if we pay attention to how gender and sexuality are threaded into the narrative? What differences emerge? These are the key questions I want to address in this chapter. Despite widespread assumptions, Catholicism has *not* disappeared in Western Europe, even in the most putatively secular of countries, France. Indeed, the church is playing a prominent role in an international, deeply political movement rallying against what has been called the "theory of gender."[9] More than most realize, because its activism is often behind the scenes, the church in secular Europe and around the globe plays a prominent role in international efforts to defend the primacy of the heterosexual, reproductive nuclear family, and to advance the anthropology of gender complementarity, rooted in the differences between men and women at the biological, psychological, and even ontological levels. It aims not only to influence the sphere of sexuality and gender relations among the faithful but also secular law.[10] Like the mid-century Catholic advocates of human rights, these Catholic gender activists today draw on the philosophy of Catholic personalism, espoused originally by Jacques Maritain and Emmanuel Mounier from the 1930s to the 1950s. But as Camille Robcis has recently shown, Catholic personalism, a central feature of the intellectual renaissance that laid the foundations for Vatican II, is filtered in today's political climate through the ideas of John Paul II.[11] It is appropriated for an agenda very different from what personalists such as Maritain had in mind. I am not concerned about the purity of Catholic personalism, for ideas often go on to have complex and surprising afterlives. But if we look at how the conceptual features of personalism such as relationality, the person, communion, and love were used from the 1930s to the 1950s, and see how they are marshaled today in "secular" Europe against what is disparagingly called "the theory of gender," suddenly the current Catholic approaches to women, gender, and sexuality on the far right do not seem so inevitable or natural; they actually seem odd and deeply ironic.

Illuminating the depth of the irony requires digging into the theological sources from the 1930s to the 1950s, and what the sources reveal is that heterosexual, procreative matrimony was not the primary site of Christian relationality, as current movements would have it. I have found instead that it was actually friendship. And here lies the heart of my argument: despite the fact they have been tethered to another agenda, it was through their intimate friendships above all that men and women of the mid-century intellectual renewal in France sought to apprehend God's presence, and felt themselves taken in, with one another, to the mystical body of Christ and live out the Christian vocation.[12] The intimacy among friends was more than a trope or a symbol of another, more real kind of love: it was a fundamental, experiential way of communing with one another and most importantly, with God. The complimentary of differences between men and women and heterosexual marriage instrumentalized biologically for children, were not prioritized. If anything, they were denigrated as Protestant. Unearthing this "archive of love" among friends, as I call it, is not an answer to every question we have today about secularization, religion, gender, and sexuality, but it undeniably opens up possibilities to imagine other forms of Catholic intimacy besides the one constantly paraded before us on the international political and religious stage as a "Catholic" reaction to secular modernity. It also breaks apart secularism's triumphal narrative that, on the one hand, sees religion as the problem for women, gender, and sexuality, and, on the other hand, secularism as the only solution. However, none of these insights are available to us unless we include women in our telling of the story of religion and secularism. Despite the fact that the narrative of secularism is regularly rehearsed as if it could be, it will never be complete without attention to women, gender, and sexuality.[13]

Women, Gender, and Sexuality: Rethinking Catholicism and the Secular

Placing women, gender, and sexuality at the center of an analysis of Catholicism and secularism does not merely diversify the otherwise largely male and clerical intellectual world (although it does this of course) but it actually gets to the heart of religion and secularism itself. For instance, as

Tracy Fessenden, Linell Cady, and Janet Jakobsen have argued, secularism's privatization of religion constrained religion to find expression in the private sphere and locate its disciplinary, regulatory power exclusively in that domain.[14] The private sphere not only includes conscience and belief but also signifies women's bodies, family life, normative relations between men and women, and intimacy. As the church intervenes in contemporary movements regulating gender and sexuality, it is perfectly fulfilling its assigned role, defending the narrow turf secularism has allotted it. The fixation on regulating the sphere of women, gender, and sex is the church's compliance with the plan of secularism.

Today, the church defends this ground with far-reaching critiques that extend beyond the particular issues of contraception, abortion, and gay marriage. In 2013, for example, the French Catholic activist organization Manif pour Tous (Protest for All) organized a massive rally in Paris with three hundred thousand people protesting France's Mariage pour Tous (Marriage for All) legislation, extending marriage to same-sex couples.[15] In the case of Catholic activists in Europe associated with Manif pour Tous, their campaigns, for example, focus on a much broader critical assessment, what they call the "theory of gender" (*théorie du genre*).[16] In the movement's founding document published in November 2013, *L'idéologie du genre: La Manif pour Tous*, they explained that their activism had to be directed to something much more foundational and philosophical rather than the immediate, political issues. One pillar they targeted in particular was individualism ("*l'ultra-individualisme*"), which pulls families out from their natural, relational setting where their bonds of intimacy are heterosexual and familial, and sexuality remains tethered to its biological procreative ends.[17] Their critiques also gather around social constructionism, which aims, according to their literature, "to deny the rootedness of femininity and masculinity in the natural, sexed body." It generates a "dangerous" notion that "the pure, given body has no intrinsic value."[18] The putative individualism/atomism (rather relational or communal anthropology) and its denial of biological reality is "an ideology that is destructive, obscurantist, anti-social, anti-people, just as it is anti-natural."[19] These are two key underpinnings that animate what Bruno Perreau calls the "fantasy of invasion" by "gender theory" in France.[20]

Humanistic, universalistic language challenging the theory of gender—in terms of nature, sociality, relations, and reality, rather than recognizably Catholic justifications—appears throughout France's active *blogosphère catholique* as well. On May 29, 2013, the popular priestly website padre-blog wrote about the future of Catholic political activism after Mariage pour Tous with a claim that "We must return to *reality* . . . this reality, undermined by a law that institutes the lie of artificial parentage by suggesting that a child can have two moms or two dads."[21] Many activists connect their conservative gender and sexuality activism with Pope Francis's ecological message, and this shared language around nature, biology, reality, ecology floats between these two modes of political protest. On social media, one group, L'Avenir Pour Tous, an offshoot of Manif pour Tous, held up the notion that the "Pope calls us to see our common home the way it is: natural," in an all-encompassing discussion of Pope Francis's writings on the family *and* the environment.[22] This kind of universalistic, natural, and relational language keeps the particularism of Catholicism in the background, but as scholar Danielle Tartakowsky recently put it, "The movement is inconceivable without Catholicism," and crucially, "its success is partly dependent on keeping its religious roots out of sight."[23]

This approach drawing on universalist language of personhood, relationality, nature, communion, and reality as a Catholic approach to politics was promoted with great success by the Vatican II pioneers and Jacques Maritain in particular. Maritain was one of the most prominent Catholic philosophers in the world during the period from the 1930s to the 1950s. A neo-Thomist, he advocated a return to a Catholic philosophy of natural law and "critical realism." He sought to ground philosophy in the sensible world as it is (independent of our mind), and so to offer a critique of idealism. In addition to a realism grounded in natural law, Maritain also put forward an anthropology that was at its core deeply relational rather than individualist. In *The Person and the Common Good* (1947), Maritain described the "fundamental distinction between personalism and individualism." Mere individuals, he wrote, are isolated units of society, but persons by their very nature are made by and for others. The "essence of personhood" is its need for communion with others, it "requires with *other* and *the others* . . . it requires a dialogue in which souls really communicate." Relationality is rooted in the persons' dignity as made in the image of God, which means resembling the other-oriented God of love in communion. Communion with others and with God is therefore, according to Maritain and the personalists, a fulfillment of the fundamental nature of personhood.[24] Maritain's realism, grounded in the sensory world as it is (natural law) *and* an anthropology that is thoroughly relational, would become an influential way that European Catholic intellectuals and activists would approach politics in the years to come. Pope John Paul II, for example, lists Maritain among the "great Christian thinkers" in his 1998 encyclical *Fides et Ratio* (Faith and Reason).[25] By the late 1990s, John Paul II had been engaging Maritain's concepts of Catholic personalism—its relational anthropology and its realism rooted in nature—for decades, particularly in his writings on women, gender, and sexuality: *Love and Responsibility* (1981) and *The Theology of the Body: Human Love in the Divine Plan* (1997). John Hellman sees in Pope John Paul II a "reincarnation" of Jacques Maritain, and Brooke Williams Deeley, in her introduction to a collection of John Paul II's writings on women, argues that the pope "advances discourse in continuity with groundwork laid by Maritain . . . on the centrality of *relation* to our understanding of the person."[26] John Paul II, she writes, is "following in the footsteps of Maritain" while also moving "in a new direction."[27] Sr. Prudence Allen states it more strongly in an essay showing how Maritain, in his anthropology and in his own marriage, provided the ideal blueprint for Catholic teaching on sexuality and gender, particularly gender complementarity, which John Paul II later perfected and carried out.[28] Scholars across the spectrum draw a fairly straight line from Maritain to the pope's teaching on women, gender, and sexuality.[29]

To be sure, Pope John Paul II drew deeply from Maritain's relational anthropology and realism, but what these scholars miss, and what Camille Robcis has so usefully highlighted, is that by the 1980s, in response to the changing political and cultural scene, John Paul II began to weave sexual difference and gender complimentary into his relational anthropology, and move the procreative ends of sex closer to the center of his understanding of communion. This was quite new. John Paul II sexualized the personalism of earlier decades, or more specifically he heterosexualized it. As Robcis puts it, "he redefined the social as fundamentally heterosexual."[30] Maritain's relational self became now a "unity of two," as Pope John Paul II wrote in his 1995 *Letter to Women*, written on the occasion of the World Conference on Women in Beijing. The pope's "unity of two" is the one to whom "God has entrusted the world of procreation and family life, and the creation of history itself."[31] The person finds its full realization not only

in relation with another and with God, but through, "the duality of the
masculine and feminine." This duality is founded on complementarity and
difference: "Womanhood and manhood are complementary not only from
the physical and psychological points of view, but also from the ontological."[32] This intricately woven matrix of procreation, family, and gender
complementarity at the very *ontological* heart of selfhood, God's design,
and history itself undergirds the church teachings on marriage, contraception, and abortion rooted in this particular theology of personhood and
love. This emphasis is simply absent in the early personalists.

But unlike almost any other kind of abstract theological anthropology,
this one actually materialized in the international organizations Pope John
Paul II founded to promote his vision of intimacy among Catholic families
around the world, and to advance its legislative protection in law. Its power
is felt at the United Nations where, because of the territory it oversees in
Vatican City, unlike all other religions, which are only entitled to limited
privileges of nongovernmental organizations, the Catholic Church enjoys
considerable political power, almost on equal footing with nations. The
Holy See has the right to participate in and formally address General Assembly debates, to intervene in discussions that proceed through consensus, participate in all meetings open to nations, can circulate proposals as
official documents, and cosponsor resolutions. Again and again, the Holy
See has participated in international conferences on population, development, women, and global health and has obstructed measures that challenge church teachings on these topics.[33] Its power too is felt around the
world when Catholic leaders vote on legislation that enshrines church teachings in secular law, as in the Philippines and El Salvador.[34] The church
also supports more than three hundred thousand health facilities around
the world, mostly serving the poor, and has made it clear that they would
close facilities before succumbing to external pressures to offer contracep-
tive services.[35]

When we look at women, gender, and sexuality in an analysis of secularism and Catholicism, we see neither the total disappearance of the church
nor its irrelevance but an astounding fulfillment of its promise to be a "sign
of contraction" with secularism on issues of gender and sex, as promised
in *Humanae Vitae* [1968].[36] But it does so by drawing on, and modifying,
the universalistic language of nature, relationships, sociality, intimacy, and
reality supplied by postwar personalists such as Maritain.

Imagining Other Possibilities: Love and Friendship in the French Catholic Revival

The political power of these ideas has made it so that some ways of thinking about Catholicism and intimacy seem inevitable, and others seem completely inconceivable. It is embedded in everyday habits of thinking that religion, and Catholicism in particular, is the problem for women, gender, and sexuality, and secularism is the only answer. We tend to frame secularism and religion as adversaries over who controls policies affecting women, sexuality, and gender.[37] So where might we look for thinking and practices outside this old logic? Can we imagine other forms of personhood and intimacy, beyond those supplied by the secular or the conservative Catholic imagination?

In looking for alternatives, we can even stick with the intellectual vitality of Catholicism and personalism in the 1930s, 1940s, and 1950s that laid the foundation for Vatican II. To enter into this theological world, we have first to recognize that this was a robust intellectual community that included both men and women. My research on this community began years ago with Raïssa Maritain (1893–1960), the scholar, poet, contemplative, and wife of Jacques Maritain. The Maritains were married in 1904 but in 1912, the year they became Benedictine oblates, they took a vow of celibacy that held for the remaining forty-eight years of their marriage, a loving relationship that only ended after Raïssa's death. They never had children. As the Catholic definition of marriage becomes more and more about physical complementarity and procreation, was the marriage of the Maritain's even sacramental? The notion of forgoing sex in a marriage for higher ideals of the love of God was called at the time a *"mariage blanc."* It was not entirely uncommon, and most of the intellectuals in this network were highly skeptical of both Protestantism and the secular state, and they saw in Protestantism a compulsion toward marriage and reproductive sexuality in a directly focused opposition to the Catholic monastic and clerical ideal. For Luther, "be fruitful and multiply" was more than a command from God; it was a divine ordinance built into our very selves, as impossible to overcome as the need for sleep, and the celibacy of monks and nuns was indeed "wretched by its very nature."[38] Luther's theology of sexuality and marriage was a target of Maritain's critiques in *Three Reformers: Luther, Descartes, Rousseau* written in 1928, sixteen years into his and Raïssa's vow of celibacy.[39] In addition to Luther, they also recoiled at French acquiescence to this ideal in the 1930s and 1950s when the nation invested in campaigns promoting marriage and children the site for rebuilding a postwar nation.[40] In contrast to the sexually reproductive matrimonial ideal, the Maritains instead formed what they called "a little flock" (*le petit troupeau*) of three, and their household included Raïssa, her sister Vera, and Jacques. They lived by a strict daily program of prayer, meditation, mass, spiritual reading and silent recollection, all carefully organized by Raïssa. They were not alone. Many deeply religious, intellectual men and women in their network also refused the directive tracks of family and children, including their friends the medievalists Marie Magdeline Davy (1903–1998) and Marie-Thérèse d'Alverny (1903–1991), both students of Étienne Gilson, and the philosopher Simone Weil (1909–1943), Catholic sculptor Marek Szwarc (1892–1958), the novelist Julien Green (1900–1998), not to mention the countless celibate clergy and members of religious orders in their friendship circle.[41]

The intimate communities I have studied included men and women, mostly laypeople, but it was only by looking at women's writings alongside those of men that brought the spiritual significance of friendship to the surface. Raïssa Maritain, for example, chose friendship as the way to organize the retelling of her spiritual autobiography that appeared in 1942 as *Les grandes amitiés* (*Great Friendships*).[42] I quickly discovered that this was merely the tip of the iceberg; it was everywhere in this community. The idea that the most powerful setting for the Christian to live out her personalist vocation for communion would be friends came to many intellectuals in this context through the controversial Catholic novelist Léon Bloy (1864–1917), the Maritains' godfather. Bloy had a major role in the cultivation of religious sensibilities in this community. When spiritual seekers came to Bloy (and there were many, he was a well-known Catholic in the early twentieth century), he advised that the first step for the spiritual seeker was to leave one's blood family to forge a "*nouvelle famille spirituelle*" based on friendship.[43] Bloy orchestrated these friendship circles among adult Catholics in his life, giving people new "brothers and sisters," forging a "strong spiritual kinship" that constituted a "spiritual initiation" to Christianity.[44] One friend wrote about the friendship circle Bloy cultivated for him in a 1917 memoir, "Bloy's wife Danish, my own wife Flemish and French, Raïssa and Vera, Russian Jews, Jacques Protestant French, and we formed together one great big family [*une seule grande famille*]." Within the setting of new kinship forged outside of the confines of marriage and birth (a "core spiritual family"), "apparently life was as it was before," one friend recalled, "but everything was transformed. It was extraordinary! Every idea, every attitude, inner or outer, every action, even the most common and daily activity, was totally different. All things now had meaning, and operated in a climate far more exhilarating and more real."[45] Moreover, it was not merely the women who were in charge with loving due to their nature or some "feminine genius"; in his letters to Raïssa, her sister, and Jacques, Bloy too, as would other men, lavished his affections on his friends. "I want to take you into my lion paws, you, Vera, and Jacques, and devour you lovingly," he wrote.[46] He signed his notes with "Tender kisses to my spiritual children."[47] Intimacy among friends forged the material out of which religious experience was enacted. It was more than learning *about* Christianity from a friend. The intimacy of friendship was the apprehension and realization of Christianity. Bloy had set the stage from 1900 to 1917.

Countless letters and memoirs from the next generation of Catholics reveal the prominence of affectively charged communities of friends rather than the nuclear family whose explicit aim was to inculcate both Love and God in community. One example is found in the massive corpus of beautiful letters we have between Jacques Maritain and the fiction writer Julien Green.[48] Green met Jacques in 1926 and the two had a close bond for almost fifty years, until Maritain died in 1973. Green, like so many, had come to Maritain with religious questions. Green immediately felt his friend to be *the* galvanizing force for his own faith. Maritain kept trying to send Green to a priest for his religious questions, but Green only wanted Maritain. "For me as for so many others, *you* have been God's friend and witness!"[49] Again it is not just that Maritain as his friend taught Green "about" God or about Catholic belief. Their relationship *created experiences* of God for him. As Green confessed to Maritain, "It is God Who has placed us on one another's path, so that you might speak to me, and speak to me in His place. Of that I am very sure."[50]

Over the decades, the experiences grew more and more mutual. Maritain, a man celebrated as the radiating center for so many mid-century Catholic friends, wrote to Green in 1970, "At the end of life, I see more clearly than ever what grace and what sweetness from heaven your blessed friendship is for me. You are constantly in my heart and in my prayers. I would gladly give my life for you if it were worth anything."[51] The sacred media of Christianity—sweetness, grace, gifts from Heaven, blessings—came to

Maritain *through* Green. What or who is in Jacques's inner life (his prayers and heart)? "You are" he tells Green, "constantly." When Jacques Maritain died, Greene, who was gay but lived with his sister all his life wrote, "Maritain is dead. His hand will never again cover mine affectionately; he will never again throw kisses to me, when leaving in the street."[52]

Religiously significant love between friends, to be sure, took work. In addition to face-to-face meetings and signs of affection (hands touching, blowing kisses), friends sustained their love and communicated its spiritual worth through letters to one another, photos of one another, and little sacred objects tucked in the letters they exchanged. These material objects created a visible, tangible climate of religiously meaningful relationships. When friends went to the home of the Maritains, framed photos of friends were placed within group frames of recognizable holy figures, such as Thomas Aquinas, Teresa of Avila, the pope. When Green received a long-requested photo of Jacques, he proclaimed that the portrait "captures those traits of the inner man which has had an influence on all of us. It too, it is a faithful reflection of your physical presence which is so dear to us."[53] The handwritten letters themselves, according to Green, were "full of treasures, treasures of grace." Raïssa Maritain often mailed friends letters containing spiritual advice and prayer cards, pictures of saints, a written transcription of prayers in Latin. These letters too were "treasures," according to one friend, which he "guarded with his life."[54]

The letters exchanged between friends separated by war give particular testimony to the spiritual sustenance friendship provided through the pain of exile. The Cardinal Charles Journet (1891–1975) and Jacques Maritain had a close friendship for over fifty years and began writing letters in 1920. We have access to their bond in a six-volume series of their correspondence containing 1,774 letters.[55] During the war, Journet remained in Europe while the Maritains were in exile in the United States, where they would remain until Raïssa's death in 1960. After the war, Journet wrote to the Maritains, remembering their times together: masses in Paris, Meudon, and Versailles. "Of these memories of us, they are like stars in the dark night," he wrote. "Your love has always been that you saw me as God wants me to be. . . . Your kindness is a sweet gift from heaven and I want to become every day less unworthy."[56] For his part, Jacques wondered how he and Raïssa could ever explain the joy they received from Journet's letters, which "are graces from God, God, who has given us your marvelous friendship."[57] The feeling was mutual: "I thank you Jacques," because through their relationship, and through their shared relationships with the saints, Journet claims to have learned to "love Love" [*aimer l'Amour*]. Ideals of Love and Friendship were often capitalized, elevating them to the heights of the sacred.[58] "You," Jacques had confided to him a few months earlier, "are our consolation, you are Friendship itself, you are Love itself, [*vous êtes pour nous l'Amitié même*],"[59] Journet, Jacques, and Raïssa regularly signed off their letters with "I embrace you in Jesus Christ," or "sweet friendship in Jesus."[60] For the Maritains, *these* were the bonds that enabled the person to "commune with another and ultimately, with God," to cite Jacques's personalism. Gender complementarity and procreative sexuality were simply not part of this rich and layered world of spiritual kinship.

The religiously significant love between friends helps us envision new ways of thinking about kinship and family in the Catholic responses to secularism. Although the church continues to flex its massive organizational muscle to keep the traditional center and margins of the family circle (the procreative nuclear family in the center, and everything else on the margins) exactly as it is, we have to ask: can we imagine other possibilities of arranging intimate lives, even for Catholics? Judith Butler has described the popular assumption that "kinship does not work, or does not qualify as kinship, unless it assumes a recognizable family form" and cautions against habits of thinking in which "sexuality, kinship, and community" become "unthinkable" if they are outside this familiar frame.[61] Creative imagination for difference helps break apart these routinized ways of thinking.

From the perspective of people such as the Maritains and Bloy, friendship may have been a perfectly natural way to live out their vocations as Christians who were drawn to a relational understanding of the person. They drew from scriptures such as Matthew and Mark's Jesus, who "demanded a readiness to forsake marriage and family" (Mt 10:37). These were Catholics for whom saints and mystics from the medieval period were extraordinarily energizing sources of spiritual and moral rejuvenation, and as Mary Dunn's work has recently shown, the overwhelming tradition in Christianity rejected marriage, reproductive sexuality, and motherhood.[62] Other scholars, such as Brian McGuire, Alan Bray, and Jodi Bilinkoff, have shown that in the medieval and early modern periods in Christian history, friendship in particular provided a rich alternative for spiritually significant intimacy outside the nuclear family, which was for the most part, denigrated.[63] Bray's book gives the most vivid image of the spiritual friendship: priests who had been close friends in life, wanted to lie together in death and share a grave, like John Henry Newman and his friend John St. Ambrose.[64] Today these kinds of spiritual bonds are lost to our imaginations.

Despite the way in which Maritain continues to be marshaled for John Paul II's anthropology, recent research on Maritain's previously unpublished correspondence with Charles Journet reveals Maritain's deep reservations about the church's ban on contraception and insistence on the procreative ends of intimacy, in as early as 1930. But like so many sympathetic male Catholic scholars, Maritain was worried that publically challenging church teachings on sexuality would compromise his authority on issues he deemed more important, such as democracy and human rights.[65] Journet and Maritain "did not dare to make their reservations public," according to the research of Bernard Doering. In the later years surrounding the publication of *Humanae Vitae* in 1968 (five years before Maritain died), Maritain felt "horrified at the thought of butting into something that is not my business," and later decided against writing to his friend Pope Paul VI.[66] But with Maritain's well-known high regard for authority, he accepted the final word of the pope and never published anything on the topic.[67] Catholic teachings on love, gender, and sexuality developed in the subsequent decades under John Paul II, and came to undergird and govern the fundamental issues of theology including anthropology, personhood, relationality, and ontology. This would have been almost too impossible to imagine during Maritain's lifetime.

Conclusion

Upon seeing images of protesters from France in 2013, carrying signs depicting a man, woman, and their baby declaring, "we want sex, not gender!" or "Don't touch our stereotypes!" one can see them as paradigmatic Catholic responses to secularism: its fixation on gender and sexuality, and its insistence on being a force of countercultural critique in this sphere. But bringing to mind figures such as the Catholic personalists—celibates who spent their lives forging "spiritual families" among friends—and knowing that they have become part of the philosophical and anthropological underpinnings of the movement for heterosexuality, biological complimentarity, and procreative sexuality, the word irony came to mind. But as I consider who now suffers under the enormous power of the church's battles to keep intimacy heterosexual, matrimonial, and procreative, I know that a much more somber term is needed. I think of the women throughout Catholic countries in Latin America and the Philippines, who are, in the words of Jennifer Hughes, "on the edge of a reproductive cliff" without access to desperately needed contraception.[68] I think about the women in prison right now in El Salvador who have been found guilty of having abortions in contradiction of national law (sometimes wrongly, having suffered a miscarriage).[69] Or I think of the young girls, undocumented migrants crossing the US border from Central America, who were sexually abused on their journey and denied emergency contraception by the Catholic relief organizations that met them at the border.[70] Catholic teachings on women, gender, and sexuality *have* a power over the world, but a power felt mainly on the bodies of the powerless. An affluent Filipino family has no trouble affording contraception, which is outrageously expensive because the Catholic government will not subsidize it.[71] Wealthy young girls from Central American cities are not on the migrant trail, vulnerable to sexual predators. It is only from the perspective of incredible wealth and privilege that one can see conservative Catholic teachings on intimacy as purely ideological or irrelevant (something that merely "you pretend to preach, and we pretend to obey" in the secular West).[72]

Like so many other Catholics, I too felt huge relief when Pope Francis said we have spent too much time as a church, talking about sexuality, about women, about gender ("it is not necessary to talk about these issues all of the time," he said, in one of his first published interviews.)[73] Pope Francis brought immigration, mercy, and the environment to our conversations about faith and politics. But if we ignore issues of women, gender, and sexuality, they become more hidden, less open to critique. It remains captive to those activists on the right who use it to advance their limited notions of intimacy and men and women's nature. Under the guise of moving on, progressive Catholics unwittingly accept the assumption that thinking about Catholicism and intimacy is the domain of conservative religious regulation. Arguing for attention to more robust "public issues" such as the economy and war, they become complicit in the secularist and conservative religious binaries of private and public.

Admittedly, the friendships I have described do not provide us with a straight line to all the answers, but they help open our imaginations to other models of Catholic love beyond the heterosexual and purely procreative, a kind of love that has nothing to do with gender complementarity. These alternative models of Catholic intimacy, even kinship—Maritain blowing kisses to Green, Bloy devouring them in his lion paws of love—remains illegible on the contemporary religious and sociopolitical landscape. Their bonds of love have faded into obscurity. A resuscitation of these "soul mates" might provide life and energy to those who see the power of some Catholic approaches to modernity, but who dare to imagine the possibilities that might emerge from a larger, more expansive sense of the bonds of affection that make us whole. Now may be the just the right time to rescue them from oblivion.

Notes

Many thanks to John Seitz, Mara Willard, Rachel Smith, and Tamsin Farmer for their invaluable feedback and encouragement on this essay. I also am grateful to the participants of the "Tradition, Secularization, and Fundamentalism" conference sponsored by the Orthodox Christian Studies Center of Fordham University in June 2016, and to organizers and friends Aristotle Papanikolaou and George Demacopoulos. I also thank Mary Kate Holman for her research assistance on the *blogosphère catholique* for this essay.

1. See Joseph A. Komonchak, "Modernity and the Construction of Roman Catholicism," *Cristianesimo nella Storia* 18 (1997): 353–85.

2. See Étienne Fouilloux on the "unbearable" intellectual atmosphere of Rome that persisted well until 1962 in Étienne Fouilloux, *Une église en quête de liberté: La pensée catholique française entre modernisme et Vatican II, 1914–1962* (Paris: Desclée de Brouwer, 1998), 301.

3. For an overview of *la nouvelle théologie*, see Gabriel Flynn and Paul Murray, *Ressourcement: A Movement for Renewal in Twentieth-Century Catholic Theology* (Oxford: Oxford University Press, 2014).

4. A Catholic genealogy of human rights has been celebrated by many Catholics—see, for example, Mary Ann Glendon, "The Influence of Catholic Social Doctrine on Human Rights," *Journal of Catholic Social Thought* 10, no. 1 (2013): 69–84—but for Samuel Moyn and others, it betrays the deep conservatism of human rights discourse and policy; see Samuel Moyn, *Christian Human Rights* (Philadelphia: University of Pennsylvania, 2015).

5. Viggo Mortensen, "From Confessional Ecumenics to Theology of Religions," in *European and Global Christianity: Challenges and Transformations in the 20th Century*, ed. Katharina Kunter and Jens Holger Schjørring (Berlin: Vandenhoeck and Ruprecht Academic, 2011), 365.

6. Matthias Koenig and Wolfgang Knöbl, "Religion, Nationalism, and European Integration," in *Religion and National Identities in an Enlarged Europe*, ed. Willfried Spohn, Matthias Koenig, and Wolfgang Knöbl (New York: Palgrave Macmillan, 2015), 120.

7. Leila Marchand "Plus de la moitié des Français ne se réclament d'aucune religion," *Le Monde,* May 7, 2015, accessed May 10, 2016, http://www.lemonde.fr/les-decodeurs/article/2015/05/07/une-grande-majorite-de-francais-ne-se-reclament-d-aucune-religion_4629612_4355770.html#ehOHTel3KP611Drg.99.

8. John Allen, *The Future Church: How Ten Trends Are Revolutionizing the Catholic Church* (New York: Random House, 2009), 16.

9. Camille Robcis, "Catholics, the 'Theory of Gender,' and the Turn to the Human in France: A New Dreyfus Affair?" *Journal of Modern History* 87, no. 4 (December 2015): 892–923.

10. Mary Ann Case, "The Role of the Popes in the Invention of Complementarity and the Vatican's Anathematization of Gender," *Religion and Gender* 6, no. 2 (2016): 155–72; University of Chicago Public Law Working Paper 565, accessed May 5, 2016, http://papers.ssrn.com/sol3/papers.cfm?abstract_id=2740008.

11. Robcis, "Catholics," 900–23.

12. I explored this theme in Brenna Moore, "Friendship and the Cultivation of Religious Sensibilities," *Journal of the American Academy of Religion* 83, no. 2 (May 2015): 237–63.

13. Women are absent from many of the massive analyses of Christianity and secularism; see, for example, Charles Taylor, *The Secular Age* (Cambridge, MA: Belknap Press, 2007); Thomas Pfau, *Minding the Modern: Human Agency, Intellectual Traditions, and Responsible Knowledge* (South Bend, IN: University of Notre Dame, 2013); and Brad Gregory, *The Unintended Reformation: How a Religious Revolution Secularized Society* (Cambridge, MA: Harvard University Press, 2011).

14. Linell E. Cady and Tracy Fessenden "Gendering the Divide: Religion, the Secular, and the Politics of Sexual Difference," in *Religion, the Secular, and the Politics of Sexual Difference*, ed. Linell E. Cady and Tracy Fessenden (New York: Columbia University Press, 2015), 9.

15. Robcis, "Catholics," 892–93. Céline Béraud and Philippe Portier, "Mariage pour tous: The Same-Sex Marriage Controversy in France," in *The Intimate: Polity and the Catholic Church; Laws about Life, Death and the Family in So-Called Catholic Countries*, eds., Karel Dobbelaere and Alfonso Pérez-Agote (Leuven: Peeters, 2015), 90–124.

16. Often in French activist literature, the term remains Anglicanized and untranslated as "theory of gender," and the activism slides easily into long-standing French anti-American sentiment, signaling native kinship relations are also in danger of "Americanization." For a useful analysis of the French activist literature citing English rather than French, see Robcis, "Catholics," 907. Judith Butler also offers a reading of French anxiety around

the Americanization of French gender norms in "Is Kinship Always Heterosexual?," *differences* 13, no. 1 (2002): 37.

17. *L'idéologie du genre: La Manif pour Tous* (November 2013), 19, accessed August 3, 2016, http://www.laici.va/content/dam/laici/documenti/donna /culturasocieta/francois/LMPT-L-ideologie-du-genre.pdf.

18. *L'idéologie du genre*, 8.

19. *L'idéologie du genre*, 17.

20. Bruno Perreau, "The Power of Theory: Same-Sex Marriage, Education, and Gender Panic in France," in *After Marriage Equality: The Future of LGBT Rights*, ed. Carlos Bell (New York: New York University, 2016), 335.

21. "Manif pour tous: et maintenant?," accessed August 3, 2016, http://www .padreblog.fr/et-maintenant.

22. See, for example, the social media account of *L'Avenir Pour Tous* following the Pope's publication of *Amoris Laetitia*, accessed August 1, 2016, https://twitter.com/AvenirPourTous/status/719442858374262789.

23. Quoted in Alexander Stille, "An Anti-Gay Marriage Tea Party, French Style?," *New Yorker*, March 18, 2014.

24. Jacques Maritain, *Person and the Common Good* (South Bend, IN: University of Notre Dame Press, 1977), 19–22.

25. Pope John Paul II, *Fides et Ratio*, para.74.

26. John Hellman, "The Humanism of Jacques Maritain," in *Understanding Maritain: Philosopher and Friend* (Mason: Mercer University Press), 131; Brooke Williams Deeley, "General Introduction," in *Pope John Paul Speaks on Women* (Washington, DC: Catholic University Press of America, 2014), 10; my emphasis.

27. Williams Deeley, "General Introduction," 10.

28. Sr. Prudence Allen, "A Life Shared: The Complementarity of Jacques and Raïssa Maritain," in *The Wisdom of Youth: Essays Inspired by the Early Work of Jacques and Raïssa Maritain*, ed. Travis Drumsday (Washington, DC: Catholic University Press of America, 2016), 23–48.

29. See the essays in *The Vocation of the Philosopher: From Maritain to John Paul II*, ed. John P. Hittinger (Washington, DC: Catholic University Press of America, 2010).

30. Robcis, "Catholics," 922.

31. Pope John Paul II, *Letter to Women*, para. 8.

32. Pope John Paul II, para. 7.

33. Center for Reproductive Rights, "The Holy See at the United Nations: An Obstacle to Women's Reproductive Health and Rights," briefing paper, August 2000, 7.

34. See the 2014 Amnesty International Report, *On the Brink of Death: Violence Against Women and the Abortion Ban in El Salvador* (2014), 11–13. See also Ana Santos, "Ending a Marriage in the Only Country that Bans Divorce," *Atlantic*, June 25, 2015; and "Birth Control in the Philippines," *Religion and Ethics Newsweekly*, June 12, 2015.

35. Center for Reproductive Rights, "The Holy See at the United Nations," 7.

36. *Humanae Vitae*, para. 18.

37. Cady and Fessenden, "Gendering the Divide," 8. Joan Wallach Scott, "Secularism and Gender Equality," in *Religion, the Secular, and the Politics of Sexual Difference*, 32.

38. Luther, "The Estate of Marriage," [1519] in *Faith and Freedom: An Invitation to the Writings of Martin Luther,* ed. John F. Thornton and Susan B. Varenne (New York: Random House, 2002), 251. During their marriage, the Maritains guarded their vow of celibacy with secrecy, but after Raïssa died, Jacques opened up in Jacques Maritain, "Love and Friendship," in *Notebooks* (New York: Magi Books, 1984), 228.

39. Jacques Maritain, *Three Reformers: Luther, Descartes, Rousseau* (New York: Sheed and Ward, 1928), 9, 171–75.

40. Claire Duchen, *Women's Rights and Women's Lives in France 1944–1968* (London: Routledge, 1994), 64–66. For more on the Catholic promotion of the nuclear family as a response to secularism, see James Chappel's discussion of what he calls "paternal Catholic modernism," in *Catholic Modern: The Challenge of Totalitarianis and the Remaking of the Church* (Cambridge, MA: Harvard University Press, 2018), 59–107.

41. For more on sexuality in this context, see Stephen Schloesser, "'What of that curious craving?': Catholicism, Conversion and Inversion au temps du Boeuf sur le Toit." *Historical Reflections / Réflexions Historiques* 30, no. 2 (2004): 221–53.

42. The first volume of the memoir was published as *Les grandes amitiés* (Paris: Éditions de la Maison Française, 1941), and then translated into English by Julie Kernan as *We Have Been Friends Together* (New York: Longmans Press, 1942). The second volume was issued separately in an English translation by Julie Kernan as *Adventures in Grace (Sequel to We Have Been Friends Together)* (New York: Longmans Press, 1945).

43. See the memoir by Pierre van der Meer de Walcheren, close friend of the Maritains and Bloy, *Journal d'un converti* (Paris, France: Georges Cres, 1917), 22.

44. Pierre van der Meer de Walcheren, *Rencontres* (Paris: Desclée de Brouwer, 1961), 37.

45. van der Meer de Walcheren, *Journal d'un converti*, 22.

46. Léon Bloy, *Lettres à ses filleuls* (Paris: Stock, 1928), 139.

47. Bloy, 139.

48. Jacques Maritain and Julien Green, *The Story of Two Souls: The Correspondence of Jacques Maritain and Julien Green* (New York: Fordham University Press, 1988).

49. Maritain and Green, 141.

50. Maritain and Green, 149.

51. Maritain and Green, 149.

52. Maritain and Green, 270.

53. Maritain and Green, 270.

54. Maurice Sachs and Jacques and Raïssa Maritain, *Correspondance Maurice Sachs/Jacques et Raïssa Maritain, 1925–1938* (Paris: Éditions Gallimard, 2004), 33, 111.

55. Charles Journet and Jacques Maritain *Journet-Maritain Correspondance (1960–1973)*, 6 vols. (Fribourg: Editions Saint-Augustin, 1996–2008).

56. Charles Journet and Jacques Maritain, *Journet-Maritain Correspondance (1940–1949)*, vol. 3 (Fribourg: Editions Saint-Augustin, 1998), 386.

57. Journet and Maritain, 303.

58. Journet and Maritain, 386.

59. Journet and Maritain, 152.

60. Journet and Maritain, 466.

61. Judith Butler, "Is Kinship Always Already Heterosexual?," 14, 40.

62. Mary Dunn, *Cruelest of All Mothers: Marie de l'Incarnation, Motherhood, and Christian Tradition* (New York: Fordham University Press, 2016), 97–99.

63. Brian Patrick McGuire's *Friendship and Faith: Cistercian Men, Women, and Their Stories, 1100–1250* (Farnham: Ashgate, 2002); Jodi Bilikoff, *Related Lives: Confessors and Their Female Penitents, 1450–1750* (Ithaca, NY: Cornell University Press, 2005); Constance Furey, *Erasmus, Contarini, and the Religious Republic of Letters* (Cambridge: Cambridge University Press, 2006); and Alan Bray, *The Friend* (Chicago: University of Chicago Press, 2003).

64. Bray, *Friend*, 294–95.

65. Bernard Doering, "Jacques Maritain and Charles Journet on Human Sexuality," *Theological Studies* 62 (2001): 597–606; Bernard Doering "Maritain, Journet, and *Humanae Vitae*," in *Redeeming Philosophy: From Metaphysics to Aesthetics*, ed. John J. Conley, SJ (South Bend, IN: University of Notre Dame Press, 2014), 150–62.

66. Doering, "Maritain, Journet, and *Humanae Vitae*," 154.

67. Doering, 154.

68. Nancy Scheper-Hughes and Jennifer Scheper Hughes, "The Final Conversion of Pope Francis," *Berkeley Review of Latin American Studies*, Spring 2015, 12–17.

69. Amnesty International Report, *On the Brink of Death: Violence Against Women and the Abortion Ban in El Salvador* (2014).

70. "Suit Challenges U.S. Over Abortions and Birth Control for Immigrant Minors," *New York Times*, June 24, 2016, accessed August 8, 2016, http://www .nytimes.com/2016/06/25/us/suit-challenges-us-over-abortions-and-birth -control-for-immigrant-minors.html.

71. Jamie Manson, "Church's Ban on Contraception Starves Families and Damages Ecosystem," *National Catholic Reporter*, February 6, 2012, accessed August 8, 2016, https://www.ncronline.org/blogs/grace-margins/churchs-ban -contraception-starves-families-and-damages-ecosystem.

72. Peter Steinfelds, *People Adrift: The Crisis of the Roman Catholic Church in America* (New York: Simon and Schuster, 2004), 275.

73. Pope Francis, *A Big Heart Open to God: A Conversation with Pope Francis* (New York: HarperCollins, 2013), 34.

THE SECULAR PILGRIMAGE
OF ORTHODOXY IN AMERICA

Vigen Guroian

The newness to Orthodox Christianity of its cultural station in America cannot be denied. With the notable exception of the Russian mission in Alaska, for the most part the Orthodox Church did not come to America as a mission but followed its people's departure from the homeland often under extremities of war, social upheaval, or natural disaster. There was no preparation for coming here. Whether Orthodox people arrived in America from Russia, Greece, the Middle East, or Armenia, in virtually every case the relocation was something akin to an out-of-body experience. They left behind historical Orthodox cultures and were immersed immediately into a society that the Orthodox faith had no role in shaping, a secular society that bafflingly was also religious, although not in a familiar way.

Perhaps more than any other Orthodox theologian in America of his day, the late Fr. Alexander Schmemann, in his lectures and writings, endeavored to make sense of America's secularism and religiosity: how is it that in America the churches themselves become carriers of secularism? Schmemann described the Orthodox Church's encounter with American secularism as a crisis of faith, even "more radical and decisive," he judged, "than the one brought about by the fall of Byzantium in 1453. The Turkish conquest was a political and national catastrophe, [but] it was not the end, . . . of the 'Orthodox world,'" in other words, "of a culture, a way of life, a world-view integrating religion and life."[1] In America that culture, that integration of religion and life, was gone; no matter the imaginative and sometimes fantastical efforts to keep the old world alive in ethnic conclave or church building.

This anachronistic adherence to regional and national identities ironically, matches Protestantism's divisiveness. For in America both behaviors lend themselves to denominationalism, a phenomenon Orthodoxy has condemned as in conflict with the church's unity in Christ. Schmemann worried about the Orthodox Church's failure to resolve the canonical problem of overlapping dioceses in America, not just because rules are broken but also because this division fosters the perception that Orthodoxy is itself denominational. "It is our betrayal of Orthodoxy, in our *reduction* of it to our petty selfish 'national identities,' 'cultural values,' 'parochial interests,'" Schmemann writes, "that makes it look like another denomination with limited scope and doubtful relevance."[2]

Preceding their arrival in America, the Orthodox churches had experienced nothing comparable to the peculiarly American phenomenon in which a religious body is neither an established church nor a sect but something in between. "Inside" the new denomination there might persist for a time the belief that in the new world it is still a church as it was in the old world; however, in view of an aggregate of other "churches," it can never aspire to be a national ecclesiastical institution as it was in Serbia, Bulgaria, or Greece.[3]

Impressions grow into something akin to a dogma. The belief catches hold that a multiplicity of religious communities is good for America because each represents some part of the truth of Christianity, none the whole of it, or alternatively that each "religion" is true in its own fashion. In any case, the result is that conviction in the catholicity of the church fades even among believers, a telling sign of secularization.

Religion in Secular America

My teacher Will Herberg's classic mid-twentieth-century study of religion—*Protestant, Catholic, Jew*—was among the first books of its kind to analyze the role of denominationalism in evacuating Catholic convictions from churches and relativizing religious belief. Although Schmemann rarely cites Herberg, there is little doubt that he learned from him. Nor does Schmemann tell the entire story of the secular pilgrimage of Orthodoxy in America. How could he? Why would he? He was, after all, first and foremost a liturgical theologian. And although the theme of secularism appears frequently in his writings, Schmemann does not explore in detail theories of secularization. I cannot do much better in this brief space. Nonetheless, in order to better understand the secular pilgrimage of Orthodoxy in America, something needs to be said about the meaning of such pivotal terms as secularization, secularity, and secularism.

Some religionists and social scientists have argued that a distinction must be made between secularity and secularism. They maintain that the *secularity* of America is neutral about religion and affords space for religious belief and practice without intrusive state interference within a religiously pluralistic environment, and that this is a good thing. *Secularism*, they argue, is, by contrast, an ideology opposed to religion or belief in anything transcendent.

I do not think that social reality bears up this distinction. Rather, secularity and secularism go hand in glove; there is no such thing as a secularity that is neutral about religion, here in America, or anywhere else. Nevertheless, secularism is not always antireligious. American secularism, unlike some European varieties, is not antireligious, at least not in the hard sense of that term.

This is another way of saying that secularity is inevitably ideational. I do not see how it could be otherwise. Wherever one finds it, secularity makes claims about the structure of the world and meaning within it, which may or may not be reflected in law and social arrangements. A philosophy of life inevitably accompanies secularity. The *ism* belongs to secularity as the germ to the grain. The *ism* in secular is, as Schmemann writes, "a worldview, and consequently a way of life, which attributes to the basic aspects of human existence such as family, education, science, profession, art,"[4] and the like, an autonomy that may or may not leave room for organized religion.

Talcott Parsons on Secularization

The 1960s was rich in reflection on secularism and religion. The twentieth century sociologist Talcott Parsons was an important contributor to this study. In the mid-1960s, Parsons penned an influential essay titled "Christianity and Modern Industrial Society." In it he dissented from a view commonly held that secularization indicates a decline of religious belief. He argued, instead, that secularization could be, as in America, a process by which religious values become "differentiated" from their core, original communities and spread into society at various levels where they gain autonomy, an independence from the sanction of traditional religious authority. On this basis, Parsons confidently proposed that "in . . . a variety of respects modern society is more in accord with Christian values than its forbearers have been."[5]

I first read Parsons as an undergraduate at the University of Virginia. I was not persuaded by his arguments, although my professors seemed to be. Perhaps this was because, like Parsons, they were Protestants. To begin, the title of Parsons's essay is misleading—"Christianity and Modern Industrial Society" is not about Christianity in general. Parsons's perspective is distinctively Protestant; his suppositions about what a church is are Protestant. To my mind, Parsons sets out to reconstruct Protestantism in order to account for secularity and make a case for Christianity's continued influence, even in the wake of a receding role of the churches in society. His method and analysis reduce the Christian faith to morality. He assumes that a Christian ethos can thrive loosened, separated from the ecclesial body, its sacraments, and the worship that body offers to God. Then again, I doubt Parsons was thinking along these lines when writing. Liberal Protestants such as Parsons might be content with the emulsification of Christianity, even the church itself, into the secularist order. Orthodoxy, at least in its classical expression, cannot.

I have paused to consider Parsons because today one still hears echoes of his argument among church people and from within the academy. More important, Schmemann and Orthodox theology have a very different view on the matter. Pace Parsons, Schmemann does not argue that secularization is a measure of the decline of religion or morality, but he does insist that secularization is incompatible with the Christian vision of life. He maintains that Christian identity originates from and is sustained by worship, in the *lex orandi*, and that secularism is quite simply the *negation* of worship.

This, however, does not mean that secular people are ipso facto irreligious, and that they are not attracted to religious ritual. Many are religious and belong to churches. Some are highly attracted to religious ritual, and dedicated to creating new, more "relevant" forms of worship. Yet, if one digs further, says Schmemann, one finds more often than not that these same persons cling to an understanding of what it means to be human, which precludes any need to pray, and worship becomes not much more than a form of audiovisual assistance to comprehension of religious ideas.

A secularist, on one level, may ascribe to the idea of God that God exists, even that God is the Creator and that God governs the world, yet, on another level, share with nonreligious secular counterparts full confidence in the autonomy of human existence and the self-sufficiency of the world. A secularist of religious belonging might even believe in life after death, allowing that this belief has little or nothing to do with worldly projects of care for the sick or material assistance to the poor. Nor will one find this kind of religious secularist praying for the dead, unless perhaps as prescribed by liturgical forms that he or she is likely to believe are antiquated and need revision.

One might say: "Why, you see, all that I know I know through my senses. I can see the hungry child in front of me. I know what hunger is like. I am connected to the hungry person in front of me by my own experience of the same. I can feed this person. The dead I don't know about." I have heard just this sort of sentiment expressed in a church that prays for the dead at every liturgy.

The opposite of autonomy is theonomy. This is the belief that the fulfillment of human existence, although it begins in this world, is nonetheless wholly dependent upon grace and communion with God. Genuine worship, Schmemann constantly reminds his readers, is not merely a referral of ourselves and the world to God. Secular people that often define themselves as "spiritual" think of worship as an aid to success in their aspirations for worldly happiness and prosperity and their efforts to make this a more just and peaceful world. Both American religion and secularism frequently affirm this serviceableness of religion and prayer.

Rather, worship is the action by which human beings freely submit and dedicate their lives and the life of the world to God. The perfection of our humanity is holiness, the holiness of God, which God communicates to us through the sacraments of baptism, penance, and the Eucharist, especially. Holiness transcends the values of toleration, social justice, and brotherhood held so high by secular America. Secularists and religious people alike will support these values with no need or thought to invoke divinity. Holiness and union with God, which is worship's true aim, is alien to the secular man or woman.

Stated somewhat differently, secularity is the negation, the evacuation from life, of the experience of the world as sacred reality, "participant" in divine reality and "participated in" by the divine. This is the full meaning of what Schmemann means when he says that secularism is "the *negation*

of worship." Orthodox anthropology defines man "as a worshipping being, as *homo adorans*: the one for whom worship 'posits' his [or her] humanity and fulfills it,"[6] Schmemann states. Only through the prayer that
affirms and establishes our and the world's relationship to God is theonomy restored and renewed. Only in this theonomy, which by definition
secularism denies, is human nature completed, or perfected.

The name for this completion or perfection is deification (in Greek:
theosis). From this high standard and goal, one can see how the secular
pilgrimage of Orthodoxy is as great a challenge to the church as was its
struggle in antiquity to define the right belief over against the classical
heresies that threatened the truth of salvation. That struggle was not just
about being linguistically correct. It was about ensuring that the church
be of right mind, be properly prepared to receive and accept the gift of
salvation through Jesus Christ.

For these reasons, Schmemann insists, "Secularism is . . . the greatest
heresy of our time, [and] requires from the Church not mere anathemas,
and certainly not compromises, but above all an effort of understanding
so it may ultimately be overcome by truth."[7] And he adds, "The unique-
ness of secularism, its difference from the great heresies of the patristic age,
is that the latter were provoked by the encounter of Christianity with Hel-
lenism, whereas the former is the result of the 'breakdown' within Christianity itself."[8] Secularism is a "stepchild" of Christianity.[9] It imitates the
Christian virtues. But this is only an imitation because the virtues have
been stripped from the ascetical and spiritual disciplines that remind those
who exercise them of their complete dependence upon God and need to
repent that they may be made holy. Secularism in a religious mode misin-
terprets Christ's promise to his disciples, "Peace I leave you, my peace I
give to you" (Jn 14:27) as a plan for peace in this world. It forgets or over-
looks Christ's admonition that the peace he gives is "not as the world giveth"
(Jn 14:27). The progressivisms of our day owe their inspiration to Christianity. Christianity planted in our Western culture a hope for perfection
by a participation in God's holiness. In a secular age, this is translated into
the expectation that by humanity's efforts alone this perfection, this peace
will be achieved. A belief in history and progress replaces a belief in God
and Providence.

In his best-known book, *For the Life of the World*, Schmemann advises,
"It is indeed one of the grave errors of religious anti-secularism that it does
not see that secularism is made up of *veritas chretiennes devenues folles*, of

Christian truths gone mad, and that in simply rejecting secularism, it in fact rejects certain fundamental Christian aspirations and hopes."[10] Or as G. K. Chesterton put it in *Orthodoxy*: "The modern world is not evil; in some ways the modern world is far too good. It is full of wild and wasted virtues. When a religious scheme is shattered (as Christianity was shattered at the Reformation), it is not merely the vices that are let loose. The vices are, indeed, let loose, and they wander and do damage. But the virtues are let loose also; and the virtues wander more wildly, and the virtues do more terrible damage. The modern world is full of the old Christian virtues gone mad."[11]

Will Herberg's "The American Way of Life"

In *Protestant, Catholic, Jew*, Will Herberg famously introduced the locution "American Way of Life."[12] It is his shorthand way for speaking of the secular religiosity or, viewed from a slightly different perspective, the religious secularity, of America. Herberg's "America is at once the most religious and secular of nations" has been cited a countless number of times since he first made this declaration almost seventy years ago. Herberg explained that the American Way of Life is "not an overt philosophy; [but instead] . . . an underlying, often unconscious, orientation of life and thought. [It] is essentially . . . thinking and living in terms of a framework of reality and value remote from the religious beliefs simultaneously professed."[13] Nor, according to Herberg, is the American Way of Life "a 'common denominator' religion. It is not a synthetic" or syncretistic system, not a composite of beliefs drawn or selected from the major religions in America. It is, rather, "an organic structure of ideas, values, and beliefs" constituting "a faith common to Americans."[14] This "common faith" is the default position of many, if not most, Americans when they are challenged to describe what in religion they believe. Can there be much doubt," Herberg asks rhetorically, "that, by and large, the religion which actually prevails among Americans has lost much of its authentic Christian (or Jewish) content?"[15]

The God of the American Way is "unknown," so he may take many names. There are many idols in the land. The god of the American Way is not the Trinitarian God of Christian Orthodoxy. In its advanced state, the faith of the American Way is a "faith in faith itself." Herberg adds: "Of course religious Americans [may] speak of God and Christ, but what they . . . regard as really redemptive is religion, the 'positive' attitude of *believing*."[16] This is secularism, and the churches in America carry it in their very "bodies."

As I have suggested already, Herberg helped Schmemann to understand the Orthodox experience in America. And, yet, Orthodoxy is virtually absent in *Protestant, Catholic, Jew*. In 1973, as a graduate student in theology at Drew University, I queried Herberg about this. He responded that when, in the 1950s, he was putting together *Protestant, Catholic, Jew*, he judged that the Orthodox had not as yet drawn fully under the aegis of the American Way of Life. They remained in most essentials still an immigrant church not wholly integrated into the familiar American religious panoply.

Herberg makes but one reference to Orthodoxy in *Protestant, Catholic, Jew*. This belongs to a footnote that cites an article whose author is Russian Orthodox. He protests: "'We Orthodox . . . are indignant each time we hear of Three Great Faiths. We know it should be Four, and individually we have tried to convince our fellow-Americans of this. But we have gotten nowhere.'" Herberg interjects: "It would be interesting to discover how Mr. Lewis knows that Orthodoxy 'should be Four'; obviously he takes the American scheme of the three great faiths for granted, and merely wants to add his own as the fourth." Evidently, even as he was writing *Protestant, Catholic, Jew*, Herberg had detected in this writer's frustration a sure sign that Orthodox Americans had begun to conceive of their faith as a worthy adjutant to the American Way. He might easily have added that Mr. Lewis's statement demonstrates how exactly the American Way transforms historical religious identity into its own idolatrous image.

Herberg also told me on this occasion that were he to write a second edition of *Protestant, Catholic, Jew*, he would include Orthodoxy in it much more prominently. Yet he was quite clear, speaking as teacher to student, that this would not be an honor the author bestowed but rather an objectively obligatory amendment to his thesis about how the secularism of the American Way dissipates the confessional muscle of the great religious traditions, Orthodoxy now included.

Peter Berger's "Heretical Imperative"

During the 1980s as I set out to record some of my own thoughts on the subject of religion and secularity in America, I happened upon a small book in the Alderman Library of the University of Virginia by the religious sociologist Peter Berger. It bore the intriguing title *The Heretical Impera-tive*. Like virtually all of the notable books on the subject of religious be-longing in America since *Protestant, Catholic, Jew, The Heretical Imperative* says hardly a word about Orthodoxy, except for one paragraph. In that paragraph Berger muses: "One can only speculate at this point what will happen to . . . Orthodox Christians as they move, with their icons and vestments, onto the centerstage of American religion. [But] one will be on safe ground if one assumes that they will encounter . . . what their prede-cessors, from Puritans to Jews, have encountered—pluralization and *ipso facto* the existential as well as cognitive dilemmas of the Protestant para-digm."[17] Berger already has told the reader that the Protestant paradigm *is* the "heretical imperative" and explained that he is not using the word *heretical* pejoratively or negatively as in historical and dogmatic theology. He points out to the reader that the core meaning of heresy is "to choose," taken from the Greek verb *hairein*.

He then proceeds to demonstrate on historical grounds, which I have no room to enumerate here, that Protestantism, much more so than Roman Catholicism, has had to confront straight on modernity's pressure to deviate from tradition in making *choices* that best serve the prospering of individu-als and the religious community.

Indeed, the heretical imperative arose within the historical circumstances that in Europe gestated Protestantism during the fifteenth and sixteenth centuries. These decisions to deviate from standing tradition and author-ity were made in a landscape filled with churches, monuments, and mem-ories of the saints, memories that were in no way abstract but, rather, constantly confirmed by geography and history. America, however, is a very different landscape. In America, religion lacks the supports of the old world. In America, traditions are experienced not as "destiny," as they were in the old world, but as the products of necessary choices. Thus, according to Berger, in America the heretical imperative is "normalized;" to choose what to believe, to choose one's religion, becomes the almost instinctive thing to do.

In America, Berger further explains, religious traditions lose their hold on both institutions and human consciousness. In the past, people could feel secure within a religious tradition because there was little that ordinarily competed with it. Modernity is different because modern people—presumably he means those who live in advanced industrial socie-ties—are faced with a plethora of competing "plausibility structures":

"Heresy, which is to say 'picking and choosing' from these 'plausibility structures' becomes a necessity."[18] Before modernity the normal condition was faith; in modernity the normal condition is religious uncertainty or, at the very least, instability of religious belief. Before modernity secularization was unlikely because traditional authority stood up. In modernity, religious traditions succumb to skepticism and voluntarism. There is a "pluralization" of religious beliefs and institutions. As not one "plausibility structure" is able to legitimate the social order, secularity—not necessarily religious disbelief—takes hold.

Berger rightly warns against misdirected objections to "pluralization" and secularization, objections that seek cover under hardened neo-orthodoxies or a rigid fundamentalism. There has been a pluralism of religions in the past, and people made choices. The story of St. Paul speaking on Mars Hill and addressing people of many different religious and philosophical persuasions testifies to this. His speech about the unknown or unnamed God reminds us, however, that he lived in an age in which religious belief was the norm. It is not that religious pluralism is new, but that secularization brings about also the cognitive possibility of choosing not to believe in a god. More recently Charles Taylor has gone to great lengths in order to make a similar argument in his *The Secular Age*.

Of course, the other side of this is the possibility of adhering to a belief in God. When Schmemann pleaded for a conscientious effort to understand the nature of secularism, he was calling upon the Orthodox to fully comprehend and intelligently confront the novelty of the Orthodox Church's situation in America. Berger's *The Heretical Imperative* troubled me on first encounter because I found its analysis of modernity plausible, and his speculation that Orthodoxy would eventually come under the influence of the heretical imperative persuasive as well. I also was reminded of Herberg's profound insight about the hegemony of the American Way over even the much-celebrated religious pluralism that proliferates beneath its broad and encompassing "sacred canopy."

Conclusion

Last, I return to the title of my essay, "The Secular Pilgrimage of Orthodoxy in America." I have brazenly borrowed the locution "secular pilgrimage" from the essay "A Secular Pilgrimage" in *A Continuous Harmony* by the American essayist and fiction writer Wendell Berry, published in 1970.

I have thought that the locution and the proposal that Berry makes in his essay about the path taken by several contemporary American poets might light a way past Berger's perplexing "heretical imperative." However, I am sufficiently chastened by the writers mentioned in the course of my remarks not to propose what the exact outcome of Orthodoxy's secular pilgrimage will be.

In his essay, Berry defines *secular* and *pilgrimage* in quite specific ways through his discussion and analysis of the quest of several contemporary American "nature poets" to articulate a positive vision of the human encounter with nature. Berry discovers in these poets' endeavors an account of their experience of nature that reveals a spiritual, even religious, dimension to the encounter. In particular, he mentions the poets Gary Snyder, Denise Levertov, and A. R. Ammons, and explains that he describes their pilgrimage as secular "because it takes place outside of, or without reference to, the institutions of religion." No shrines or holy places populate their poetry.[19] This secular pilgrimage, he says, with palpable irony on his lips, may also be described as a religious quest, for through their reflection on nature these poets reclaim a sense "of wonder or awe or humility," a "presence of mystery and divinity."[20] They do not find "a world of inert materiality that is postulated both by the heaven-oriented churches and the exploitative industries" but rather a "*created* world in which the Creator, the formative and quickening spirit, is still imminent and at work."[21] There is something profoundly Orthodox and deeply sacramental in these observations of a born and bred Baptist.

For Berry, like Schmemann and Herberg, secularity and secularism amount to one and the same thing. Secularity connotes an absence of the kind of experience that human beings need in order to truly thrive, not merely as animals but also as spiritual beings. Berry does not call secularism a heresy, but were he to adopt more explicitly theological speech, he might. Berry insists that secularism misrepresents the world as being autonomous, a world in which spirit is absent. By misleading us about the nature of the world, by misleading us about the human condition within this world, through its dualism of the sacred and profane, secularism denies the Incarnation and prevents salvation, or the healing of our diseased humanity and a world wounded by sin. Berry admires these poets for piercing through secularism's false vision of a world in which God is not present and active.

Berry is not about the business of reclaiming institutions and religious sites which often are, in his view, anachronisms in the world in which we live. Nonetheless, he recognizes that in some real sense there is a disadvantage in not having them. How can the Christian faith be plausible without them? I have found in Berry's description of the poet's secular pilgrimage an analogy to the situation of the Orthodox churches in America. Having left behind "organic" Orthodox worlds that were filled with reminders of sacred reality, having entered a culture in which those reminders do not exist for them, Orthodox Christians are indeed on a kind of secular pilgrimage, like the nature poets Berry admires. America's secularity is subtler than its European counterparts but, nonetheless, more disorienting, disordering, and disarming precisely because of the relative absence of venerated holy places, churches, ancient shrines, and monasteries long associated with the Christian faith. Absent are not only these markers of God's presence but also the geography, history, and language by which Orthodox Christians identified themselves ethnically or nationally as Orthodox Greek, Serbian, or Ukrainian. This helps to explain the relentless efforts of the Orthodox to project the old world onto the new American social reality—efforts that, rather than renewing tradition, flag the slow death of the religious community. This is because these efforts, rather than open up, hinder a life-giving and redemptive comprehension of what it means to be the Orthodox Church in America.

The secular pilgrimage of Orthodoxy commences with this dislocation, this separation, from the geography, culture, and "material" history with which it has identified for millennia. But obviously that is not all. Whereas in Greece, Russia, or Romania the Orthodox faith was in some real sense co-coextensive with the people, or the nation as a whole, in America this is not possible. It is not simply a matter of religious pluralism or of the sheer diversity of American life that blocks the way. More important, the people *interpret* pluralism as the norm of religious life, much as they *interpret* the separation of church and state as almost a divine mandate, an eleventh commandment.

For the first time in its history—or, more accurately, histories—Orthodoxy lives in a secular culture where free expression of religion is protected but religion is not permitted to claim the whole of life. In Greece, Russia, Ukraine, and other countries, Orthodoxy was the symbol of the unity of the people. "The American Way of Life is the symbol by which Americans define themselves and establish their unity," Herberg states.[22]

Schmemann observes that "in spite of all formal rectitude of dogma and liturgy," Orthodoxy in America has lost something essential from its past, a "living interrelation with culture, a claim to the *whole* of life." "This," he conjectures, "explains the instinctive attachment of so many Orthodox, even American born, to the 'national' forms of Orthodoxy, their resistance, however narrow-minded and 'nationalistic,' to a complete divorce between Orthodoxy and its various nationalistic expressions."[23]

This behavior, however understandable, holds little promise for a future in which Orthodoxy prospers and the truth of the Gospel on which it stands becomes attractive to fellow Americans. Nor is it possible, Schmemann rightly maintains, "simply to 'transpose' Orthodoxy onto American cultural categories."[24] To strive to be the "fourth major faith" of the American Way amounts to a rejection of the freedom that American culture and polity give the church to dissent where dissent is called for, to criticize where the truth about God and humanity is jeopardized, and to proclaim God's saving grace in a public square where there remain few reminders of the kingdom of God that was for millennia the unifying symbol of Western culture.

Can Orthodoxy, so habituated to legitimating culture, act counterculturally? That is a big question. If, as Berger muses in *The Heretical Imperative*, the Orthodox were to move their icons out beyond the church building into the culture, is it possible that the power of Christ and the Holy Spirit within the icons could not only lay bare the idols of commerce and advertising, entertainment, celebrity, and politics that hold captive the imaginations of people but also awaken those who hold up the icons to a new religious mission in a post-Christian America?

Notes

1. Alexander Schmemann, *Church, World, Mission* (Crestwood, NY: St. Vladimir's Seminary Press, 1979), 9.

2. Alexander Schmemann, "Problems of Orthodoxy in America III: The Spiritual Problem," *St. Vladimir's Seminary Quarterly* 8, no. 4 (1965): 193.

3. See Will Herberg, *Protestant, Catholic, Jew* (Garden City, NY: Doubleday, 1960), 85–86.

4. Schmemann, "Problems of Orthodoxy," 173.

5. Talcott Parsons, "Christianity and Modern Industrial Society," in *Secularization and the Protestant Prospect*, ed. James F. Childress and David Harned (Philadelphia: Westminster, 1970), 64.

6. Alexander Schmemann, *For the Life of the World* (Crestwood, NY: St. Vladimir's Seminary Press, 1973), 118.

7. Schmemann, 128.

8. Schmemann, 128.

9. Schmemann, 127.

10. Schmemann, "Problems of Orthodoxy," 171.

10. Schmemann, *For the Life of the World*, 111.

11. G. K. Chesterton, *Orthodoxy* (Garden City, NY: Image Books, 1959), 30.

12. In the 1960s, the religious sociologist Robert A. Bellah renamed this the American Civil Religion.

13. Herberg, *Protestant, Catholic, Jew*, 2.

14. Herberg, 77.

15. Herberg, 3.

16. Herberg, 265.

17. Peter L. Berger, *The Heretical Imperative* (Garden City, NY: Anchor Press/ Doubleday, 1980), 54–55.

18. Berger, 25.

19. Wendell Berry, *A Continuous Harmony: Essays Cultural and Agricultural* (New York: Harcourt Brace, 1970), 6.

20. Berry, 5.

21. Berry, 6; my emphasis.

22. Herberg, *Protestant, Catholic, Jew*, 78.

23. Schmemann, "Problems of Orthodoxy," 78.

24. Schmemann, 192.

Saeculum–Ecclesia–Caliphate: An Eternal Golden Braid

Paul J. Griffiths

The title of this essay includes three terms of art that I would like to define first.

Saeculum is a Latin word that by the fifth century in the Latin-using West had come to mean the time that begins with creation and ends with the general resurrection.[1] The adjectival form, *saecularis*, secular in English, therefore means anything—good, bad, or indifferent—belonging to that temporal period. I will use the adjective to refer to the politics of any state whose laws, norms, and practices limit themselves to the *saeculum* by prescinding from any explicit reference beyond the this-worldly, and thus also from any reference to the god of Abraham.[2] Such politics are secular, and such a state is a secular state. It is a form of political association defined by an absence; the only explicit presence in its authoritative sources and its making and enforcement of laws is reference to what belongs to the spatiotemporal manifold.

Ecclesia is a Latin (and Greek) word that denotes the church understood as the community of those who have been called out from the world and incorporated into the god of Abraham by way of baptism in the triune name of Father, Son, and Spirit. The church is a form of association during the *saeculum*, but one not solely secular; its primary explicit love is for the god of Abraham. That god does not belong to the *saeculum*; rather, the world of time and creatures is itself a creature, brought into being out of nothing by that god—who is, according to Jewish, Christian, and Islamic understanding, the only god there is and, thus, the only bearer of a nonsecular name. The church, then, is explicitly and definitively a non-

94

secular association, even if one located in the *saeculum*, at least for the time being.[3]

Caliphate is an English word, derived from Arabic, and I will take it to denote an Islamic polity ordered by sharia and administered by a single successor to Muhammad. It is an association of those who submit to (what they take to be) the revealed political will of the god of Abraham. That revealed will, together with its authoritative interpretation and development, is, for caliphates, determinative of politics. If the identification of Muhammad's god with the god of Abraham is accepted—and I will argue that Christians should entertain that identification with deep speculative seriousness—then a caliphate (there have been many), too, is explicitly and definitively a nonsecular association, although one that, unlike the church, recognizes no sovereignty other than its own.

Each of these three forms of association—the secular state, the church, the caliphate—is in its own way aspirationally universal; each can easily be divided into subkinds; and there are tensions among the political principles of each, often sufficiently deep that the polities formed by them cannot easily coexist.

Political Theology

Catholic political theology—at least since Leo XIII, who died in 1903, and arguably for much longer than that—has understood the church to be a form of association in some respects subsidiary to and dependent on the state, whether or not that state is secular. This entails that the state has responsibilities and purposes other than those of the church; it entails, too, that the church has no ambition to exercise sovereignty in all matters that have to do with the common good. Some of those matters properly fall under state sovereignty, and others under the sovereignty of nonecclesial associations and nonstate associations—families, unions, guilds, political parties, professional associations, sports teams, and the like. The state's essential purpose, on this Catholic view, is to nurture the common good, sometimes by what its own agents and functionaries do, and sometimes by supporting, or at least not obstructing, subsidiary associations (including the church), which themselves nurture the common good in particular ways.[4]

The church, however, is also, and indeed primarily, a transnational association. This means that it lives now, as usually in the past, as an association locally subsidiary to states of many different kinds: late-capitalist democracies; expansionist empires-in-the-making of many stripes (post-Stalinist, post-Maoist, post-Fordist); small-scale dictatorships; Islamic monarchies; transnational federations; and so on. Few of these forms of political order, perhaps none, take very seriously what the church would like them to think is their reason for being, which is the nurture of the common good; each of them in one way or another, directly and explicitly offends in its laws and actions against what, from a Catholic viewpoint, are nonnegotiable elements of a properly ordered commitment to the common good. This state of affairs makes tensive the relation between the church and any particular state; it also provides a partial explanation of the ambivalence about the state, and especially the secular state, evident in the church's political theology and in its relations with particular states.[5] The state is always, for the church, a lamentable necessity in much the same way as the monarchy was for ancient Israel; and the late-modern nation state provides occasions for lament of a peculiarly intense kind.[6]

There are some 185 states in the world at the moment, and evident among them are half a dozen or so deeply, and sometimes violently, incompatible understandings of how the common life of citizens ought be ordered. These facts provide Catholic political theology with some things to think about in addition to tensions between what the church understands to be the common good of citizens and the norms and laws of particular states. I have two such topics in mind: First, the fact that the world's states have different interpretations and understandings of political order and sovereignty evident—Has Catholic political theology anything to say about this? Is this variety, by itself, a good, perhaps a contribution to the common good of humanity? Or is it something to be criticized and, if possible, abrogated? And second, the possibility of ranking or ordering particular forms of political order as more or less supportive of the common good—Has Catholic political theology anything to say about that? Should, for instance, Catholic political theologians advocate constitutional democracy as a form of political order more conducive to the common good than, say, sharia-ordered oligarchy? Answers, however speculative, to these two questions bear on one another. If, for example, it is possible to rank forms of political order, does this mean that less-good polities ought to be abolished in favor of better ones? If recalcitrant political variety is itself a political good, then the possibility of ranking may not yield the conclusion that the less-good should be abrogated or erased in favor of the better.

I do not intend to answer these questions. Instead, I will engage them by way of two broadly Augustinian axioms, and by doing that present a trajectory of Catholic political theology about them. I intend what I write as stimulus and provocation rather than as conclusion—that, after all, is the main purpose of speculative theology, which is the genre to which this essay belongs.

The first broadly Augustinian axiom is that there are political goods—goods that serve the common good, that is—proper to the active and continued presence in the world of states that embody and advocate rival forms of political order. Variety on this matter is itself a good. The second such axiom is that among the principal indicators of service to the common good on the part of a particular state's laws, policies, and norms is that they explicitly honor and respond to the god of Abraham. Versions of these axioms are to be found explicitly in Augustine as well as in the long Augustinian and more broadly Catholic tradition. How might they provide answers to our questions?

The Advantages of Global Political Pluralism

I will start with the first axiom. It claims that global political pluralism is a good because it conduces to the common good; and that its reduction to a political monism in which there is at play in the world a single understanding of political order and, therefore, a single form of the state, loses that good. Suppose, for example, that the world were to contain among its states only constitutional democracies; and, to make the thought-experiment clearer yet, that there were just one of these—that the world's democracies have coalesced into one, the United States of the World. Or, suppose that the only state in the world were a global caliphate, administered by an accredited successor of Muhammad and ordered by sharia—that ISIS's current ambitions for a local caliphate stretching from Pakistan to Morocco have successfully become global. What political good would be lost by these monisms, or by any other political monism you care to imagine?

This is not a question about the degree to which these, or any other, particular understandings of the *polis* serve the common good. It is a question, rather, about how active political differences embodying rival understandings of the common good in fact serve the common good. It is also a question about why the imperial drive toward establishing, worldwide, a single political form and a single political understanding—the global export of state socialism or late-capitalist democracy, for example—loses something of deep importance to the (political) common good.

Catholic political theology has something to say about these questions. States, particular local political forms, are always—in a devastated world like the one produced by the fall from grace that ejected us from Eden—characterized by a passion for domination. They always want, though not always with the same degree of intensity and certainly not always with the same likelihood of success, to extend their power until they have no rivals. This is among their defining characteristics, and the passion in question (Augustine calls it *libido dominandi*) becomes more evident and more active as the power of a particular state grows. On this understanding, every particular state is aspirationally a universal empire and acts on this aspiration to the degree that local variables make such action possible. This characteristic of states is formally and functionally like the passion for sin evident in all human creatures. Just as we, individually, inevitably seek the lack that is sin's goal, so states seek the emptiness that political power without rivals provides. Both gestures are solipsistic: they want to extinguish everything other than themselves, and that is exactly the characteristic feature of the sin of Satan, and thereby of all sin. Pride and envy, among the sins, show this fundamental feature of sin with particular clarity; and *libido dominandi* is pride and envy intertwined in the sphere of politics.[7]

That is the first move. What follows from it at once is a characterization of the way in which the continued existence of genuine political rivalries serves the common (political) good. It does so by restraining and constraining the desire for political power whose end is the extinction of all political difference, all political rivalry. All states are aspirationally universal; were any one to achieve its goal in this respect, by Europeanizing the earth, as the British Empire once wanted to, or by Americanizing the earth, as the American imperialism now does, or by Islamizing the earth, as some versions of the caliphate now may, it would thereby subsume whatever political and common goods it had sought and served into the service of itself. It would have become a Lord—a *dominus*—to itself, and would therefore be, politically speaking, strictly autonomous, a law to itself. That is, it would no longer be a political entity, no longer capable of serving the common good, but capable only of self-contemplation. States, in this view, require the recalcitrance of rivals in much the same way that humans require the recalcitrance of others. The degree to which states erase this recalcitrance is the degree, in a fallen world, to which they cease to be cities and become places in which political lament is impossible because political ambition has been realized.[8]

Augustine's instance of this point is a principled objection to Rome's extinction of its major rival, which was, in the republican period, the Carthaginian state; he objects to this not because he values the political norms of Carthage or excoriates those of republican Rome; he objects to it because Carthage's extinction makes Rome effectively politically unrivaled and thus a global arena for the exercise of self-serving political violence.[9] Similarly, in some important respects, the United States seeks now the erasure of its principal political rivals, which include the nascent caliphate. *Carthago delenda est* was the refrain repeated in session after session of the Roman senate by Cato the Elder as the Punic Wars approached their end. We have our equivalents: Democrats and Republicans in the United States are almost equally excitable and almost equally repetitive about the importance of destroying our political rivals, especially ISIS because we especially do not like it; Catholic political theology has the tools for a potent critique of this position.

The critique amounts to this: Any state, whether secular in the sense earlier given or not, should understand itself as subject to, indeed in part defined by, an ambition for universality that involves the erasure of its political rivals and should understand this ambition as a failure of politics. It should enshrine these understandings in its laws and norms and should encourage its functionaries and representatives to remember them frequently. It should remind its citizens of them, too, and will most effectively do so by instituting public liturgies of lament for the state's inevitable failure to constrain its ambitions in this direction, and by finding all possible means to remind its citizens of the goods present in polities external to itself, however deep the failings of those polities may be. The burden of proof for the desirability of extraterritorial adventures aimed at erasure of rivals should be made very heavy, almost too heavy to bear. That is because the damage to which all states are subject is deep: however heavy the burden of proof is made and however frequent the public liturgies of lament for the state's failures to restrain itself, the state will try to find a way to do what states do—which is attempt to erase its rivals and universalize itself. Catholic political theology can at most offer a reminder and a warning about these things; but it is a warning worth attending to.

For Catholics who are also citizens of the United States, one aspect of the reminder and the warning would have to do with ISIS. The Islamic

State—among the polities at the moment active in the world and (from some perspectives) threatening to the United States—is at the moment the principal object of actions aimed at its extinction by the United States and its allies. It is also the principal object of political rhetoric that advocates its erasure. Representatives and functionaries of ISIS reciprocate some of this, but to a lesser degree; they are more concerned with the establishment of a caliphate unsullied by US and European economic norms, military power, and social habits than with the erasure of rivals; their violent excursions into rival territory—New York, London, Madrid, Paris, and Istanbul, among others—are not intended to erase those rivals, but, rather, to persuade them that they cannot maintain colonial dominance without cost, and ought to abandon the attempt.[10] Considerable violence has been done by both sides in this conflict, with more, and worse, on the horizon; but the violence is unequally distributed. In body count, which ought always be the first (though not the last or the only) measure in matters of violent conflict among states, the United States and its allies are the worse offenders. But I am less concerned with assessing the degree and kind of violence at play in this conflict than with thinking about the aspiration to erase political rivals; and even in that matter, largely with the Catholic-theological view that there are political goods proper to the active presence in the world of rival understandings of how states ought to be governed and the common life of their citizens ordered. From that angle, the recommendation is clear. Catholic Christians in the United States should certainly lament all violence done in the conflict between the United States and ISIS's version of the caliphate; but they should also resist, publicly and with vigor, advocacy of erasure and policies aimed at that end. That is the yield of the first Augustinian axiom. It commends a stance to the church in the United States, one that, as far as I can tell, is being advocated by almost no one.

Polities and the God of Abraham

The second Augustinian axiom is that among the indicators of service to the common good on the part of a particular state is that its laws, policies, and norms explicitly honor and respond to the god of Abraham. Nonsecular polities incarnate and represent a political good that secular ones lack. Why should this be true? For the broadly Augustinian tradition it is true because political order is most fundamentally a matter of love. There are properly political loves, and all states necessarily have them: every body of law and every set of norms shows its loves. The scope and directedness of political loves is evident, more or less, in laws, norms, and policies—in, that is, the public documents and effective practices of states. A state whose political loves are explicit in naming the god of Abraham as the one for whose glory and in whose service it nurtures the common good—and is also explicit in articulating the ways in which its particular laws respond to the god of Abraham's desire for human flourishing—has, from a Christian point of view, a political advantage that secular states, and others whose laws do not explicitly respond to the god of Abraham's name, lack. It is the advantage of knowing the god of Abraham as the source and goal of the common good, and of knowing something, at least, of the particular history of that god with the peoples of the earth, and of what that history means, politically. This is not to say that there are no political goods evident in secular states; neither is it to say that nonsecular states have nothing to learn about the common good from secular ones; neither is to say that nonsecular states should always be ranked above secular ones in a putative hierarchy of political goodness. But it is to say that nonsecular states have a first-blush advantage over secular ones because they incarnate and represent a political good that secular states lack. And this advantage provides a provisional and partial answer to my question about the possibility of ranking particular forms of political order as more or less supportive of the common good.

The United States is a secular state in the sense given to that term at the beginning of my remarks. It makes a constitutional virtue of prescinding from explicit response to the god of Abraham. The god present in its founding documents, while arguably the god of Abraham, is largely offstage, and is used, even when onstage, as a distant guarantor of what reason can show. The laws and norms of the nation are not arrived at by way of engagement with the revealed will of that god, and much less by way of exegesis of and commentary upon texts taken to reveal that god's political will. The caliphate, whether the one represented by ISIS or some other, is, by contrast, exactly a nonsecular state. Its laws, norms, and policies are explicit in their response to the god of Abraham, and the particulars of those laws are frequently and typically articulated with the particular history of that god with the Muslim people and, by extension, with the Jewish and

Christian peoples. On this matter, then, Catholic Christians in the United States should judge that the caliphate has a first-blush political advantage over secular states such as the United States.

But even this modest suggestion might be wrong. Suppose, for example, that the god Muslims worship, the one whom the architects of the caliphate and the regents and successors of Muhammad advert to in their making and administration of laws, is not the god of Abraham but, rather, some other. Some Catholic theologians argue this line, as do many other Christians in the United States, Protestant and Orthodox.[11] This is a large question, and one on which Catholic Christians have no determinative magisterial teaching. There is, however, some teaching that suggests the possibility, even the likelihood, of an identification of the god of Islam with the god of Abraham;[12] and there is much in the texts and traditions of Judaism, Christianity, and Islam that shows deep affinity in identifying and thinking about Abraham's god. It is also true that there is much disagreement among Christians and Muslims about what that god is like and wants of us, politically and otherwise; but such disagreement, although important, is entirely compatible with the view that Catholic Christians and Muslims are together thinking about and responding to the god of Abraham. This is because giving a different sense to an expression, even a significantly different one, does not by itself force the conclusion that what is being referred to is also, and thereby, different. We call the same planetary body the morning star and the evening star, thus using two expressions with different sense that refer to the same thing. Discerning difference in sense (in, perhaps, the list of predicates that Muslims and Christians use of the god of Abraham) requires, by itself, no conclusions about whether the same god is being referred to.[13] My own speculative view, not without magisterial support, is that Catholic Christians should adopt as a working hypothesis the view that Muslims and Christians are responding to and thinking about the same god. If that position is adopted, then this objection to the thesis that the caliphate has a significant first-blush advantage as a political order over secular states stands to one side.

Even if it is true that ISIS's version of the caliphate orders its laws in explicit response to the god of Abraham, might it not be the case that those laws and norms and policies, in their particularity, are deeply and horrifyingly mistaken about the common good? Might it not be the case that the caliphate's laws deform rather than serve the common good? Might it not yet be the case that these deformations render null the first-blush political advantage of explicit service of and response to the god of Abraham?

It might. But the case that it is has yet to be made. It is certainly the case that the caliphate, in its nascent form as ISIS, sponsors in its laws and practices many things that, from a Catholic Christian viewpoint, oppose rather than serve the common good. There is execution and bodily mutilation of criminals; there is suicide bombing; there is the refusal of education to women and the practice of sexual violence upon them; there is extraterritorial assassination; there is wanton destruction of historical monuments; and there is deep and systematic violence practiced upon those who are not Muslim, including Jews and Christians. These are all terrible things. Every drop of blood shed in these ways and every act of violence performed in these ways should be mourned by Christians. But the United States and other secular states are in the same situation. We too, and I write now as an American as well as a Catholic, execute some among our criminals; we imprison a vastly higher proportion of our population than does ISIS; we abort our babies at a much higher rate; we probably have a higher civilian murder rate than in any ISIS-administered territory; we, like them, practice extraterritorial assassination, and on a considerably larger scale, and, by now, we celebrate, in public, the fact of it much as they do (the public and official celebrations surrounding the assassination of Osama bin Laden in 2011 marked an important transition on this matter); we are a direct military threat to their continued existence while they are not to ours; we are, as I write, actively engaged in the slaughter of people in their territories; and, we are, as a nation, founded upon genocide and fattened by slavery, a double legacy with the violent results of which we still live. Are we better than them, politically speaking? Are they worse than us? It is not easy to say.[14] It is certainly much less easy to say than our forty-fifth president thinks (although he has been more forthcoming than his predecessor about the degree to which the United States itself performs the horrors it publicly opposes). All states do terrible things. The caliphate does. Secular states do. The United States does. That the caliphate does cannot serve, then, as an easy way to overcome the first-blush political advantage they have over us, which is that their laws explicitly respond to the god of Abraham while ours do not.

Catholic political theology affirms that renunciation by states of the ambition to erase political rivals is a properly political good. It is the good of the continued presence of political rivalry as a check upon the otherwise unrestrained tendency of states to seek, solipsistically, to make their preferred form of political order be the only one available. Catholic political theology also affirms that explicit responsiveness to the god of Abraham in the making and administration of laws is a political good, which is at least to say that states that do it are to be preferred, at first blush, to those that do not. Catholic Christians in the United States ought to take these affirmations seriously, as might, I hope, other Christians. Were we to do so, the form and content of public witness by Christians in the United States to our present difficulties would be deeply, and encouragingly, different from what it is.

I end on a final speculative point. Some forms of Islamic polity are especially damaging at the moment to Christians and Jews, so much so that there is a real possibility that large areas in the Middle East that traditionally have had communities of Christians and Jews might before long be emptied of them.[15] This is something Christians should lament and protest; it is also something that does, or should, create a bond between Jews and Christians. But it is not something that should bring into being any special animus on the part of Christians toward Muslims in general or advocates of the reestablishment of a caliphate in particular. Nor should it yield the conclusion that an Islamic caliphate should be avoided by Christians. The church's presence in the world is geographically uneven, now as it has always been; regions once substantially Christian now are not, and regions once largely empty of Christians are now replete with them. This fluidity is an ordinary part of life in the devastation, and nostalgia for a particular geographic distribution of the visible church's presence is not a Christian virtue. It may be that Christians in some Islamic polities will find martyrdom at a higher rate, at the moment, than is the case for Christians elsewhere. What should be said about that is what should always be said about martyrdoms: they are dreadful; they are artifacts of the fall; they are to be lamented; and, at the same time, they are to be celebrated as witness to the power and presence of the triune Lord in the world, participatory in and dimly reflective of the death of Jesus on the cross.

Notes

This is a revised and expanded version of a talk given under the same title at a conference on tradition, secularization, and fundamentalism at Fordham University on June 24, 2016. The conference was sponsored by Fordham University's Orthodox Christian Studies Center, and I am grateful to Aristotle

Papanikolaou and George Demacopoulos for the invitation, and for the lively discussion the talk received on the day. I am grateful, too, for comments on an early draft of the piece, to Lauren Winner, Carole Baker, Philip Porter, and Brendan Case. More distantly, I have learned a good deal about political theology from Chuck Mathewes, Eric Gregory, James Wetzel, Stanley Hauerwas, and John Milbank. Most of them would, I am fairly sure, cordially disagree with the line here taken.

1. This, for example, is Augustine's preferred usage. See my "Secularity and the Saeculum," in *Augustine's City of God: A Critical Guide*, ed. James Wetzel (Cambridge: Cambridge University Press, 2012), 33–54. See also Robert A. Markus, *Saeculum: History and Society in the Theology of St. Augustine*, 2nd ed. (Cambridge: Cambridge University Press, 1988); and *Christianity and the Secular* (South Bend, IN: University of Notre Dame Press, 2006). There are, of course, many and lively debates about the proper use of *secular* and cognates not here accounted for—the definition offered here is stipulative.

2. By "the god of Abraham," I mean the triune Lord who calls Abraham, makes beloved the people of Israel, becomes incarnate as Jesus of Nazareth, and inspires the church. This is a Christian mode of identification. It assumes, as a dogmatic commitment, that the god the people of Israel are covenanted to is the same as the god the church worships. It leaves open the question of whether the god who spoke to Muhammad is also the same. More on this below. For a different perspective, see Rémi Brague, *Du dieu des chrétiens* (Paris: Flammarion, 2009).

3. In using this phrase, I have in mind W. H. Auden's *For the Time Being: A Christmas Oratorio*. For a recent edition, with an excellent introductory study of the poem, see Auden, *For the Time Being*, ed. Alan Jacobs (Princeton, NJ: Princeton University Press, 2013).

4. This trajectory of thought is among the principal facets of the idea of subsidiarity, which has become a central commitment of Catholic social doctrine in the twentieth and twenty-first centuries and can be seen clearly at work in papal teachings from Leo XIII's *Rerum Novarum* (1891) to Francis I's *Laudato Si'* (2015). It is especially clear in Benedict XVI's *Caritas in Veritate* (2009), because it is applied there with great clarity to particular forms of association and particular matters of public policy.

5. On this ambivalence (perhaps a stronger word is necessary), see Russell Hittinger, "Toward an Adequate Anthropology: Social Aspects of *Imago Dei* in Catholic Theology," in *Imago Dei: Human Dignity in Ecumenical Perspective*, ed. Thomas Albert Howard (Washington, DC: Catholic University of America Press, 2013), 39–78. Among Hittinger's concerns in this essay are the ways in which corporate rather than individual entities may be taken to image the Lord. He is clear that the modern state has a strong tendency to usurp all such

---

imaging for itself, and thus to reduce other forms of association to nothing. Typically, the modern state understands the entities that count in the world to be only itself and individuals, with the existence of the latter predicated exclusively on the existence of the former. For a structurally similar line of thought, albeit with quite different antecedents, see Giorgio Agamben, *State of Exception*, trans. Kevin Attell (Chicago: University of Chicago Press, 2005); *The Time That Remains: A Commentary on the Letter to the Romans*, trans. Patricia Dailey (Stanford, CA: Stanford University Press, 2005); and *The Church and the Kingdom*, trans. Leland de la Durantaye (London: Seagull, 2012).

6. It is of course true that the Catholic Church has not always lamented every particular state, secular or otherwise, to the same degree. States are more or less lamentable. But it remains true that, according to Catholic theology, the need for states is an artifact of the fall, and that therefore each of them—every member of the class—is to that extent to be lamented.

7. I borrow here, gratefully, from Jean-Luc Marion. See, notably, *Prolégomènes à la charité*, 2nd ed. (Paris: La Différence, 1991), 12–42; and *Au lieu de soi: l'approche de Saint Augustin* (Paris: Presses Universitaires de France, 2008), passim.

8. On the importance of lament to the proper constitution and ordering of the state, see Gillian Rose, *Mourning Becomes the Law: Philosophy and Representation* (Cambridge: Cambridge University Press, 1996). Rose is, in my judgment, among the more important political theorists of the twentieth century (she died in 1995).

9. See Augustine, *De Civitate Dei*, 1.30.

10. ISIS is, beyond reasonable argument, an aspirational caliphate motivated principally by opposition to the violent presence of the United States and its allies in various parts of the Middle East. On this, in the instance of ISIS's presence in Gaza, see Sarah Helm, "ISIS in Gaza," *New York Review of Books* 63, no. 1 (2016): 18–20. On the longer history behind ISIS, see William McCants, *The ISIS Apocalypse* (New York: St. Martin's Press, 2015). See also Jessica Stern and J. M. Berger, *ISIS: The State of Terror* (New York: Ecco, 2015); and Joby Warwick, *Black Flags: The Rise of ISIS* (New York: Doubleday, 2015). The theorists of al-Qaeda, including Osama bin Laden—see the speeches collected in Bruce Lawrence, ed., *Messages to the World: The Statements of Osama bin Laden* (New York: Verso, 2006)—as well as those of ISIS, such as Abu Omar al-Baghdadi and Haji Bakr and those belonging to other Islamic groups, differ in the emphasis they place on freeing the Islamic world from Western influence, on the one hand, and destroying their (perceived) opponents, on the other. But the weight generally lies on the former.

11. See Brague, *Du dieu des chrétiens*.

12. See, for example: "the plan of salvation also embraces those who acknowledge the creator (*qui creatorem agnoscunt*), and among these the Muslims are first; they profess to hold the faith of Abraham (*fidem Abrahae se tenere profitentes*) and along with us they worship one merciful God (*nobiscum Deum adorant unicum*)" (*Lumen Gentium*, from no. 16). See also: "They [Muslims] worship one God (*unicum Deum adorant*), living and subsistent, merciful and almighty, creator of heaven and earth, who has spoken to humanity and to whose decrees, even the hidden ones, they seek to submit themselves whole-heartedly (*toto animo se submitteres student*), just as Abraham, to whom the Islamic faith readily relates itself (*ad quem fides islamica libenter sese refert*), submitted to God" (*Nostra Aetate*, from no. 3).

13. It is Catholic dogma that the god the people of Israel worship is the triune Lord. This provides a splendid illustration of the sense-reference distinction. Jews and Christians do not agree about how the Lord should be identified and described, and some of those disagreements reach the level of prima facie contradiction (e.g., the Lord is incarnate/the Lord cannot be incarnate). But these differences do not require the conclusion that the god the Jews identify and worship is distinct from the one Christians identify and worship. So, perhaps, *mutatis mutandis*, for the god of Jesus Christ and the god of Muhammad.

14. The indexes of flourishing just mentioned are partly drawn from and have a deep affinity with those developed by Amartya Sen, in, for example, *Development as Freedom* (Oxford: Oxford University Press, 1999) and Martha Nussbaum in *Creating Capabilities: The Human Development Approach* (Cambridge, MA: Harvard University Press, 2011). The Sen/Nussbaum approach to capability has significant theoretical problems; but its fundamental intuitions—that there are conditions necessary for humans to flourish of a general and widely agreed kind and that these are largely amenable to empirical measurement (per capita/per annum rates of death by violence, imprisonment, and death from hunger and thirst and treatable sickness, for instance, can be measured easily)—appear to me both right and important. Assessing states by applying these measures does not yield the conclusion that any particular form of political order is demonstrably better than any other.

15. See Jonathan Sacks, "On Creative Minorities: 2013 Erasmus Lecture," *First Things*, January 2014, accessed February 18, 2019, https://www.firstthings .com/article/2014/01/on-creative-minorities. See also his *Not in God's Name: Confronting Religious Violence* (New York: Schocken, 2015).

A Secularism of the Royal Doors: Toward an Eastern Orthodox Christian Theology of Secularism

Brandon Gallaher

> Beyond courage, it is also possible to live in the ancient faith, which asserts that changes in the world, even if they be recognized more as loss than a gain, take place within an eternal order that is not affected by their taking place. Whatever the difficulty of philosophy, the religious man has been told that process is not all. Tendebantque manus ripae ulterioris amore [They were holding their arms oustretched in love toward the further shore (Aeneid, 6.314)].
>
> **George Grant, _Lament for a Nation_**[1]

I n a famous passage, Dietrich Bonhoeffer (1906–1945) mused that society was moving toward a "completely religionless time." This, he wrote, would prove revolutionary for Christianity as a religion, for it would have to disrobe itself from its religious garments, which include "the temporally conditioned presuppositions of metaphysics" and "inwardness" and envision a means by which Christ can become the Lord of the "religionless." Such a "religionless Christianity" would require a re-meaning of all that formally had been taken for granted as established Christian realities—church, community, the homily, the liturgy, the Christian life and, above all God himself. "How do we speak," he asked, "in a 'secular' way about 'God'?"[2] This is strong and beautiful stuff. There is only one small problem with this musing, it is false.

A Completely Religionless Time?

Religion has not disappeared but actually grown in form, diversity, and strength of voice in all the major world religions, including Christianity.[3] Christianity is expected to grow globally from 2.2 billion in 2010 to 2.9 billion in 2050 (31.4 percent). Nearly one in three people worldwide will be Christian in 2050.[4] However, as has been often noted, and here one remembers Bonhoeffer, Christianity is declining in Western Europe.[5] The greatest growth of Christianity tends to be in the Evangelical Protestant churches (Charismatic Christianity and Pentecostalism) as found mostly in Africa and Asia,[6] and, it should be noted, the share of the overall Christian population is decreasing for the Orthodox.[7] With the result of increased migration from the developing world, especially among Muslims (whose numbers are projected to increase by 73 percent by 2050),[8] liberal democracies in the West have had to face in recent years how to incorporate religious voices in the public sphere. The end of Christendom has not meant the end of religion worldwide, let alone religiosity, but its postmodern metamorphosis.

The Western Exceptional Case

Yet Bonhoeffer was not that wrong in arguing for the coming of a "religionless time" if we look at the decline of Christendom or a culturally hegemonic Christianity in the West, that is, the rise of "secularization" in all its complexities. In some parts of Western Europe and North America the public sphere has indeed developed in a globally exceptional fashion with the marginalization of organized religion. For example, in Canada, in the 2011 National Household Survey, 24 percent of the population reported no religion. In British Columbia, where I was raised, 44.1 percent of the population said they had no religious affiliation. This was the second highest level in the country after the Yukon (49.9 percent).[9] It is no surprise, therefore, that the public square (including the media, government, schools, universities, and local community centers) in the Greater Vancouver area can often seem extremely hostile to organized religion, especially, Christianity. Religion in this context is very much a private matter, and those who are religious are considered idiosyncratic, if not downright odd.

I want to propose in this sort of late modern context, the minority context in a global perspective, that what is called for theologically is neither

another secular post-death-of-God account of religion.[10] Nor is what is
needed for God-talk another account of how the secular realm hides a
covert and corrosive political theology requiring in response a radically
orthodox Christianity.[11] Rather, what may contribute to the upbuilding of
the church's present witness in this religionless, secular and Western context is a positive account of the theological status of the secular, secularization, and secularism.

My aim is not to develop a practical model for "Orthodox Christian
nations" and "cultures" which might be "helpful" in articulating issues such
as particular church-state models and the presence of the church in a secular cultural context. My object is actually quite "impractical." Instead this
essay sketches a positive theological vision of the secular from the basis of
the Orthodox Christian tradition, that is, it envisions an Eastern Orthodox Christian theology of secularism that might then broadly inspire a new
proactive approach in Orthodox theology to the phenomenon of secularism in a context that mostly rejects it completely as a Western aberration.
After the Holy and Great Council of Crete of June 2016, there is the need
in Orthodoxy to develop antinomically a positive and creative response to
Western secular culture to balance off the characteristic Eastern Orthodox critique of secularism and the West. Crete was, arguably, the beginning of an attempt to articulate an Orthodox world after Byzantium but
firmly enmeshed within Western culture. It was the first universal conciliar attempt to acknowledge that Orthodoxy now finds itself in a new
modern Western order, the context of secularism, that it has not created
but which it now must respond to creatively as a premodern Eastern
Church.[12] While retaining its premodern liturgical and spiritual consciousness, its salt and light, its difference, its Easternness, Orthodoxy is called
as a religious and civilizational minority to envision how it may witness in
its majority secular Western context. This is the challenge and necessity of
articulating an Eastern Orthodox Christian theology of secularism.[13]

Eastern Orthodox Opposition to Secularism

Modern Orthodox theology has a tradition of antisecularism. In recent
years, it has become known for its opposition to secularism as a political
ideology. Rowan Williams has called such an ideology, found in France
and Kemalist Turkey, "programmatic secularism." With programmatic secularism, the public sphere is seen as a strictly patrolled religionless free

space. The aim of the creation of this ostensibly neutral and universal secular sphere is to create a "clear public loyalty to the state unclouded by private convictions" which are "rigorously banned" from the public arena. Williams distinguishes this from "procedural secularism," which can take many different forms (as I will discuss), where a neutral state oversees a wide variety of religious communities and only intervenes to keep the peace.[14]

The Russian Church, seen in the speeches and writings of Patriarch Kirill (Gundiaev) of Moscow (b. 1946) and his assistant Metropolitan Hilarion (Alfeyev) of Volokolamsk (b. 1966), vigorously has opposed programmatic secularism, which it tends to collapse with procedural secularism, usually described as "militant." Other placeholders for secularism are *liberalism* and *the West*. Various "postsecular conflicts" abound,[15] from nurses being told not to wear crosses to Christian-run bakeries refusing to make pro-gay marriage cakes. The Moscow Patriarchate is well known in the Western media precisely for such conflicts, from the Pussy Riot affair to opposition to gay rights. In reaction to secularism and the West, Patriarch Kirill, in particular, has articulated a form of neoconservatism. It is a quasi-phyletist, anti-Western and pro-family values state-church ideology, often termed *Russkii Mir* (the Russian World).[16] *Russkii Mir* has formed the ideological basis for the strategic collaboration of the Russian state and church with rightwing transnational moral coalitions such as the World Congress of Families, the Western European far right (e.g., Hungary's Viktor Orban, France's Marine Le Pen and Austria's Karin Kneissl) and the evangelical wing of the Republican Party (including, the engagement of Putin and the Moscow Patriarchate with Donald Trump).[17] What we see, arguably, with *Russkii Mir* is programmatic secularism turned on its head: an ever greater union between the Russian state and church with ecclesial forms filled with Soviet content; a near collapse of Russian ethnic, national, and even civic identity with Orthodox identity; and the largely quixotic attempt by the Orthodox Church through education and catechesis to turn a secular post-Soviet culture into an idealized "Holy Rus'."[18] Russian Orthodoxy has ironically been secularized by its own self-nationalization. One is reminded of the nationalization of Shinto in post-1868 Japan with the creation of the state ideology of "Shinto secular."[19]

Yet there is another form of Orthodox antisecularism, which is less well known in the West: "spiritual" or "theological" antisecularism. Some of the Russian Church's animus toward political secularism is simply that it subscribes to this deeper antisecularist critique. We see this position in the documents of the Holy and Great Council of Crete of June 2016.[20] Secularism is said to be an "ideology" that seeks "the full autonomy of man from Christ and the spiritual influence of the church," whose "conservatism" is said to oppose all progress.[21]

In this context, secularism is understood as an anti-theological theology that splits off the sacred from the secular by cutting humanity's links to Christ and the church. Humanity and the world are meaningful only on their own terms with the transcendent ruled out entirely. Orthodoxy, as Alexander Schmemann (1921–1983) argued, objects to a false autonomy being given to the secular sphere. Life and the world are only meaningful by symbolically manifesting the divine, what is beyond itself and elsewhere. The secular, then, is secular only as also sacred because it is the "sacrament of the divine presence" who is Jesus Christ, life in all its fullness (Jn 10:10). Christ is only known in and through *this* world and in *this* life.[22] When one portions off a material world from a spiritual and religious realm then one loses what is the basic priestly vocation of humanity which is to transform the world into life in God by filling it with meaning and spirit.[23] To carve out of the world a secular sphere (which is *merely* material and profane) that is said to be wholly distinct from the religious (as the spiritual and the sacred) is, for the Orthodox, a "monstrous lie."[24] Christ is the life of that world, and through his Spirit he is its secret sanctifying power (Col 3:3), the "force that through the green fuse drives the flower,"[25] both blessing and baning. With secularism, instead of the church bringing together humanity and creation into one body, with Christ as its head and focus of worship, as symbolized in the Eucharist, a secular sphere is strictly delineated from the sacred with the erection of its own false secular idols as centers of unity. The world is then depersonalized, made into an object whose meaning is found only within itself. Secularism is the "negation of worship" as it rejects the sacramentality of creation.[26]

An Eastern Orthodox Christian Theology of Secularism?

Orthodox antisecularism, however, does not take into account the plurality of modernity and secularism. In this way, it misses the opportunity of theologically reenvisioning secularism with precisely the sort of sacramental vision it espouses. Contemporary sociology of religion has now largely abandoned older totalizing narratives of modernity that argued that religions inevitably wither on the vine once societies enter into the full growth of the modern ("the disenchantment of the world") and are emancipated from magical thinking.[27] There exist, as Schmuel Eisenstadt (1923–2010) wrote, "multiple modernities" with "multiple institutional and ideological patterns" moved forward by multiple different social actors pursuing "different programs of modernity, holding very different views on what makes societies modern."[28] But if there are multiple forms of the modern, then there must also be multiple forms of the secular, secularization and secularism, as is the case with procedural secularism, from the United States, Turkey, and Italy to the United Kingdom, Indonesia, and Germany with different constellations and relationships between separation of church and state and forms of the differentiation of law, morality, and religion.[29]

Here, in this postsecular context of extreme secular hybridity, enters a theological opportunity for Orthodoxy. One might argue for the plausibility of hypothesizing an Orthodox Christian theology of secularism, and with it a new form, an alternative Orthodox modernity, just as Shinto, Buddhism and Islam may play a role in the public life of the secular nations of Japan, Laos, and Indonesia, respectively. An Eastern Orthodox theology of secularism might see the secular and the sacred, the church and the world, as existing in a creative tension, in Bonhoeffer's phrase, "a polemical unity."[30] In such a unity, and here one is reminded of the sacramental vision we described in articulating Orthodox theological antisecularism, the church lives in, by, and through the world in which it dwells as its home and the world through it. The church itself founds, undergirds, and then, by kenotically withdrawing to remain present, sets free the world to be itself and develop independently in the secular space, which is then far from being "neutral."

Dialectical Sacramentality

Any Orthodox Christian theological vision of secularism if it is to be sacramental must be dialectical or polar in its structure, for the secular as a reality only lives in and by the sacred and the sacred depends on the world in which God has given himself up in Christ. Both realities, therefore, live in, by, and through one another and imply the other in a perpetual creative tension, a unity-in-difference that generates both cultural creativity and the mission of the church in witnessing in the world to Christ. Yet one should neither obliterate the difference between the two—so that we must argue for the secular and the sacred remaining unconfused and in some fundamental sense unchanged insofar as they retain their identities and do not become incommensurable—nor should they in this way be divisible or in some sense separable from one another.[31]

Richard Kearney (b. 1954) argues for an approach to the transcendent and belief whereby one can believe again (lit. *ana-theism*) after the death of God, after Auschwitz, as it were, through a continuous movement that includes a critical and purgative atheism as an integral part of theism which is "second faith beyond faith." One never chooses once to believe in God but again and again as we speak in his name and ask him, like Christ, why he has abandoned us.[32] In this movement of second faith, one is encountered by God in the form of the stranger,[33] Kearney tracing this movement in a variety of world religions, and one is forced to enter into an existential wager as to whether one will offer the stranger divine hospitality and change one's life or remain unchanged in hostility. This stranger, paradoxically, depends on us, for God to be in the world he needs us to offer him welcome, requires our openness to host him and indeed save him. God, in his freedom, chooses to be God for us as a God in need.[34] God, then, is not the remote omnipotent deity of theodicy, Pascal's God of the philosophers, the God of "ontotheology" and metaphysics, but God on the cross, God on trial and hung by his creation yet reigning from that tree. This is not simply about God but about how we live with difference. More concretely, it is about how we live with moral and religious diversity ("reasonable accommodation") and how the ethical and political postsecular conflicts that arise from such difference might be managed in a secular liberal society.[35] What Kearney shows us is that you cannot manage difference effectively in the long run unless you allow for the spiritual possibility that the Other is one's life. Simply keeping people from rhetorical and physical violence in a society is not enough. One needs, as Gianni Vattimo (b. 1936) says in speaking of Derrida's thought, to offer hospitality to the guest by putting oneself in his hands, entrusting oneself to him and in this way acknowledging that when we speak to him applying the principle of charity, the Christian to the Muslim, the atheist to the Hindu, that he may be right.[36]

Since God is God for us only as he gives himself to us in the world, in its beauty and in its brokenness, we come to see, Kearney argues, that the "sacred is *in* the world but not *of* the world" for the "sacred inhabits the secular" but "it is not identical with it."[37] Secular and sacred exist in a "fertile" or "fecund" tension that avoids a dualism that opposes them and a monism that collapses one into the other—exclusive humanism or Byzantium. This leads Kearney to contend for a "sacred secularity" or, as it were, a secular sacrality that is a two-way process of sacralizing the secular, which is ever supplemented by the secularization of the sacred. One cannot return to God letting him in unless one first has abandoned him like Peter who betrayed him thrice. And the God returned to is not the God of death, the God of metaphysics, but the incarnate God of life given in the face of the stranger who is, above all, this stranger whom his creation hated and delivered unto death as a stranger. In such a vision of secularism, he argues, we reinsert the hyphen back between the secular and the sacred.[38] We approach secularism as sacramental. Kearney argues that anatheism avoids a sterile atheism that wishes to purge God from the world rejecting the sacred in favor of a narrow understanding of the secular. This is the vision of secularism of the New Atheists. He also swears off the religious fundamentalism of an Osama bin Laden or a Jimmy Swaggart that would obliterate the secular in favor of the sacred. Lastly, he rejects pantheism, say the New Age, that collapses the polarity of secular and sacred into one monism so denying any distinction between the transcendent and the immanent, which forestalls true otherness: "Anatheism does not say the sacred *is* the secular; it says it is *in* the secular, *through* the secular, *toward* the secular. I would even go so far as to say the sacred is inseparable from the secular, while remaining distinct. Anatheism speaks of "interanimation" between the sacred and the secular but not of a fusion or confusion. They are inextricably interconnected but never the *same* thing."[39]

But this renewed understanding of secularism as a dialectic of secular and sacred, of the secular in the sacred and vice versa, is precisely the sort of sacramental vision one sees in Orthodox who critique secularism. Sergii Bulgakov (1871–1944), like his student Schmemann, strongly critiques secularism but he comes to a conclusion about the world in relationship to the sacred not that different from Kearney. Bulgakov speaks of two false poles in the Christian attitude to life that exist in a bad dialectic of unresolved contradictions as both are equally one-sided. There is a world-denying Manichaeism, which sees salvation as a flight from the world. For this "anti-cosmism" there is a vast gulf between the world (secular) and God (sacred) making "Divine-humanity," Christ and his church, ontologically impossible. Against anti-cosmism, there stands the "cosmism" of "secularization" or the "secularization of life."[40] Christianity has created this false attitude to the world and life, which emerged during the Reformation and Renaissance.[41]

The secularization of life accepts the world as it is, "worships the status quo," because, it is alleged, Christianity is powerless to direct or control life so it sets up the world and its life as its own standard of values. Life and humanity become completely mechanized, dead, un-free since they are bound by a tight scheme of necessitous cause and effect. This sort of modern atheist position deifies the world, so it is a specific form of pantheism. It is not the "zero of religion" but simply the lack or "minus" of a lifeless Christianity that so fetishizes transcendence that it deprives the world of God.[42] The only solution, Bulgakov argues, is a new *askesis* in and for the world which "struggle[s] with the world out of love for the world,"[43] seeing the creaturely world as "sophianic," primordially blessed, united with the divine world in the divine Sophia or God: "Heaven stoops toward earth; the world is not only a world in itself, it is also the world in God, and God abides not only in heaven but also on earth with human beings."[44] In other words, in the metaphor of the one Sophia, divine and creaturely,[45] we see an alternative image of Kearney's interanimation of the sacred and the secular. The purpose of an Orthodox theology of secularism, insofar as it is a form of dialectical sacramentality, is the transfiguring of creation, elevating it in the worship of its Creator who was transfigured on the cross so that that world becomes transparent to the Spirit of Christ.

Grounding Secularism in Christ

Yet, the interanimation between the sacred and the secular of which both Kearney and Bulgakov wrote for the Christian must, as we alluded to earlier, find its home in Christ. Thus, Bonhoeffer argues against a view that would see two spheres in perpetual conflict: one is divine, holy, supernatural, Christian, that is, the sacred, and the other is worldly, profane, natural, un-Christian, that is, the secular. For the next move is to put Christ on one side of this divide thereby alienating him and us from the world he created and redeemed. This forces man to seek Christ without the world in which he was incarnated, which is a sort of docetism, or to go the way of an angry atheism and seek the world without Christ. There are not two realities but one reality of God in Christ in and for the world. In being with him we stand as the church both in God and in the world since the church is *in* but not *of* the world. As Bulgakov reminded us, God abides in

Christ and the church (divine-humanity)—in heaven but also on earth. Christ contains within himself the world, he embraces within his very life as the Son of God the secular and the sacred and the world "has no reality of its own, independently of the revelation of God in Christ."[46] The opposites, then, sacred and secular, are in an original or polemical unity in Christ and do not have their reality except in him in a polemical attitude toward one another bearing witness in this way to their common reality and unity in the God-Man. History's movement consists of divergence and convergence from and toward him. One cannot, therefore, understand secularism and the secular and secularization apart from the fact that the secular is what is continuously being accepted and becoming accepted by God in Christ.[47] The human vocation, echoing Schmemann,[48] is priestly, insofar as it is divine-human and imaged after our "great high priest who has passed through the heavens, Jesus, the Son of God" (Heb 4:14). We are called to lift up the secular in thanksgiving so that it becomes a vehicle for the Spirit—unifying in ourselves what is disparate. If in Christ, then, God entered into the world so too what is Christian is only found in the secular, the supernatural in the natural, the holy in the profane and the revelational in the rational. To be a Christian, then, is to be a secular person but always in Jesus Christ in his body in the world, the church.[49] It is not inconceivable, then, if all of history is in Christ diverging and converging in and toward him in the world in him, that the movement in history that is the end of Christendom and the rise of the secular or secularization could be viewed not as a divergence from him but a tacit and mysterious convergence that is identical with God's own self-kenosis in Christ. In order that Jesus can be more fully in the world he redeemed, he must withdraw his body from its domination of the secular space in order that that space may in freedom develop of its own accord and the church may sit in that space witnessing to the life of Christ and coax the world to turn toward the one in whom it is upheld, freed, and even validated in its pluralism. Thus, an Orthodox theology of secularism must not only be sacramental, insofar as it is a dialectic of secular and sacred, but it must be grounded in Jesus Christ as the sacrament of the world, but to be Christoform, it also must be cruciform and involve a radical self-emptying of God in Christ in his body the church.

Secularization as Kenosis

Vattimo, with his *pensiero debole* (weak thought), refers to secularization as a providential form of kenosis insofar as beginning with the death of Christ, then moving to the rise and then decline of Christendom, one has the long slow death of the metaphysical concept of God as objective abstract Being. Being is in an inexorable movement toward enfeeblement, dissolution, the declination or distortion (*Verwindung*) of metaphysics, which Vattimo likes to call Being's lightening or its losing weight (*alleggerimento*).[50] This is the overcoming of metaphysics (*Überwindung*) through its distortion and gradual dissolution/declination,[51] which leads to the lack of any stable structure of Being which is equivalent to Nietzsche's famous word that "God is dead."[52] The "God" that is dying only existed as the ground of a pietistic morality. It was the god of the philosophers, not the god of Abraham, Isaac, and Jacob.

In slowly withdrawing, weakening, and self-emptying, Being's absence is, in a strange way, a sort of presence. The absence of Being is a presence because by withdrawing itself, Being illumines beings, the things themselves, and generates the multiple meanings in interpretation. Being is confirmed as that which illumines all without being those things themselves, just like a lamp that illuminates a chair so that it "is there" is not the chair itself. Being is itself kenotic or self-emptying in character forever subsisting by diminishing just as Christians hold that all things increase because Christ decreases on the cross. Vattimo here cites a line from Bonhoeffer's *Act and Being*: "A God who is, is not [*Einen Gott, den es gibt, gibt es nicht*]."[53] With the weakening of Being, which roughly tracks with the slow death of the old God of Christendom and Christendom itself, is the beginning of a free secular order of a plurality of interpretations of how to live one's life, its meaning in community, and this new consciously constructed order—call it "modern-liberal-socialist-democratic thought," the secular age[54]—is ruled, limiting the chaos, by a respect for the other, which he calls "charity."[55] The future of Christianity is to become a nondogmatic religion of pure charity moving ever more toward its own dissolution through its own desacralization in the process of secularization. Vattimo likes to quote Augustine here: "Love and do what you will."[56]

Secularization as the kenosis of God is salvation, which is the end of religion and the consummation and death of Christianity, in Being fulfilling its weakening religious vocation.[57] Vattimo plays with Heidegger's famous words from the 1966 *Der Spiegel* interview, "only a god can save us" and says instead that "only a relativistic God can save us"—"relativistic" for him is identical to "kenotic."[58] What Christ does, therefore, in dying on the cross, in his self-emptying, his kenosis, is reveal the death of the strong metaphysical God (Vattimo likes to say: "Thanks be to God I am an atheist") and Christ incarnates, as it were, Being now seen as the non-violent non-absolute God of our post-metaphysical age in his weakness and lightening. Quite simply, Christ reveals that God/Being has a vocation for weakening and the decline of the church's cultural rule over the West is part of this providential process.[59]

Secularization as Providential

Now, this all clearly is highly problematic and, how shall we say, a little overwrought. It rather uncritically and unhistorically glorifies secularization as the master narrative of the West at the same time as it claims there are no master narratives and—this is its greatest flaw—leaves "charity" free from the process of dissolution in a sort of ahistorical haze.

But I want to appropriate constructively some of Vattimo's thoughts and take them a little further, suggesting some possible lines toward a new positive theology of the secular, secularization, and secularism for the Orthodox. Vattimo is helpful in seeing secularization and the end of Christendom as in some sense providential. Modern culture, despite its great dangers, as Charles Taylor (b. 1931) has argued, can be viewed as providential to the extent that with its breaking with "the structures and beliefs of Christendom" certain aspects of Christian life, its gospel ethic, such as in a more humane attitude to women and now sexual minorities, were taken forward and developed, penetrating human life and society, in ways that would simply not have been possible within a purely Christian culture.[60] The church illumines things in the world by its very withdrawal, its self-emptying, via secularism. In this way, the church's light then can spill out far ahead onto the path society treads without it obscuring that light by its dogmatic and historical bulk. Secularism is then seen as a tacit, providentially guided evangelism. Vattimo, as I mentioned earlier, identifies this providential aspect of secularization and the decline of Christendom, with God's self-emptying in Christ, and I want to take this idea further in articulating a positive Eastern Orthodox theology of secularism. In what follows, I want to pursue a theological experiment, a Trinitarian reverie on civil society and secularism bringing together some of the threads just mentioned stretching out to the far shore of an Orthodox Christian theology of secularism.[61]

Secularization as Trinitarian

When it is said that secularization is a form of kenosis, I mean that in Christ we see the culmination of a divine-human movement of God's complete self-gift to creation and then to civil society where he relativizes himself, emptying himself of all claims to centrality, to being the foundation of truth and morality. He withdraws to illumine so that his creatures can freely choose to follow him or not, organize their communities in light of him or not, choosing to do so not because it is natural and the end of their nature but merely as they are struck by the witness of his love, his coaxing them forward through the persuasion of the Spirit who ever turns them more deeply to his weakening grace on the cross. We are created in God's image, but, more particularly, in the image of Christ,[62] who is the image of the invisible God (Col 1:15) in whom "all things hold together" (1:17). What it means to be formed after Christ is both for him to make room for us in his creation of which we form the apex and to gift us with a share of being insofar as humanity is a portion of God.[63] This share of Being is a space given to us to be ourselves—freedom and the creativity which derives from that; and in being free, God cannot—indeed, has bound himself, emptying himself of all power—and will not, overwhelm us. He will not force us into particular moral decisions, he will not compel us to structure our communities after his law of love but gently coaxes us and persuades us through his Spirit toward the way of truth in growing up into the measure of the stature of the fullness of Christ (Eph 4:13). Christ's self-emptying in creation and redemption is a holy withdrawal of the sacred to make room for the secular—the human in the image of God—to be itself. It is a withdrawal that undergirds that space as free and valid in its own right because it is a gift of God and so it is an absence that allows for the presence of the secular in the bosom of the sacred. But if we can say that God reveals himself paradoxically by withdrawing and weakening himself to leave room for the secular, albeit a secular upheld and allowed to be by the sacred as both are contained in Christ himself, then are we not saying that divine transcendence exists in an interanimation with its immanence in the world? What sort of God would give himself to us in this way?

If Being/God has a weakening vocation, then could we not apply this sort of theology to the Trinity? Here we might read the life of God, in light of the cross, as a movement of perfect charity, respect, tolerance, and embrace of the Other in all his difference and particularity where each of the divine persons lets the Other be by letting the Other go.[64] The Father pours himself out in birthing the Son even unto his complete self-exhaustion, a sort of spiritual death, and he spirates the Spirit, breathes it out eternally as the gift of his self-denying joy that rests on his Son. In turn, the Son affirms his Father as source and the nonfoundational ground of his own Being, so allowing the Father to be as Father and from their mutual self-giving and self-acknowledgment the Spirit binds them together in love, cutting back his own voice in order that he might mediate the particularity of another.

One image of this self-emptying, self-giving, self-receiving and self-withdrawing to expand beyond itself divine life is found in Andrei Rublev's icon of the Trinity with the three angels, mysterious strangers that visited Abraham at Mamre. At its heart, as Kearney has pointed out,[65] is a space, a *khora* or space which is not a space,[66] an altar around which they are gathered as if for a dance into, through, and outside of one another. On top of this space lies a chalice in which there is an immolated calf. This symbolism of the icon allows one to generously interpret it (using Rv 13:8 with its "Lamb slain from the foundation of the world") as depicting an eternal sacrifice of love in the weak God of the Trinity as the pre-eternal foundation of the act of creation and redemption in Christ. But might we follow this thought experiment through yet further?

Can we understand this *khora* as an altar, the basis of sacrifice, as the space of otherness whereby each person grants out of a weakening self-sacrificial love, a realm of freedom to let the Other be himself, free to be different in his particularity as different yet united around this space which is not a space? This space, we might argue, is the space of God's Being as free weakening and self-emptying love that eternally gifts otherness. But if on top of this space of Being is a chalice with the "Lamb slain" (Rv 13:8), can we then not see the very foundation of creation which God gifts to us—and, by extension, civil society, that place in which we agree to order our lives together as citizens of a commonwealth for the end of human flourishing—as a space to be free in our otherness? We then could argue that God creates his world just as he exists as Trinity, that is, by pouring himself out into nothingness, dying to himself in weak Being and in this way relativizing himself and in a sense being born as "God" for a "world" (as divinity is a relational concept), and no longer being merely the "Absolute" but also "Absolute-Relative."[67] This is the eternal death of God as Absolute, the God of the philosophers, for if we want to climb up to see who God is, what the foundation of reality may be, we will only see the very same suffering and weakening God who relativized himself by giving himself to us on a cross, having lived and died by girding himself as a slave becoming no one and nowhere. By granting creation a space to be itself, albeit one eternally founded and undergirded in God in Christ, God refuses to determine the end of creation's nature and, therefore, its actions. This self-emptying in creation obtains its consummation, its completion, and the fullness of its presence to the world in the weakness and withdrawal of the Creator and Savior God dying on the cross. In perhaps Bonhoeffer's most famous words: "The God who lets us live in the world without the working hypothesis of God is the God before whom we stand continually. Before God and with God we live without God. God lets himself be pushed out of the world on to the cross. He is weak and powerless in the world, and that is precisely the way, the only way, in which he is with us and helps us . . . only the suffering God can help."[68]

How shall we apply this thinking to a theological vision of civil society and secularization? The weak God's self-giving on the cross is twofold: (a) in dying for us on the cross he creates the world to be holy in its secularity which is upheld by him as it exists by virtue of his self-emptying and self-giving, his withdrawal so that it might be itself; and (b) he establishes a base, a community of the crucified, from which he may witness to his weak love—his body the church. But in establishing this space within the free space of creation, the church, all of this reality being, of course, held together in God in Christ, he moves even further back into himself. Yet this move back into himself, this self-limitation, contraction of the divine,[69] as God is eternal, invisible and infinite is a move where he never leaves us at all. He spreads himself open in vulnerability as an invisible empowering and all-pervasive foundation to allow the creation of civil society, a secular commonwealth of agreed and common ends ordered to peace, order, and government, but which is in, by, and from the church as the body of the living Christ. In this idea of civil society there reigns a free albeit bounded plurality of interpretations on what constitutes the good. Although there exists one commonality which underpins its pluralism, as in God himself, which is equality of respect and embrace of the Other in their difference, so honoring their freedom of conscience and allowing peace and harmony to order human relations as well as the good of just governance balancing the different ends of all citizens. Society, then, is left to itself to find its own coherence that needs not be aligned with that of his body, although God ever coaxes and persuades it deeper into himself so that it might discover the eternal and invisible foundation of its basic and common life. Thus, tolerance, human rights, freedom of conscience, care for creation, and even the separation of church and state all can be traced to the body of God, built up in love by Christ Jesus whose image we bear, a body that withdraws itself in order to be present to creation and civil society. Secularism is not only a kenotic reality that is grounded in Christ, but, because it is kenotic, it is also Trinitarian, sacramental, and ecclesial in character.

The church does have a space in creation and, within creation itself, a space and voice in civil society. I am not advocating political quietism. Yet its space is a space to witness, reaching out beyond itself, and, therefore, is not a platform to lecture or tell the different parts of society, the different portions of the human organizations that make up a political commonwealth; they should not be in and of the world, although it can and should at times critique aspects of civil society that are counter to the gospel ethic. As Bonhoeffer said, the church's space is one that exists "in order to prove to the world that it is still the world, the world which is loved and reconciled with him."[70] In this Orthodox theological vision of secularism, all of creation is tacitly taken up, embraced, and borne within the body of the church, the body of God, and called from its foundation to acknowledge God's radical acceptance and honoring of it in Christ. Indeed, all creation and, in creation, civil society itself, crowned by humanity, shares in the humanity of Christ whose body is the church so that in essence the limits of the church do not exist at all and creation is, in Bulgakov's words, simply the "cosmic face of the Church."[71] This means politically that there do not exist two separate cities—the church and the secular world organized into its varied political forms—with two sets of mutually incompatible values. Rather, secular society and secularism, rightly understood, are an unmanifested or tacit version of the church where what is secular or worldly has divine-human roots. By withdrawing from society, a withdrawal which is its form of presence, ever witnessing to its Lord, the church emphasizes that "the world is relative to Christ, no matter whether it knows it or not."[72]

This witness is best viewed in terms of the church persuading the world that at the points where the world's values align with the church, indeed, may be tacit developments of the gospel ethic, they find their true incarnation in Christ crucified. The place of witness of the church can be viewed as akin to the Royal Doors at the center of the Orthodox iconostasis. These Holy Doors of the Kingdom are swung wide open during the whole of the "Bright Week" following Easter or Pascha. The church in the public sphere simply points, as it were, in between these doors to the altar, a space that has its foundation in God himself, on which lies the sacrificed Lamb of God which is the true fulfillment of secularism, the weakening God that lies secretly at the center of creation and of secular society: *Ecce homo! Behold the man!* (Jn 19:5). Here at the center of creation, at the center of civil society, is its true meaning: the body of the Living Christ, the church as the earthly manifestation of the union and communion of the Holy Trinity. As Christians, we are called to lift high the Lamb of God and let the light of Christ illumine all so that all may come and taste and see that the Lord is good. But this uplifting is always persuasive and never reactive and coercive, or we will contradict the very image in which we are made.

New Paths of Political Theology

It is time to balance antinomically Orthodox antisecularism with a positive Eastern Orthodox Christian theology of secularism. Such a new experimental theology tries to see how Orthodoxy might boldly bear witness to Christ in the modern pluralistic and secular West, to respond to the contemporary challenges the West presents to Eastern Orthodoxy.[73] All the while, Orthodoxy must continue to critically keep in mind the West's numerous failures, its departures from the Christian message and Orthodoxy's premodern difference, for lack of a better term, its "Easternness."[74] New paths of Orthodox political theology need to be beaten through the overgrown wood, trying to see how the light of Christ which illumines all might be working in a space of a modern society that at first looks simply Godless, dark, and chaotic so that the mission of the church, its premodern sensibility, and witness to One by whose pinned palms the world is embraced in himself, is not lost to view.

Notes

1. George Grant, *Lament for a Nation: The Defeat of Canadian Nationalism* (Montreal: McGill-Queen's University Press, [1965] 2005), 94–95.

2. Dietrich Bonhoeffer, "Letter to Eberhard Bethge, [Tegel] 30 April 1944," in *Letters and Papers from Prison*, enl. ed., ed. Eberhard Bethge and trans. Reginald Fuller et al. (New York: Macmillan, 1972), 280.

3. See "World Christian Database at Centre for the Study of Global Christianity, Gordon-Conwell Theological Seminary," World Christian Database, accessed April 12, 2019, http://www.worldchristiandatabase.org/wcd/home.asp.

4. "The Future of World Religions: Population Growth Projections, 2010–2050: Christians," Pew Research Center, accessed April 12, 2019, http://www.pewforum.org/2015/04/02/christians/.

5. See Grace Davie, *Europe: The Exceptional Case—The Parameters of Faith in the Modern World* (London: Darton, Longman and Todd, 2002); and Hugh McLeod and Werner Ustorf, eds., *The Decline of Christendom in Western Europe, 1750–2000* (Cambridge: Cambridge University Press, 2003).

6. "Global Christianity—A Report on the Size and Distribution of the World's Christian Population," Pew Research Center, accessed April 12, 2019, http://www.pewforum.org/2011/12/19/global-christianity-exec/.

7. "Orthodox Christianity in the 21st Century," Pew Research Center, accessed April 12, 2019, http://www.pewforum.org/2017/11/08/orthodox-christianity-in-the-21st-century/.

8. "The Future of World Religions: Population Growth Projections, 2010–2050: Muslims," Pew Research Center, accessed April 12, 2019, http://www.pewforum.org/2015/04/02/muslims/.

9. "No Religion by Census Mapper," accessed April 12, 2019, https://censusmapper.ca/maps/59.

10. See, for example, Mark C. Taylor, *After God* (Chicago: University of Chicago Press, 2007); and John D. Caputo, *The Folly of God: A Theology of the Unconditional* (Salem, MA: Polbridge, 2015).

11. See, for example, John Milbank, *Theology and Social Theory: Beyond Secular Reason*, 2nd ed. (Oxford: Blackwell, 2006).

12. See Brandon Gallaher, "The Orthodox Moment: The Holy and Great Council in Crete and Orthodoxy's Encounter with the West: On Learning to Love the Church," *Sobornost* 39, no. 2 (2017): 26–71; and "Orthodoxy and the West—The Problem of Orthodox Self-Criticism in Christos Yannaras" in *Polis, Ontology, Ecclesial Event: Engaging with Christos Yannaras' Thought*, ed. Sotiris Mitralexis (Cambridge, UK: James Clarke, 2018), 206–25.

13. See Brandon Gallaher, "Eschatological Anarchism: Eschatology and Politics in Contemporary Greek Theology," in *Political Theologies in Orthodox*

Christianity, ed. Kristina Stoeckl, Ingeborg Gabriel, and Aristotle Papanikolaou (London: T and T Clark-Bloomsbury, 2017), 146–49.

14. Rowan Williams, *Faith in the Public Square* (London: Bloomsbury, 2012), 2–4.

15. See the Postsecular Conflicts project at the University of Innsbruck led by Kristina Stoeckl, accessed April 12, 2019, https://www.uibk.ac.at/projects /postsecular-conflicts/.

16. See Brandon Gallaher, "A Tale of Two Speeches: Secularism and Primacy in Contemporary Roman Catholicism and Russian Orthodoxy," in *Primacy in the Church: The Office of Primate and the Authority of the Councils*, vol. 2, *Contemporary and Contextual Perspectives*, ed. John Chryssavgis (Crestwood, NY: St. Vladimir's Seminary Press, 2016), 807–37; and "The Road from Rome to Moscow," *Tablet*, February 20, 2016, 8–9.

17. See Kara Fox and Valentina Di Donato, "In Italy's city of love, global far-right groups join forces under a 'pro-family' umbrella," *CNN*, March 31, 2019, accessed April 12, 2019, https://edition.cnn.com/2019/03/31/europe /verona-world-congress-of-families-intl/index.html; Kristina Stoeckl, "The European Culture Wars," *ZOiS Spotlight*, April 3, 2019, accessed April 12, 2019, https://en.zois-berlin.de/publications/zois-spotlight/the-european-culture -wars/; Mark Silk, "The Other Russian Collusion Story," *Religion News Service*, March 25, 2019, accessed April 12, 2019, https://religionnews.com/2019/03/25 /the-other-russian-collusion-story/; Paul Glader, "Are American Evangelicals Using Russia to Fight Their Culture War?," *Religion Unplugged*, March 28, 2019, accessed April 12, 2019, https://religionunplugged.com/news/2019/3/28 /are-american-evangelicals-using-russia-to-fight-their-culture-war; Anton Shekhovtsov, *Russia and the Western Far Right: Tango Noir* (Abingdon, Oxon/ New York: Routledge, 2018); Christopher Stroop, "Between Trump and Putin: The Right-Wing International, a Crisis of Democracy, and the Future of the European Union," *Political Research Associates*, May 11, 2017, accessed April 12, 2019, http://www.politicalresearch.org/2017/05/11/between-trump-and-putin -the-right-wing-international-a-crisis-of-democracy-and-the-future-of-the -european-union/#sthash.yabTSawE.cvjvDDWy.dpbs; Christopher Stroop, "Pence Meets with One of Putin's Top Clerics: Strange Bedfellows at BEGEA's World Summit in Defense of Persecuted Christians," *Religion Dispatches*, May 12, 2017, accessed April 12, 2019, http://religiondispatches.org/pence -meets-with-one-of-putins-top-clerics-strange-bedfellows-at-bgaes-world -summit-in-defense-of-persecuted-christians/; and Casey Michel, "The Rise of the 'Traditionalist International': How the American Right Learned to Love Moscow in the Era of Trump," *Right Wing Watch*, March 2017, accessed April 12, 2019, http://www.rightwingwatch.org/report/the-rise-of-the

-traditionalist-international-how-the-american-right-learned-to-love-moscow
-in-the-era-of-trump/.

18. See Sergei Chapnin, "A Church of Empire: Why the Russian Church Chose to Bless Empire," *First Things*, November 2015, accessed April 12, 2019, https://www.firstthings.com/article/2015/11/a-church-of-empire. Cf. John P. Burgess, *Holy Rus': The Rebirth of Orthodoxy in the New Russia* (New Haven, CT: Yale University Press, 2017).

19. See Jason Ananda Josephson, *The Invention of Religion in Japan* (Chicago: University of Chicago Press, 2009), 19–20 and 132–63; and cf. Cyril Hovorun, *Political Orthodoxies: The Unorthodoxies of the Church Coerced* (Minneapolis, MN: Fortress Press, 2018).

20. For commentary, see Gallaher, "The Orthodox Moment."

21. "Encyclical of the Holy and Great Council of the Orthodox Church," para. 10, accessed April 12, 2019, https://www.holycouncil.org/-/encyclical-holy -council; and see "Message of the Holy and Great Council of the Orthodox Church," para. 5, accessed April 12, 2019, https://www.holycouncil.org/-/message.

22. Alexander Schmemann, *For the Life of the World: Sacraments and Orthodoxy*, 2nd ed. (Crestwood, NY: St. Vladimir's Seminary Press, [1963] 1988), 100.

23. Schmemann, 18.

24. Schmemann, 76, see also 112.

25. Dylan Thomas, "The Force That through the Green Fuse Drives the Flower" in *Dylan Thomas: The Poems*, ed. Daniel Jones (London: J. M. Dent and Sons, 1978), l.1, 77.

26. Schmemann, *For the Life of the World*, 118 and 124.

27. Max Weber, *Max Weber's Science as a Vocation*, ed. Peter Lassman and Irving Velody with Herminio Martins (London: Unwin and Hyman, [1918] 1989), 13–14.

28. See S. N. Eisenstadt, "Multiple Modernities," in *Comparative Civilizations and Multiple Modernities*, 2 vols. (Leiden: Brill, 2003), 2:536.

29. José Casanova, "The Secular, Secularizations, Secularisms," in *Rethinking Secularism*, ed. Calhoun, Juergensmeyer, and Van Antwerpen (New York: Oxford University Press, 2011), 54–74.

30. Dietrich Bonhoeffer, *Ethics*, ed. Eberhard Bethge and trans. Neville Horton Smith (London: Collins, 1964), 199.

31. See Henricus Denzinger and Adolfus Schönmetzer, eds., *Enchiridion Symbolorum*, 36th ed. (Barcelona: Herder, 1976), para. 302, 108.

32. Richard Kearney, *Anatheism: Returning to God After God* (New York: Columbia University Press, 2011), 16.

33. Kearney, 17–81.

34. See Brandon Gallaher, *Freedom and Necessity in Modern Trinitarian Theology* (Oxford: Oxford University Press, 2016), 95–114, 238–49.

35. Jocelyn Maclure and Charles Taylor, *Secularism and Freedom of Conscience* (Cambridge, MA: Harvard University Press, 2011), 41.

36. Gianni Vattimo, *After Christianity*, trans. Luca D'Isanto (New York: Columbia University Press, 2002), 100–101.

37. Kearney, *Anatheism*, 152.

38. Kearney, 139–42.

39. Kearney, 166.

40. Sergei Bulgakov, *Sophia, the Wisdom of God: An Outline of Sophiology*, trans. Patrick Thompson, O. Fielding Clarke, and Xenia Braikevitch (Hudson, NY: Lindisfarne, [1937] 1993), 14–15 and 20.

41. Bulgakov, 20.

42. Bulgakov, 15.

43. Bulgakov, 21.

44. Bulgakov, 17.

45. See Gallaher, *Freedom and Necessity*, 84–94.

46. Bonhoeffer, *Ethics*, 196–97.

47. Bonhoeffer, 198–99.

48. See Schmemann, *For the Life of the World*, 15, 17, 93–94.

49. Bonhoeffer, *Ethics*, 200.

50. See Gianni Vattimo, "Dialectics, Difference, and Weak Thought," trans. Thomas Harrison, *Graduate Faculty Philosophy Journal* 10, no. 1 (Spring 1984): 157–59.

51. Vattimo, 158

52. See Martin Heidegger, "The Word of Nietzsche: 'God Is Dead,'" *The Question Concerning Technology and Other Essays*, trans. William Lovitt (New York: Harper and Row, 1977), 53–112.

53. Gianni Vattimo with Piergiorgio Paterlini, *Not Being God: A Collaborative Autobiography*, trans. William McCuaig (New York: Columbia University Press, 2010), 24.

54. Vattimo and Paterlini, 152.

55. Gianni Vattimo, *Belief*, trans. Luca D'Isanto and David Webb (Cambridge: Polity, 1999), 62–65; Vattimo, *A Farewell to Truth*, trans. William McCuaig (New York: Columbia University Press, 2011), 75–79; and Vattimo, *After Christianity*, 48, 82, 111–12.

56. Gianni Vattimo and John D. Caputo, *After the Death of God*, ed. Jeffrey W. Robbins (New York: Columbia University Press, 2007), 41–46.

57. Vattimo, *After Christianity*, 24.

58. Vattimo, *A Farewell to Truth*, 47.

59. Vattimo, *Belief*, 39.

60. Charles Taylor, *A Catholic Modernity?* (New York: Oxford University Press, 1999), 16, 18, 26, 29, 36–37.

61. For more on Trinitarian theology, see Gallaher, *Freedom and Necessity*, 238–50.

62. See Irenaeus of Lyons, *On the Apostolic Preaching*, trans. John Behr (Crestwood, NY: St. Vladimir's Seminary Press, 1997), para. 22; and see 2 Cor 4:4. For a discussion, see Brandon Gallaher, "Creativity, Covenant and Christ," in *God's Creativity and Human Action: Christian and Muslim Perspectives*, ed. Lucinda Mosher and David Marshall (Washington, DC: Georgetown University Press, 2017), 86–96.

63. See Origen of Alexandria, *On First Principles*, 1.3.6, trans. G. Butterworth (Gloucester: Peter Smith, 1973), 35 [*Sources chrétiennes* 252, 154–55, l.161]; Pseudo-Dionysius the Areopagite, *Divine Names*, in *Pseudo-Dionysius: The Complete Works*, trans. Colm Luibheid, Paul Rorem (New York: Paulist Press, 1987), 5.6 [*Patristische Texte und Studien* 33; 184, ll.17–21], 99; and Thomas Aquinas, *The Summa Contra Gentiles of St. Thomas Aquinas*, 3a.20, trans. English Dominicans (New York: Benziger Brothers, 1924), 38. See also Maximus the Confessor, *On Difficulties in the Church Fathers: The Ambigua*, 2 vols., ed. and trans. Nicholas Constas (Cambridge, MA: Harvard University Press, 2014), *Ambiguum* 7.pref. [*PG* 1068D], 1:75–78. (exegeting Gregory Nazianzus, *Oration* 14.7 [*PG* 35.865C]).

64. See Gallaher, *Freedom and Necessity*, 189.

65. Kearney, *Anatheism*, 25–26.

66. See Paul S. Fiddes, *Seeing the World and Knowing God: Israelite Wisdom and Christian Doctrine in a Late-Modern Context* (Oxford: Oxford University Press, 2013), 218–65 (esp. 249–56), 320–21, 325–26.

67. See Gallaher, *Freedom and Necessity*, 70–94.

68. Bonhoeffer, "Letter to Eberhard Bethge, [Tegel] 16 July [1944]," in *Letters and Papers from Prison*, 360–61.

69. See Gallaher, *Freedom and Necessity*, 86–87.

70. Bonhoeffer, *Ethics*, 202.

71. Sergii Bulgakov, *The Bride of the Lamb*, abridged trans. and ed. Boris Jakim (Grand Rapids, MI: Eerdmans, 2002), 267.

72. Bonhoeffer, *Ethics*, 206–7.

73. See, for example, the attempt to respond as Orthodox to LGBTQ+/sexual diversity: Brandon Gallaher, "Tangling with Orthodox Tradition in the Modern West: Natural Law, Homosexuality, and Living Tradition," *Wheel*, nos. 13–14 (Spring/Summer 2018): 50–63; and the British Council Bridging Voices joint Exeter-Fordham project led by Brandon Gallaher, Aristotle Papanikolaou, and Gregory Tucker, "British Council Awards Grants for Bridging Voices Addressing the Role of Religion on Culture and Policy," *British Council USA*,

December 20, 2017, accessed April 15, 2019, https://www.britishcouncil.us
/about/press/british-council-awards-grants-bridging-voices-addressing-role
-religion-culture-and; "Meet the Exeter-Fordham Bridging Voices Consortium,"
British Council USA, August 10, 2018, accessed April 15, 2019, https://www
.youtube.com/watch?v=AKzMDEO_e-E; and Tom Stoelker, "British Council
Awards Grant to Orthodox Christian Studies Center for LGBTQ Research,"
Fordham News, January 18, 2018, accessed April 15, 2019, https://news.fordham
.edu/university-news/83996/.

74. See, for example, the contemporary critique of transhumanism in
Brandon Gallaher, "Godmanhood vs. Mangodhood: An Eastern Orthodox
Response to Transhumanism," *Studies in Christian Ethics*, February 15, 2019,
accessed April 15, 2019, https://journals.sagepub.com/doi/10.1177
/0953946819827136. More generally see Gallaher, "Orthodoxy and the West."

Fundamentalism

FUNDAMENTALISM: NOT JUST A CAUTIONARY TALE

Edith M. Humphrey

Thus says the LORD: "Behold, I lay for the foundations of Zion a stone
that is costly, choice, and designed as a cornerstone, one to be honored for
Zion's foundations; and whoever believes on him shall by no means be
ashamed."

Is 28:16 LXX (my translation)

This verse from Isaiah, in its LXX expression, was so important to
the Christian community that it is echoed in several places in the
New Testament. In its original context, the verse depicts the LORD as prom-
ising to renew the covenant with Israel, despite her apostasy and compromised sojourn among the nations. There we hear about the inadequacy of
human schemes that in the end have become "a covenant with death" (Is
28:18) for Israel, "for the bed is too short to stretch oneself on it, and the
covering too narrow to wrap oneself in it" (Is 28:20). Over against such
short-sighted strategies, the LORD is anticipated as bringing in a surprising
era of justice and rest. Early Christians who followed the apostolic rule of
faith interpreted this prophetic assurance as a reference to the advent of
the Messiah, who was himself the true Temple, and the unique foundation not to be supplanted by any other (1 Cor 3:11). The prophetic judgment in this passage against those who were cherishing false hope made it
natural for the earliest Christian preachers to combine it with an earlier
word of Isaiah that also used the metaphor of a stone: "But the LORD of
hosts, him you shall regard as holy; let him be your fear, and let him be
your dread. And he will become a sanctuary, and a stone of offense, and a

rock of stumbling to both houses of Israel. . . . And many shall stumble thereon; they shall fall and be broken" (Is 8:13–15). When Isaiah 28 and Isaiah 8 were thus matched, Jesus was proclaimed as the true foundation that God laid in Zion for the renewal of the world, but also as the LORD himself, who will become, for those who reject Him, the "stone of offense."

Paradox, then, attends the biblical thread concerning foundations and the one true foundation—the unique divine cornerstone and foundation is also a means of scandal to those who reject him. This nuanced understanding is repeated in the gospels, in St. Paul's letters, and in first Peter (i.e., Mk 12:10; Rom 9:33; 1 Pet 2:6–8), a spread that testifies to its general proclamation in earliest Christianity.

If late nineteenth-century Christians had been content to identify the Rock as Jesus, then the term *fundamentalism* may not itself have become the scandal that it has today among Christians (although I remember in my graduate days one professor impugning those more conservative than himself for "Jesus-olatry"). That is, if the foundation had been delineated as the God-Man, then the *ism* would have implied a concentration upon that Holy One, and not "Jesus plus other things." But that was not the case. The fundamentals were understood as plural rather than singular, and as doctrinal rather than seen in the divine Person himself. And so, Anthony Gilles puts it, "Fundamental*ism* connotes a distortion—a hyperextension, one might say—of the fundamentals. Attaching -*ist* and -*ism* to *fundamental* suggests adhering to doctrines for their own sake, without seeing their purpose."[1] The bed is too short, the covering too narrow! Thus, the conference for which this paper was written centered around a question posed by one of its organizers: "How does a Christian community [for example, the Orthodox or the Catholic] that values tradition operate in an increasingly secularized world without lapsing into fundamentalism?"[2]

Our first instinct might be to think we know the exact intention and parameters of this question, since "fundamentalism" is common currency. Unfortunately, it is one of those words that evokes more heat than light: Do we mean by it a concentration upon certain beliefs to the exclusion of others? Narrow-minded dogmatism? Sectarian behavior? Rigorous adherence to marginal beliefs and practices? Careless rejection of contemporary ideas and practices? A lack of balance that tends to violence? Or is it a historical descriptor of groups in the late nineteenth and early twentieth century which gave rise to the term? In this paper, I will trace the biblical use of the term *foundation*, look at those in the early twentieth century who took on the name of *fundamentalist* (apparently without a sense of the *ist* suffix as derogatory), and consider a few groups to which the label has been attached today, rightly or wrongly. In performing this biblical, historical, and social investigation, I want to ferret out what we can learn from fundamentalism—both directly and inversely. For I am convinced that fundamentalism has something to say to us, and not simply as a cautionary tale. In the end, I will argue that the main impulses of fundamentalism—to discern and cleave to the fundamentals of our faith in response to social trends—can be salutary.

Biblical and Patristic Foundation

We begin by looking to Scriptures and Holy Tradition for an understanding of fundamentals—that which forms the foundation (*fundamentum* in Latin, or *themelios* in Greek). We have seen already, following the metaphor found in Romans, 1 Peter, the parable of the vineyard told by Jesus, and 1 Corinthians 3, that there is properly ONE foundation for the faith. Jesus is the rock rejected by humans but appointed by God, the unique cornerstone: "no other foundation can anyone lay than that which is laid, which is Jesus Christ" (1 Cor 3:11). However, a broader examination will show us that some passages do use the term in the plural, with an extension of its meaning. Indeed, in the synoptic gospels, Jesus himself implies that the "foundation" is *his words*, or better, adherence to them. Consider his concluding parable to both the Sermon on the Plain (Luke) and the Sermon on the Mount (Matthew):

> Everyone who comes to me and hears my words and does them, I will show you what that one is like: like a man building a house, who dug deep, and laid the foundation upon rock; and when a flood arose, the stream broke against that house, and could not shake it, because it had been built well. But the one who hears and does not do them is like a man who built a house on the ground without a foundation; against that house the stream broke, and immediately it fell, and the ruin of that house was great. (Lk 6:47–49, cf. Mt 7:24–27)

This parable, like the correction that James makes to a shallow appropriation of Pauline teaching, insists that true faith goes beyond naming a person with honor ("Lord! Lord!"), or holding a tenet intellectually, but puts conviction into practice. In a similar way, Ephesians 2:20 fills out what it means to have Jesus as the foundation, when it speaks of the apostles and prophets as the foundation, and Jesus as the cornerstone. To truly honor the LORD is to see the continuity between him and the prophets, and to understand who he is in the light of the apostolic preaching—he is YHWH in the flesh (cf. Col 1:19). The book of Hebrews takes a different tack, when it implies that the *themelios* includes elementary teachings and rites: one must go *beyond* laying "a foundation of repentance from dead works and of faith toward God, with instruction about baptisms, the laying on of hands, the resurrection of the dead, and eternal judgment" (Heb 6:1–2). John the seer picks up on the metaphor, picturing the foundations of the New Jerusalem as inscribed with the names of the apostles and adorned with precious stones (Rv 21:13, 19). The foundations are not bare but include within them many riches for those who inhabit the holy city. Finally, 2 Timothy 2:19 speaks of "God's firm foundation," in contrast to those who were teaching heresy concerning the resurrection. This metaphor sets the confident tone for the solemn refrain "the saying is sure and worthy of acceptance" that laces through the Pastorals (1 Tm 1:15; 1:31; 4:8–9, 2 Tm 2:11–13 and Ti 3:8) as preface or conclusion to words regarding creed, ecclesial matters, *and* godly living.

In light of these passages, it seems that Paul's urging of Jesus as the sole foundation was predicated by the personality cults which were emerging in Corinth, and the party-spirit that gave rise to the slogans, "I am of Apollos!" and "I am of Peter!" His focus upon Jesus was not intended to create an absolute minimalism but to suggest that if one declared, with understanding, "Jesus is LORD!" all the other pertinent matters for belief, action, and life were implied within that statement. The New Testament, then, sets forth a single foundation, Jesus himself, who was in the beginning with the Father; at the same time, it also uses "foundation" and "foundations" to speak about the teaching of Jesus, the apostles and prophets gathered around Jesus, various early statements of faith, and calls to ecclesial and personal action. There is a oneness *and* a complexity to the foundation, for it is interconnected with Holy Tradition. Fr. Georges Florovsky calls our attention to St. Athanasius's first epistle on the Holy Spirit as he spoke to Serapion: "Let us look at that very tradition, teaching, and faith of the Catholic Church from the very beginning, which the Lord gave (ἐδώκεν), the Apostles preached (ἐκήρυξαν), and the Fathers preserved

(ἐφύλαξαν). Upon this the Church is founded [τεθεμελίωται] ([*Quat Ep*]
ad Serap I. 28)."³

In exegeting St. Athanasius, Fr. Florovsky highlights the interplay
of unity and complexity, and connects Holy Tradition with the
"foundation:"

> This passage is highly characteristic of St. Athanasius. The three terms
> in the phrase actually coincide: (παράδοσις) [tradition]—from Christ
> himself, (διδασκαλία) [teaching]—by the Apostles, and (πίστις)
> [faith]—of the Catholic Church. And this is the foundation
> (θεμέλιος) of the Church—a sole and single foundation. Scripture
> itself seems to be subsumed and included in this "Tradition," com-
> ing, as it is, from the Lord. In the concluding chapter of his first epis-
> tle to Serapion St. Athanasius returns once more to the same point.
> "In accordance with the Apostolic faith delivered to us by tradition
> from the Fathers, I have delivered the tradition, without inventing
> anything extraneous to it. What I learned, that have I inscribed . . .
> conformably with the Holy Scriptures" (c. 33). On an[other] occa-
> sion St. Athanasius denoted the Scripture itself as an Apostolic *para-
> dosis* (*ad Adelph.*, 6). It is characteristic that in the whole discussion
> with the Arians no single reference was made to any "traditions"—
> in plural. The only term of reference was always "Tradition"—indeed,
> *the* Tradition, the Apostolic Tradition, comprising the total and in-
> tegral content of the Apostolic "preaching," and summarized in the
> "rule of faith." The unity and solidarity of this Tradition was the main
> and crucial point in the whole argument.⁴

In St. Athanasius, Fr. Florovsky discerns a single tradition, teaching, and
faith that forms the foundation for the church—something "total and integral" that is complex but also wholly unified, for it is summarized in the
apostolic *regula fidei*, or *kanōn aletheias*, the norm of faith and truth. In
speaking of this single "focus (*skopos*) and character of Scripture," as interpreted and proclaimed by the apostles, St. Athanasius upholds the "double account" of Christ, both divine and human, which some did not discern
in their interpretation of Scripture, since they had rejected the apostolic
preaching (*Discourses against the Arians* 3:28–36). One must have an idea
of the focus and the guiding direction of the story, when trying to understand it in its entirety: it is helpful to bear in mind that the word *skopos*

was used for a target, or a goal. This "churchly scope" is championed by the theologian as "an anchor for the faith" (*Discourses* 3:58), of use to those who are misled, those who are trying to resist heresy, and those who are trying to rescue others from such mistakes. It is to this foundation that the theologian appealed when helping Serapion sort through the heresies of the Arians (who denied that the Son was God) and of the Tropici (who denied that the Spirit was God). This understanding of a common norm, Fr. Florovsky says, is typical of patristic teaching as a whole, and so he also mentions St. Basil's reliance upon the "ecclesial mind" (φρόνημα ἐκκλησιαστικόν) and the "solid foundation of the faith of Christ" (τό στερέωμα τῆς Χριστοῦ πίστεως).[5] In the end, the foundation is understood as singularly gathered around Christ, yet richly textured, and as providing a necessary buttress against error.

Fundamentalism in the Modern Age

When we turn to the late nineteenth century, we see, among those who spoke of Christian "fundamentals," a similar concern for the center of the faith, and a similar polemical edge—this time against modernism rather than Arianism, or against those other early heretics who denied the divinity of the Spirit. Fundamentalism in its classic form was a response to modernity. However, in the beginning it was not formed in a sectarian enclave but by well-educated academics from various Protestant groups, who wrote between 1910 and 1915 a series of small booklets eventually brought together in several volumes, entitled *The Fundamentals: A Testimony to the Truth*. A perusal of those volumes shows that the authors—from America, Canada, and Britain—although shaped by their Protestantism, were neither ignorant of their subject matter nor narrow in their approach. Designed for the educated nonacademic, the essays included forays into higher criticism, biblical inspiration, various books of the Bible, archaeology, the existence of God, the virginal conception, incarnation and resurrection of Christ, the atonement, evangelism, socialism, the Sabbath, prayer, science and the Bible, evolution, the second advent of Christ, "Romanism," and various popular cults. The initial essay on higher criticism is explicit in saying that Christians need not fear historical-critical study of the Bible per se, but the rationalist presuppositions of those who were currently engaging in it.[6] Although the topics are fairly wide-ranging, it is clear that the earliest challenge for this group was the way that most scholars pursued higher criticism, particularly the German school. Only later were scientific questions, such as evolution, broached. Even there, we see that the quarrel was particularly with rationalism: "The worst foes of Christianity are not physicists but metaphysicians. Hume is more dangerous than Darwin."[7] In all this, the emphasis was upon theology more than practice.

Concurrently, the public discussion among various Protestants, especially Presbyterians and Baptists, was proceeding apace. In 1910, the General Assembly of the Northern Presbyterian Church highlighted five essentials that it saw under attack in its day, paring down the foundation from the fourteen that had been suggested in an earlier forum. In taking this decision, it blended the common Protestant impulse of minimalism with the desire for a manifesto, calling upon its members to affirm the inerrancy of the Bible, the virginal conception of Christ, the atonement described in terms of substitution, the bodily resurrection, and the miracles of the NT. (We may observe that this decision to narrow and specify the battle lines led to a hardening of positions, so that the challenges of higher criticism would now be countered by a newly formulated view of "inerrancy" rather than a more general confidence in the faithfulness of Scriptures.) When four years later the World Christian Fundamentals Association was founded by the Baptist William Bell Riley, a sixth essential was listed—the second Advent of Christ. About the same time, a group called the "Fundamentalist Fellowship" was organized by Northern Baptists, in which Riley initially took a leading role. Many of its members were concerned about the vulnerability of that denomination and its educational institutions because both lacked a formal confession, and they pressured the denomination to take appropriate action. They were, however, unsuccessful, and Baptists today remain attached to the notion of "soul liberty," in which individuals interpret the New Testament for themselves. During this time, the Northern Presbyterians went through similar discussions, actually affirming the first five essentials in their 1923 General Assembly. However, four years later, during a disciplinary controversy in New York, the more rigorous were disappointed that the decision proved to have no "teeth." By 1929, some key players had left Princeton to found Westminster Theological Seminary. The next decade saw much foment and division among Presbyterians and Baptists, as well as an increased concentration upon the increasingly accepted teaching of evolutionary theory. Only part of the discord can be attributed to the usual distinctions that we make between "liberal" and "conservative" thinking: some of it also pertained to the appropriate place of confessional statements and unified social action in the various denominations.

The two contrasting motives—to minimize obligatory doctrines and to defend the faith against various perceived incursions—meant that fundamentalism was unstable and did not easily retain its original complexity. Within twenty years, the term was applied pejoratively to various conservative, separatist, and anti-intellectual forms of Protestantism. A little later in the 1950s, conservative Protestants associated with the new Fuller Seminary, Billy Graham, and the publication *Christianity Today*, defined themselves over against those then smeared by the label. They were only partially successful, however, since in popular parlance *fundamentalism* started to be used to describe anyone more conservative than the user of the term—a trend that has continued to today.[8]

What can we glean from this brief survey? First, the original fundamentalists were responsive and educated writers, seeking to influence minds in their own day by careful tractates, not sloganeering. Second, the Protestant impulse to minimalism (pairing down fundamentals for the sake of individual freedom) figured strongly in their strategy to respond to these specific challenges. These two impulses sometimes ran counter to each other: What if the particular concern lay in an area not found in the discerned center, although connected with it, as is arguably the case with the discussion of evolution? When they stipulated essentials, were these to be construed as a manifesto or a soberly constructed credo? Even what emerged from the original publications and the church movements that followed demonstrates the tension: their five or six fundamentals were not exactly *tangential* to the ecumenical creeds but, not taken in their historical context, had the ability to skew what St. Athanasius called the *skopos* of the faith. For example, the virginal conception (although significant) arguably is not as foundational as the incarnation. Similarly, insistence upon inerrancy begs the question of the nature of inspiration and accepts the positivistic terms of those whom the fundamentalists were trying to refute. Such problems were nearly unavoidable for Western Christians responding to the challenges of modernity after the epistemological turn of Kant: indeed, many of the initial papers involved the relation between the Scriptures and the discipline of history. How we know something, especially how we know and understand events in the past, is a central question to the faith: "he suffered *under Pontius Pilate.*" However, there was little in the continuous Christian tradition to help them with this challenge. The relation of the faith to history is a key matter but had not been systematically under scrutiny prior to the Enlightenment—at least since the time of the Gnostic movement. The original papers and selected foci of the "fundamentals" as enumerated demonstrate an intuitive and laudable awareness of this question, and its significance. An adequate response, however, was ironically hampered by the unrecognized Protestant "tradition" of *sola Scriptura* ("by Scripture alone") that had replaced the apostolic *regula fidei* ("rule of faith"). Whereas the search for *skopos* includes a unity and complexity that may be held together, the marriage of fundamentals (however discerned) with the Protestant *sola* proved itself inherently unstable.

Christian Groups Called Fundamentalist Today

Protestant Examples?

Those who consider the scholarly use of the term *fundamentalism* today may be surprised by the careless use of the term in James Barr's two books, *Fundamentalism* and *Beyond Fundamentalism*, although these have been used as an authority by a number of sensible people.[9] Barr's visceral reaction, that "fundamentalist" scholars do their work hampered by "a pathological condition of Christianity" characterized by "acute anxiety,"[10] has not served him well. Unfortunately, he does not match such judgments with a careful analysis of their work. For example, K. A. Kitchen's actual arguments are never rehearsed, although he is described as "fully breathing the spirit of total fundamentalism."[11] Similarly, J. I. Packer's work is selectively cited to show that he considers propositional truth significant to biblical theology,[12] without acknowledging his imaginative approach to visionary and poetic biblical literature, his appreciation of mystery, and his easy concourse with those in other Christian traditions. It appears that any scholar more conservative than Barr receives the label "fundamentalist," which he sees as significantly overlapping with *evangelical*. His own approach to the Scriptures emerges clearly toward the end of the first volume, where he opines that "there will now probably never be sayings of which we can say with certainty that Jesus of Nazareth actually spoke these;" he concludes that the laity should be encouraged to develop an appreciation for the Bible "*not* based on real incidents and authentic sayings."[13] In *Beyond Fundamentalism*, he attempts to demonstrate from the Scriptures that the Protestant core of "justification by faith" cannot be supported,[14] nor the divine nature of Jesus,[15] nor depravity, atonement and other doctrines: "Many such ideas are lacking in clear and abundant biblical foundation."[16] Having questioned the biblical foundation, he then appeals to "inference" and "tradition," making it clear that his aim is not to destroy these doctrines, but to show their reliance on tradition.[17]

Barr's appeal to tradition is welcome, for the Achilles' heel of fundamentalism is its dependence upon the unacknowledged tradition of the *solas*. However, his offhand treatment of those who prioritize proposition and historical statements and his driving a complete wedge between Scripture and tradition are disturbing. Moreover, as a Protestant himself, he cannot offer a coherent alternative approach—for example, like many biblical exegetes of his day, he takes no notice of the ancient *regula fidei* as a lens, since this would go counter to his historical-critical sensibilities.[18] In the end, the brushstrokes are too broad to offer us anything but a caricature, and "fundamentalism," whatever it means, is more vilified than carefully explained or answered.

Fundamentalism in Catholicism?

We move on to fundamental tendencies in Catholicism. Although there are ample popular-level treatments of so-called Catholic "fundamentalism," including some shallow psychologizing pieces,[19] it would seem that by far the most careful work on this has been done as part of the Fundamentalism Project by the duo William Dinges and James Hitchcock.[20] Although the editors of these five volumes introduce their work with a defense of the term *fundamentalist* as the best that we have,[21] it is instructive that the Catholic contributors refrain from it in relation to Catholicism, even when dealing with such marginal groups as "sedevacantists"—those who believe that Peter's "seat" is now, in effect, vacant. Instead, they speak of "Traditionalism" and "Activist Conservatism," opining that the first group more nearly takes on "fundamentalist tendencies and orientations" than the second,[22] which is more collaborative with outside groups. Presumably these authors do not use *fundamentalism* because for them it conjures "serious socio-cultural implications" for public policy and the development of religion,[23] such as in sectarian Protestantism or violent forms of Islam. One helpful connection that they make between Catholic rigorists and the original Princeton group is the "highly cognitive religious orientation" of such groups, many of whom hold to a timeless Tridentine mass[24]—or to what an Anglican scholar calls "creeping infallibility" of the Pope, beyond *ex cathedra* pronouncements.[25]

Opus Dei is infamous because of its early critique by Hans Urs von Balthasar,[26] who initially used "fundamentalism" to describe this lay movement. Von Balthasar should have known better, since the founder Escriva's book, *The Way*, was not intended as a fundamentalist primer on doctrine but as a spiritual help for those seeking intimacy with God and Christian community. Later, in 1979, von Balthasar retracted his judgment, as not informed by a personal knowledge of the group, and he leveled criticism of the *Neue Zürcher Zeitung* for being anticlerical in its critique of the order.[27] Some continue to be concerned with the founder's political stance, the call to obedience among members, and the restriction of freedoms. A reading of *The Way* shows these criticisms to be overblown,[28] despite the apparently detailed analysis of some who deplore Opus Dei.[29] In fact, the book is comprised of sayings that are too gnomic to reveal the kind of oppressive regime that the detractors fear. No doubt the emphasis on personal decisions is not as strong as many of us would like: but dependence upon one's advisors is hardly a cultic or innovative feature, for it is *de rigeur* in Orthodox and Catholic monastic settings. Furthermore, the lay nature of this group in the world militates against its development into an *enclave*—a frequent charge against fundamentalism. Continued connections with the church as a whole, its sacraments, its history and its structures, also prevent full-blown "fundamentalism" (however construed) from taking root. Members of these smaller groups may choose a smaller bed and a lighter cover for various reasons, but so long as they do not repudiate their Mother, an adequate bed for stretching and a fuller covering for protection is available.

Orthodox Expressions?

The third group under consideration in this paper comprises those whose growing influence and loudly raised voices catalyzed this conference's discussion. Shrill Orthodox denunciation of the 2010 International Theological conference in Volos was the visible part of the iceberg that caused our friend George Demacopoulos to pen his warning against fundamentalism.[30] Certainly the vociferous attack against this conference on the legacy of the fathers was partially due to the ill-advised use of the term *postpatristic theology*. Perhaps Fr. Florovsky's term *neo-patristic synthesis* would have been less of a red flag to traditionalist clergy, monastics, and scholars, who made their displeasure known.[31] Beyond the opponents of Volos, we encounter "TradOx" believers across the globe and active on the Internet. These are decidedly Old Calendrist, anti-ecumenical, and maximalist in their adherence to various habits and beliefs not shared by all Orthodox:[32] sexual abstinence of a married couple after menopause, baptism for everyone received into Orthodoxy, or strict adherence to what is arguably a neo-Gnostic doctrine of demonized tollbooths. They make no distinction between schism, heterodoxy, and heresy. Indeed, the very invitation of papal representation to the Holy and Great Council in Crete is evidence to them of the compromised position of their leaders. These have made their views known clearly in a manifesto entitled "A Confession of Faith Against Ecumenism."[33]

One can see the temptation to label the supporters of this piece as "fundamentalists," for the strategy of reaction is similar. However, the slew of papers published in *The Fundamentals* was carefully conceived, over against the knee-jerk anti-intellectualism of the Confession. The Orthodox declaration, moreover, appeals to tradition, to dogmas established in the councils, and to Holy Tradition, rather than to the Scriptures per se: indeed, it castigates Protestants for *sola scriptura*, even while it describes Rome as "the mother of heresies." Some might argue that we have, *mutatis mutandis*, a similar situation to the early written *Fundamentals*, which castigated Rome and (rightly) condemned the teaching of the cults. However, the Confession actually operates in the opposite direction, for it is *maximalist* rather than concentrating on a few essentials. There is, as to be expected, a concentration upon the creeds and patristic consensus (although this consensus is exaggerated). From this foundation, the Confession roundly condemns instrumental music, uniatism, spiritual practices, women's ordination, justification by faith, sexual permissiveness, the acceptance of non-Orthodox baptism, common prayer with non-Orthodox, the use of unleavened bread for Eucharist, and a host of other practices. The haphazard linking of serious matters with cultural distinctives may seem strange in such a short document, but it does indicate a typical Orthodox way of seeing theology, life, and worship as a seamless robe. Its lack of discipline or discernment is clear, and in this way, it may be compared to later Protestant groups labeled "fundamentalist." However, its comprehensive tendency stands in strong distinction to the Protestant drive to pare down, an approach illustrated by the ludicrous but earnest title of a recent publication, *What's the Least I Can Believe and Still Be a Christian?*[34] (At times, however, the comprehensive concerns of the Confession appear to be overshadowed by its utter repudiation of ecumenical discussion, as though this were a shibboleth for Orthodoxy.)

Such traditionalist Orthodox are rigid people, to be sure, but they have as much that distinguishes them as links them with Protestants described by Barr, or the enthusiastic personal prelature members of Opus Dei. What do we gain by positing a family for three disparate groups—biblicist conservatives, mission-minded papal enthusiasts, and anti-intellectual Orthodox rigorists?

Questions and Tentative Conclusions

Our survey of the rich use of the word *foundation* in Scripture and tradition, the inception of the Princeton movement which called itself fundamentalist, and groups which since then have been attached to this term, yields several probative questions. The first most obvious question is whether the term *fundamentalist* is actually very useful today. Martin Marty and Scott Appleby have argued in their monumental study that, although the term is fraught with difficulty, it is the best that we have.[35] However, we must ask, "best for which purposes?" Certainly, the term, as used today, calls attention to certain characteristics shared by various conservative groups across religious boundaries. But, in fact, these groups show as many differences as similarities. I am reminded of the use of the term *apocalypticism*, and how many biblical scholars today think it best to avoid the term entirely.[36] It *is* possible to discern a *Gestalt* for the generic term *apocalypse*, since we have concrete examples of pieces that can be compared and judged against an emerging paradigm. But an overarching sociological phenomenon such as apocalypticism is as slippery as the concept of fundamentalism: even to speak about a working definition is to give priority to the features that one wants to highlight. It is as though we began by asking, "What is the *Gestalt* that can be traced to embrace phenomena and individuals as distinct as Jerry Falwell, Opus Dei, and the Ayatollah Kameini?" If one begins with the hunch that these are members of a single set, one is bound to discover that there is a family likeness. Furthermore, it is quite likely that those journalists of the 1970s, who possessed an understandable distaste of Falwell, were making a rhetorical point by extending using the term *fundamentalist* to terrorist groups—the move was as much an insult to these conservative Christians as an apt descriptor of the violent. The sociologist may hasten to explain that the inner dynamics between these groups are similar, and that Falwell and his ilk are not outwardly violent mostly because of the milieu in which they find themselves, which does not support activism.[37] But the explanation is only necessary because the rhetorical link between Falwell and terrorism has already been implied by using the same term for both. Finally, it is certainly unwise to use a term that has a specific historical referent, now stretched beyond its capacity, to talk about conservative groups within Catholicism and Orthodoxy. Like the Catholic scholars who wrote in the Fundamentalism Project, I remain unconvinced concerning the application of the term in connection with these, since traditionalism, naturally maximalist, does not operate in the same way as biblicism. What, then, is the best way to speak about rigorism in Catholicism and Orthodoxy?

Besides this terminological question, we also have asked, "what can we glean from fundamentalism?" Classical fundamentalism can help us see the value of a response to contemporary challenges in light of the "center." Neither Catholics nor (especially) Orthodox will go the route of minimalism nor will they concentrate upon doctrine to the exclusion of practice. There is, however, in relatively recent Eastern scholarship, a way of distinguishing between those things that are obligatory and those that are not. V. V. Boltov, in his work on the divisive matter of the *filioque*,[38] was, it seems, hospitable to this insight, suggesting different classifications for doctrine: what *must* be believed (e.g., the creeds), *theologoumena* that *may* be believed (since found in several church fathers), and what may be put forward *hypothetically* on unsettled matters. Thus, the doctrine of the two natures of Jesus is required by the faith, the *filioque* (according to Bolotov) is permissible, and a scholar considering what is meant by the Pauline statement "he became sin" might offer a suggestion for the purposes of discussion.

Although the three categories are helpful, I am uneasy about how Bolotov and others use the idea of obligation in making such distinctions.[39] Can we not instead refer to what appears as central, what is a pious *theologoumenon* connected with that center, and what is, unless shown otherwise by living tradition, tangential but possible? Concentration upon the center, and the measuring of various matters, creedal and practical, against this, is certainly a good strategy in ecumenical discussions. As William Witt puts it,

"Ecumenical dialogue that proceeds through the trinitarian, incarnational, and soteriological center will not resolve every theological disagreement, but it certainly makes such disagreements less intractable."[40] However, even to frame things in this way is to give priority to conceptual matters in a way that would have been foreign to the fathers. The apostolic *regula fidei* did not concern simply creedal statements, but a way of reading the Old Testament and a common manner of life and worship.

We may well be concerned with those Christians who major in minors, and who absolutize their own notion of Holy Tradition, frequently as a defensive response to the issues of our day. The way forward, however, is not to call them names (not even "fundamentalist") but to consider whether any of their concerns is valid, and then to show where their idea of Holy Tradition, or their way of articulating it, is too cramped or too constrained to be a remedy: the bed too narrow, the cover inadequate. Moreover, we may discover that places of convergence are to be found not only in the area of doctrine but also in praxis, worship, and general Christian living. Perhaps in living and worshipping among those whom we find too rigid or strident in tone, we will discover that they have legitimate concerns over departures from the faith that some of us would prefer not to acknowledge because of our *own* fears and our own desire to be at peace in the world. What do they have to say about life issues? About relations between the sexes? About asceticism? About devotion to a faithful community? About confusing love with tolerance in ecumenical discussion? After all, our goal is "to get a better sense of what it means to be faithful to our tradition,"[41] and beyond that, about fidelity to the God-Man who willingly plunged into our difficult world, the world that He loves. His ability to transform the rigorous and vigorous personality of St. Paul—a Torah fundamentalist, if there ever was one—should be a lesson to us that God delights in various character traits. It would seem that rigorists need irenicists and vice versa, as we together learn the relationship between truth and love, mercy and judgment. Learning not to use emotive terms in a sloppy manner and listening to each other carefully, even when we do not like the tone in which something is said, is not only a mark of good scholarship but an indication of a mature and charitable disposition. We can learn from those who are called fundamentalists—learn about passion, about engagement with our day and about cleaving to the center. For this we can be thankful.

Notes

1. Anthony E. Gilles, *Fundamentalism: What Every Catholic Needs to Know* (Cincinnati, OH: St. Anthony, 1984), 4.

2. George Demacopoulos (with Aristotle Papanikolaou) in a May 20, 2016, interview with Bobby Maddex, accessed April 1, 2019, http://www.ancientfaith .com/podcasts/features/tradition_secularization_fundamentalism_orthodox _catholic_encounters.

3. Fr. Georges Florovsky, *Bible, Church, Tradition: An Eastern Orthodox View*, in *Collected Works* (Belmont: Norland, 1972), 1:83. In comparing the citations with the actual words of St. Athanasius, I have taken the liberty of correcting minor errors, especially in the Greek, which sometimes lacks diacriticals, and, in one case, supplying the Greek verb for clarity.

4. Florovsky, 83.

5. Florovsky, 89. How to translate the Pauline phrase πίστις Χριστοῦ leads to an ongoing argument: Reformers, following Luther, have assumed it means "faith *in* Christ" whereas others have argued for the subjective or possessive genitive. I take this further, quoting the apostle, to mean the body of faith concerning Christ which the church received, which, of course, also includes an understanding of Christ's own faithfulness.

6. Dyson Hague, "The History of Higher Criticism," in *The Fundamentals: A Testimony to the Truth* (Chicago: Testimony, 1911), 1:87–122, accessed April 1, 2019, https://archive.org/details/fundamentalstest17chic.

7. G. F. Wright, "The Passing of Evolution," in *The Fundamentals: A Testimony to the Truth* (Chicago: Testimony, 1911), 7:20, accessed April 1, 2019, https://archive.org/details/fundamentalstest17chic.

8. On classical fundamentalism and its development, see T. P. Weber, "Fundamentalism," in *Dictionary of Christianity in America*, ed. D. G. Reid, (Downers Grove, IL: InterVarsity, 1990), 461–65.

9. See, for example, the Anglican William G. Witt, "Yes, Virginia, There Is Such a Thing as Fundamentalism or the Subject Matter of Christianity Is the Subject Matter of Christianity," accessed April 1, 2019, http://willgwitt.org /anglicanism/yes-virginia-there-is-such-a-thing-as-fundamentalism/.

10. James Barr, *Fundamentalism* (Philadelphia: Westminster Press, 1978), 5 and 13.

11. Barr, 131.

12. Barr, 226.

13. Barr, 335.

14. See James Barr, *Beyond Fundamentalism* (Philadelphia: Westminster, 1984), chap. 6. Barr's instincts that the Reformation doctrine is overblown beyond its appearance in Paul's letters are, in my view, correct. However, he

does not take the time to consider what St. Paul might instead have meant by the language of *dikaiosynē* and its relationship to *pistis*: an unfortunate omission by a capable exegete. Evangelicals are better served by the more detailed work of, for example, N. T. Wright and Richard Hays, than the demolition job performed here.

15. Barr, 49–65.

16. Barr, 64.

17. Barr, 65.

18. My critique may seem unfair, because in the 1970s and 1980s, the light of day had not yet dawned for either the renewed movement to theological interpretation of the Bible or Richard Hays's masterful *Reading Scripture Backwards: Figural Christology and the Fourfold Gospel* (Waco, TX: Baylor University Press, 2014). However, to appeal to tradition, as Barr does, as a means of retaining doctrine essentially banished from Scripture is a dangerous move: it leads to an incoherence between scholarship and faith, to an acceptance of Scripture and tradition as two separate and unrelated authorities, or to an idiosyncratic use of whichever tradition one needs in order to buttress a particular pet dogma. None of these options is palatable.

19. For an example, see Fr. Dwight Longenecker's engaging but overly generalized discussion, "Ten Traits of Catholic Fundamentalism," Patheos, accessed April 1, 2019, http://www.patheos.com/blogs/standingonmyhead/ten -traits-of-catholic-fundamentalism.

20. William Dinges and James Hitchcock, "Roman Catholic Traditionalism and Catholic Activist Conservatism in the United States," in *Fundamentalisms Observed*, ed. M. E. Marty and R. S. Appleby (Chicago: University of Chicago Press, 1991), 66–141.

21. Martin E. Marty and R. Scott Appleby, "The Fundamentalism Project: A User's Guide," in *Fundamentalisms Observed*, viii. The "serviceable" nature of the term is rehearsed again in the introduction to *Fundamentalisms and the State* (Chicago: University of Chicago Press, 1993), 8n4.

22. Dinges and Hitchcock, "Roman Catholic Traditionalism," 100.

23. Dinges and Hitchcock, 100.

24. Dinges and Hitchcock, 82.

25. See Witt, "Yes, Virginia."

26. Von Balthasar's first critique appeared in 1963 in *Neue Zürcher Nachrichten* and also in *Wort und Wahrheit*.

27. The drama is rehearsed by Antonio Gaspari in "A New Way for the Church?," EWTN Global Catholic Network, accessed April 1, 2019 https:// www.ewtn.com/library/spirit/newway.htm.

28. Fr. Josemaria Escriva, *The Way*, accessed April 1, 2019, http://www .escrivaworks.org/book/the_way-contents.htm.

29. Franz Schaefer, "The Unofficial Opus Dei FAQ," accessed April 1, 2019, https://www.mond.at/opus.dei/opus.dei.uo.faq.html.

30. George Demacopoulos, "Orthodox Fundamentalism," blogs.goarch.org, January 29, 2015, accessed April 1, 2019, https://blogs.goarch.org/blog/-/blogs /orthodox-fundamentalism.

31. See, for example, the critique of Metropolitan Paul (Glyfada) on the Impantokratoros website, accessed April 1, 2019, http://www.impantokratoros .gr/2BE58A08.el.aspx. In 2012, those concerned held a counter-conference in Piraeus, "Patristic Theology and Post-Patristic Heresy."

32. By maximalist, I am referring to the tendency among such Orthodox to call for unquestioning adherence to a multitude of doctrines and practices derived from a variety of sources—cultural, liturgical, patristic, devotional, or creedal. Frequently, no distinction is made here between, on the one hand, local custom, views held by some church fathers and teachings that come very late in the tradition and, on the other hand, those doctrines and practices well established in the creeds, universal liturgy, and canons. Such Orthodox believers are suspicious of the very use of the term *theologoumenon* as a Western word that smacks of the "ecumenical heresy."

33. "A Confession of Faith Against Ecumenism," Impantokratoros, October 15, 2009, accessed April 1, 2019, http://www.impantokratoros.gr /FA9AF77F.en.aspx.

34. Martin Thielen, *What's the Least I Can Believe and Still Be a Christian?* (Louisville, KY: Westminster John Knox, 2011).

35. See "The Fundamentalism Project: A User's Guide," in *Fundamentalisms Observed*, viii; and *Fundamentalisms and the State*, 8n4.

36. On the inadequacy of the terms *apocalypticism* and *apocalyptic* used as a noun, see the introduction to my *Ladies and the Cities* (New York: Sheffield, 1995; reprint T and T Clark, 2018) or Robert L. Webb, "'Apocalyptic': Observations on a Slippery Term," *Journal of Near Eastern Studies* 49, no. 2 (1990): 115–26.

37. G. A. Almond, E. Sivan, and R. Scott Appleby, for example, make this judgment: "[W]e are left with *structures* [which] tell us quite a bit about the possibilities open to fundamentalist movements. . . . The political regime under which they compete for influence and power . . . whether it is authoritarian or democratic—sets the operating rules of political competition, *thereby determining whether the struggle is to be overt or covert, the methods peaceful or violent*, and the approach gradualist or integralist." Almond, Sivan, and Appleby, "Politics, Ethnicity, and Fundamentalism," in *Fundamentalisms Comprehended*, ed. Martin E. Marty and R. Scott Appleby (Chicago: University of Chicago Press, 1995), 493; my emphasis.

38. Fr. Georges Florovsky describes Bolotov's "Thesen über das "Filioque," in his essay, "The Orthodox Churches and the Ecumenical Movement Prior to 1910," in *A History of the Ecumenical Movement*, vol. 1, *1517–1948*, ed. R. Rouse and S. C. Neill (London: World Council of Churches, 1986), 208–9. Bolotov's essay is available in German at http://www.e-periodica.ch/digbib/view?var =true&pid=ikz-001:1898:6::923#705 and (parts of it) in Russian at http:// christian-reading.info/.

39. See, for example, Stefan Zankow, *The Eastern Orthodox Church*, trans. Dr. Lowrie (London: SCM, 1929), 39–40. Some have erroneously claimed that the origin of the modern theological term *theologoumenon* is to be seen in the work of von Harnack. For example, the term is used several times without explanation, and with a slightly different meaning in his *History of Dogma*, vol. 2, trans. Neil Buchanan (Boston: Little, Brown, 1907). It was used prior to this by Bolotov, however, though it likely cannot be found in the fathers with Bolotov's meaning. It is probably telling that Bolotov used it in the context of détente with Western Christianity, but it has become current among Orthodox theologians in the past century. For a brief discussion of Bolotov's use of the term, see David Heith, "The Influence of V. V. Bolotov on Orthodox Theology," David Heith-Stade's blog, January 18, 2016, accessed April 1, 2019, https:// davidheithstade.wordpress.com/2016/01/18/the-influence-of-v-v-bolotov-on -orthodox-theology/.

40. Witt, "Yes, Virginia."

41. Aristotle Papanikolaou (with George Demacopoulos) in an interview with Bobby Maddex on May 20, 2016, accessed April 1, 2019, http://www .ancientfaith.com/podcasts/features/tradition_secularization_fundamentalism _orthodox_catholic_encounters.

Resolving the Tension between Tradition and Restorationism in American Orthodoxy

Dellas Oliver Herbel

The entire history of the Orthodox churches in America could be cast as an ongoing battle between tradition and restorationism.[1] By *tradition*, I mean the lived faith Orthodox Christians have received and changed in the face of new dynamics (whether social, political, or theological). Tradition has a content but is also constantly changing in response to new surroundings in a manner that seeks to maintain core structures and behaviors. By *restorationism*, I mean an attempt to restore a (largely imagined) past or, in the cases of many converts to Orthodoxy, a return to that imagined past. These two poles of American Orthodoxy have been in tension with one another throughout her American history, at least once Orthodoxy expanded beyond the Alaskan frontier.

Now, one might object that the history of any church would fit such an outline. Is there not always tension between addressing a current situation and "returning" to a previous standard (whether one looks to the "faith of the fathers" or whether one renounces all popes and councils and seeks the "original" books of the Bible)? In the case of Orthodoxy in America, however, I believe this tension is exaggerated, precisely because the American religious context itself is one often dominated by Protestant restorationism, at least from the Second Great Awakening (1790–1840) onward. Within American Orthodox history, restorationism has sometimes led to a committed rigidity that might well be termed fundamentalism, which opposes Orthodoxy as a lived faith enculturated in America. In this case, *fundamentalism* does not mean the Presbyterian movement arising out of Princeton in the late nineteenth century. Rather, I draw from the psychology of

152

religion,[2] wherein fundamentalism means a strict literalism and heightened concern with regard to praxis and beliefs, especially those that are not explicitly stated as necessary and central to the religion itself, as well as a concern with maintaining rather rigid ingroup and outgroup distinctions.[3]

Despite this tension, I argue that a careful look at American Orthodox Church history suggests that the healthiest way forward is one in which the restorationist moves, which are sometimes connected to fundamentalism, are incorporated and subsumed under the ongoing work of tradition. To do this, I first highlight some of the major periods in American Orthodox history in which restorationism collided with a lived tradition, concentrating on American converts to Orthodoxy. Taking into account research on mental and spiritual health and fundamentalism, I will then offer some suggestions for how we might mitigate this tension. For when successfully subsumed under a lived tradition, restorationism can avert the dangers of fundamentalism and offer something healthy, useful, and valuable to Orthodoxy as a lived tradition.

The Toth Movement

The bedrock of this tradition versus restorationism framework began in the Russian mission to North America.[4] As the Russian Mission to Alaska expanded during the eighteenth century and became the Russian Mission to North America by 1904, Orthodox concerns shifted away from how to evangelize the Native Alaskans or how to relate to the American governance beginning in 1867.[5] This shift became prominent as Orthodoxy entered the twentieth century in the lower forty-eight states. Initially, the Orthodox churches displayed questions typical to a lived tradition. One can see this in the rise of trusteeism, which derived from lay brotherhoods, wherein immigrant groups established parishes along the lines of their Protestant neighbors and only then sought out a bishop to send a priest.[6] This survival mechanism from Central and Eastern Europe was transplanted onto American soil in an American way.[7] Out of this context, however, would rise the first significant restorationist movement Orthodoxy would experience in America—that of Alexis Toth (1853–1909).[8]

Within Orthodox circles, Toth is primarily known for his run-in with Archbishop John Ireland of Minneapolis, who objected to Toth's presence in America because Toth was Eastern Catholic, which meant he was a married cleric (although by that time, he was a widower).[9] His falling out with

Archbishop Ireland led Toth to join the Russian Orthodox but the seeds for his conversion had been planted earlier. He believed Eastern Catholicism was a schism from the Orthodox Church and if the Carpatho-Rusyns returned to Orthodoxy, their conversion would end that schism. It was not enough simply to preserve their Eastern rite.

Throughout his dedicated career of service to the Russian Orthodox Mission in America, Alexis Toth consistently argued that Orthodoxy was both the Apostolic faith and the traditional religion of the Carpatho-Rusyn people. He joined this argument to the belief that the Carpatho-Rusyns were part of the Russian people, whose lives were furthered by the Tsar and the Russian Orthodox Church. In this way, Toth looked to restore the pre-*unia* Orthodox Church of the Carpatho-Rusyns. He was quite successful and late in the twentieth century, Toth would be canonized for his efforts.[10] Although Toth's efforts are often described with respect to the tensions his movement created within Eastern Catholic circles, especially with the Greek Catholic Union and its *American Russian Messenger (Amerikanskij Russkij Viestnik)*, Toth's movement created tensions within Russian American Orthodoxy as well. Bishop Nicholas assigned Fr. Sebastian Dabovich to Minneapolis, ostensibly to serve when Toth was on evangelization trips but also to speed up the Russification of the Carpatho-Rusyns in Minneapolis. Additionally, Frs. Alexander Hotovitsky and Benedict Turkevich derided Eastern Catholic liturgical traditions, Toth's paper (*Svit*), and the idea of longer sermons. Turkevich even argued that American Carpatho-Rusyns should be forced to follow the Russian imperial practice of the time and colonize Siberia. In contrast, Toth believed Carpatho-Rusyns could be both faithful Orthodox and committed Americans simultaneously.

Frs. Morgan and Irvine

At the same time that Toth's movement was spreading, two other converts began affecting the American Orthodox scene. Robert Josias Morgan (ca. 1869–1916) became Fr. Raphael, the first African American Orthodox priest, making his own restorationist journey into Orthodoxy.[11] Around the same time, the Anglican cleric Ingram Nathaniel Washington Irvine became Fr. Nathaniel.[12]

While moving within the same African American Anglican circles as George Alexander McGuire, who would go on to lead an independent

"African Orthodox Church," Morgan took a trip to Russia, where he was moved by his experience of the Russian Orthodox Church. When he returned, he established a close relationship with the local Greek Orthodox parish in Philadelphia and its clergy, and in 1907 he traveled to Istanbul where he was baptized before a crowd of three thousand people and then ordained. Although Morgan formed an "Order of the Cross of Golgotha" and openly opposed Marcus Garvey, his efforts produced few long-lasting effects on the church.[13] Morgan had begun with the primitivistic impulse to found the original church, while in the same circles with McGuire, but later came to wed that impulse to the existing Orthodox tradition, which he saw as living out a more consistent racial ethic, one he believed existed prior to the racially segregated Western Christianity he saw around him.

Ingram Nathaniel Washington Irvine's ordination made national headlines because he was an Episcopal priest who had been defrocked (many thought wrongly so) and so his ordination was viewed as a reordination by many. Irvine's conversion continued a personal trend of selecting canonical standards from the preceding tradition in order to enact something new or at odds with his received Anglican tradition. He had done this twice with Protestant Episcopal bishops and then, after being defrocked, with the Protestant Episcopal Church by returning (as he saw it) to the church of the seven ecumenical councils. Irvine understood the church of the first eight centuries to be in direct opposition to what he perceived as the "chameleon" ways of the Anglican Communion. Yet Irvine also experienced tension with his Orthodox Church. He believed the characteristics of the church of the first eight centuries meant Orthodoxy needed to overcome jurisdictional division, the loss of generations born in America, overly long services, and the lack of instrumental music.

Restorationism and Orthodox (Dis)Unity

From 1929 to 1943, restorationism helped inspire two attempts to unite the various American Orthodox jurisdictions. The first attempt, the Holy Eastern Orthodox Catholic and Apostolic Church of North America, lasted from 1927 to 1933.[14] The second, the Federated Orthodox Greek Catholic Jurisdictions, derived from a two-year (1941–1942) clash with the Selective Service but fell apart in 1943.[15] In both attempts, Frs. Boris Burden and Michael Gelsinger, two convert priests, united with cradle-born hierarchs (Afitimios Ofiesh and Sophronios Beshara for the church and primarily

Antony Bashir for the jurisdictions) to restore an alleged prior canonical unity in America. In the former, restorationism also led to aggressive and negative assessments of the Anglican Communion, whereas in the latter, the question of Orthodox immigrants communing with Episcopalians, even though no Orthodox church had been present at the time of the immigrants' settlement, caused the federation's implosion. It should be noted that both Frs. Burden and Gelsinger were former members of the Protestant Episcopal Church. In both cases, Orthodox hierarchs were held to a less committed stance vis-à-vis the Anglican Communion (Metropolitan Platon and Archbishop Athenagoras). Once again, the tension between restorationism and a lived tradition had shaped the historical trajectory of American Orthodoxy.

One of the key differences between both movements, however, was that the federation's attempt to restore union was born from a desire to engage American secularism, and this desire would continue into the 1950s as Orthodox Christians attempted to gain recognition as the "Fourth Major Faith." Orthodoxy would be successful in receiving recognition from the Department of Defense and many state legislatures, but a bill at the federal level never made the Senate floor because of, in large part, Protestant fundamentalist Carl McIntire and anticommunist sentiments at the time. Orthodoxy had to navigate both its own and Protestant fundamentalism.[16]

Moses Berry and Peter Gillquist

In the late twentieth century, Fr. Moses Berry (b. 1951) and Peter Gillquist (1938–2012), and the latter's Evangelical Orthodox Church (EOC) brought restorationist tendencies back into the Orthodox picture in rather bold ways.[17] Berry continued the legacy of Morgan in reaching out to African Americans. Gillquist's church, on the other hand, sought to find the "New Testament Church."

Concerns for multiracial and multiethnic representation and a desire for an "otherworldly" Christianity guided Berry's journey. Berry grounded his emphasis on otherworldly Christianity in early Christian Egypt. Specifically, Berry sought to return to a preracist Christianity, as exemplified in the early church's promotion of Egyptian monasticism. As such, Eastern Orthodoxy became understood as *the* Christian tradition itself, thus being able to stand as a response over and against a denominationally and racially fragmented American Christianity, even if members of that very

Orthodox Church sometimes exhibited the racial fragmentation of American society. Berry's restorationist impulse led him into the Holy Order of MANS, a new religious movement that explicitly understood itself as the reestablishment of the early church. The order later merged into Christ the Savior Brotherhood, a group that identified itself as Orthodox, although not in communion with any of the Orthodox churches. During that time, he encountered the broad ethnic and racial diversity of Eastern Orthodox saints through iconography and realized his concerns for an "otherworldly" Christianity and racial integration were found together within the Eastern Christian tradition. In 1990, he started the Brotherhood of St. Moses the Black to promote early African Christianity. When the Christ the Savior Brotherhood dissolved, he moved into mainstream "canonical" Eastern Orthodoxy.

As a leader of approximately 1,700 people who entered the Orthodox Church, Gillquist's story is probably the best known of Orthodox converts. A chief reason for this is that the book he wrote documenting that journey may well be the most successful piece of American Orthodox disinformation ever published.[18] In reality, the EOC's entrance into the Orthodox Church was rife with tension between restorationism and the lived tradition of the American Orthodox jurisdictions. A desire to be the New Testament church in the twentieth century led the EOC initially to develop into a strong, cult-like denomination. For example, the EOC developed liturgically creative (and syncretistic) attempts to reinstate the liturgy described by St. Justin Martyr (fl. 150s), embraced countercultural stances on moral and ethical questions and they employed a form of authoritarianism that might be characterized as spiritual manipulation.[19]

The EOC initially tried to enter the Orthodox Church in America and join the National Association of Evangelicals simultaneously. The church refused to accept the clerical standing of EOC clergy, and the association objected to the EOC's theology. After failing a second time to join the Orthodox Church via the Greek Orthodox Church of America (an Eparchy of the Ecumenical Patriarchate in Constantinople), the EOC leveraged Fr. Thomas Hopko's help to obtain acceptance from Metropolitan Philip of the Antiochian Orthodox Church in America. To do this, they had to let go of their desire to be a denomination within the Orthodox Church. Initially, they were brought in (in 1987) as the Antiochian Evangelical Orthodox Mission, but this was soon disbanded (in 1995) after an argument over whether priests could remarry (in which most of them opposed

Metropolitan Philip's allowance of it). Not long after that, one of the parishes (in Ben Lomond) imploded because of restorationist tendencies, which led to conflict over the issue of liturgical syncretism and a clash between strict adherence to early ascetic ideals and the realities of an authoritarian Arab episcopacy.

Conclusion

Having briefly surveyed the history of the tension between American Orthodoxy as a lived faith and restorationism, one naturally notices that a key reason for the tension revolves around the degree to which restorationism has taken a fundamentalist turn. This is consistent with studies of religious fundamentalism in which fundamentalism has been found to be a factor in feelings of shame,[20] to be a response to an irrational need for comfort or security,[21] to make one less likely to seek out psychological health,[22] less likely to help when ingroup/outgroup dynamics are explicitly present,[23] and more likely to support authoritarianism.[24]

Given that restorationism is a significant factor—and often the most significant factor for converts to Orthodoxy in America—and that it can and does attract those raised in the Orthodox Church, this should raise the concerns of both Orthodox and their ecumenical dialogue partners. The very development of Orthodox theology, especially as it relates to ecclesiology and ecumenism are at stake. The EOC entered into the Orthodox Church with a strong authoritarian flavor, with shame being used to manipulate people, and with parishes that had a history of prioritizing the alleged spiritual gifts of its clergy over all other forms of discernment. Members of the EOC in Ben Lomond retreated to the comfort of supposed early Christian expressions and standards, as did Toth with his approach to the Carpatho-Rusyn church as he understood it to exist prior to the Union of Užhorod in 1646. Fundamentalist ingroup/outgroup assessment of non-Orthodox Christians inadvertently led to the dissolution of the first two significant attempts to unite Orthodox jurisdictions in America.

So, what can be done to alleviate this tension and set a trajectory of spiritual growth for American Orthodoxy that does not get so entangled with an unhealthy, fundamentalist-restorationist approach to church life? I propose that the answer lies in precisely how the converts mentioned above underwent the process of deconverting from restorationism in order to integrate into a lived tradition. On the one end, are Toth and Morgan, whose deconversions were relatively seemless, even though Toth did maintain a strong focus on ingroup/outgroup concerns, especially with regard to Roman Catholics. Berry's would be somewhere in the middle, as he considered his entrance into Orthodoxy to be challenging and he had spent much more time living directly within a restorationist movement than Toth or Morgan. On the other end, we see the likes of Burden and Gelsinger and Gillquist and the EOC. There, the entrance into Orthodoxy was a deep and sincere struggle, a clash of two theological worlds. It is also at this end of the spectrum that we see most poignantly fundamentalist effects that can develop from restorationism. Their deconversion from committed restorationism to a lived tradition shows precisely the difficulty that fundamentalism brings forth.

So, what can we learn from those processes that can help the restorationist make her or his transition into the Orthodox tradition as it is lived and not simply imagined to have been? The first thing I think we can say is that the more a convert sees goodness and value in what his or her background was, the better the deconversion from a rigid commitment to restorationism will be. One sees this in Morgan's experience, especially in his trip to Russia.

A second factor that has been important in navigating this journey has been the degree to which a convert's restorationist view accords with behaviors, or modes of being, rather than an institutional structure. So in the case of Toth, although he emphasized Eastern things, like clerical beards or the importance of Eastern saints versus Western ones, his pre-*unia* emphasis was one that enabled him easily to accept the way the Russian Orthodox tradition was performing liturgy. Or take Morgan and Berry, who each sought a church that had a theology of racial openness each believed existed within the early church. Their approach to restorationism allowed for a flexibility that the EOC's simply did not.

If we build from these two observations, we should be able to advocate that Orthodox clergy and lay leaders strive to do two things with converts. First, they should strive hard, really hard, to help converts see, appreciate, and love the religion, church, or even atheism they are leaving. There is something of God there, too. This must be a necessary part of catechesis in all Orthodox parishes. Second, as converts enter the Orthodox Church, they must be guided to change their restorative views from being centered on ecclesiastical structures (including liturgical forms) to being centered on certain modes of being, such as traditional virtues, the ways in which changes are adapted and lived, the way evangelism and living the faith has been performed in healthy manners over the centuries.

Neither of these negates the importance of the restorative impulse. In fact, each validates it, which is important to do whenever people are seeking to come together. It is a phenomenological necessity for healthy human relationships. Yet both of these guide restorationism into a healthier expression. Both of these even guide it precisely in ways that help converts develop a deeper awareness of God's presence, for God is not most fully present in some imagined ideal. It may well be no accident that some research even suggests that deepening this awareness is one way to build spiritual and psychological resiliency within someone who has a fundamentalist mindset.[25]

Now, lest I give the false impression that all converts are fundamentalists, I should insist that not everyone who bemoans a loss of traditional values or who critiques secularism is a fundamentalist. Nor was every member of the EOC a fundamentalist at the time the EOC joined Orthodoxy. In fact, one could well argue that the EOC joined Orthodoxy the way it did in part to differentiate its spiritual growth from fundamentalism.

An even more important caveat may well be that restorationism is not just simply something enacted by converts, even if converts often have restorationist tendencies. I already noted some bishops above who were born and raised within the Orthodox Church who engaged in restorationism themselves. Furthermore, anyone who has spent any length of time online in social media is well aware that restorationism and fundamentalism are hardly a convert problem. They are Orthodox problems.

This does make the Orthodox Church's task that much more complex, for she must catechize and guide even those born in her midst away from a fundamentalist response to secularism and the religious other. In the end, though, the task, if we take our American Orthodox history seriously, remains the same and here, the same two recommendations I gave for converts applies to "cradles." In fact, that may well prove to be the bigger challenge since some cradle born Orthodox will have to confront their own attempts to restore an imagined ethno-centric past. We must teach and guide one another to see goodness and even God himself in all of our histories, backgrounds, and the world around us and we must further restorationism so that it focuses on healthy ways of living and not just particular ecclesiastical structures. Ours is a difficult task, but if we are to resolve the tension between restorationism and a lived tradition so that the former is subsumed under the latter, we must keep our hearts open to the breath of God, wherever its breezes flow.

Notes

1. A special thanks to Pam Roberts and my fellow Air National Guard clinical pastoral education participants for providing the quiet, reflective context that provided this insight. For many American Orthodox, the standard narrative had been one of unity under Russia broken by the results of the Russian Revolution and subsequent splintering of American Orthodox immigrants along ethnic lines. I published two blog posts on the topic at http://ocanews.org/Herbeljurisdiction4.22.09.html and http://ocanews.org/news/HerbelResponse5.1.09.html. Matthew Namee provided a recorded refutation of the myth, "The Myth of Past Unity," Ancient Faith Ministries, June 20, 2009, accessed March 30, 2019, http://www.ancientfaith.com/specials/st._vladimirs_seminary_summer_conference_2009/matthew_namee_historian_and_host_of_american_orthodox_history_afr. In either case, neither of us replaced the common narrative (or "myth") with a satisfactory narrative of American Orthodox Church history. Although it would take more than this essay to argue a thorough case, I believe the tradition-restorationism tension could provide a framework for discussion, and the way in which tradition expressed itself could vary significantly from place to place and decade to decade.

2. One might object to such a blatant comparison to recent studies from the psychology of religion, especially given its positivistic history. Although the studies cited here do suggest there are common psychological components to fundamentalism, my use of them does not reduce intra-Christian, restorationist conversions to Orthodoxy to merely a fundamentalistic mindset. Nor does my noting some consistencies between certain studies of the psychology of fundamentalism and Eastern Orthodox fundamentalism detract from any theological truth claim the restorationist convert may make as part of his or her conversion. Indeed, I believe that psychology of religion and theology can inform one another in much the same way that science and religion can work together without collapsing religion into positivistic science.

3. Here, I have in mind the work of Hunsberger and Altemeyer and works that have made use of their development of the religious fundamentalism scale, some of which are cited below. See Bob Altemeyer and Bruce Hunsberger, "A Revised Religious Fundamentalism Scale: The Short and Sweet of It," *International Journal for the Psychology of Religion* 47, no. 1 (2004): 47–54.

4. Greek Orthodox sometimes cite a colony, named New Smyrna, near St. Augustine, Florida, which was founded in 1768, as the first Orthodox

presence in North America. The colonists included Greeks, but they had a Roman Catholic priest. Most, if not all, the Greeks were Greek Catholic, not Greek Orthodox. Despite this, a chapel to St. Photios the Great, a pillar of Orthodoxy, has been established in St. Augustine by the Greek Archdiocese in order to commemorate those early colonists. Additionally, one might note that Philip Ludwell III (1716–67) maintained a clandestine Orthodox faith in colonial Virgina. See "Orthodoxy in Colonial Virginia," available at http://orthodoxhistory.org/2009/11/23/orthodoxy-in-colonial-virginia/ (accessed January 17, 2016). See also Nicholas Chapman, "Early Orthodox in British America," *Road to Emmaus*, no. 46 (Summer 2011): 3–25. Chapman states: "The Ludwell family, however, did not advocate a public expression of Orthodoxy but rather preserved their Orthodox faith in a manner consistent with the non-jurors and clandestine Roman Catholics at the time."

5. Literature relating to the Alaskan period is extensive. Readers interested in further exploration of this era should consult the following works: Clifton Bates and Michael Oleksa, *Conflicting Landscapes: American Schooling/Alaskan Natives* (Fairbanks: University of Alaska Press, 2011); Ted G. Hinckley, *The Americanization of Alaska, 1867–1897* (Palo Alto, CA: Pacific, 1972) and *Alaskan John G. Brady, Missionary, Businessman, Judge, and Governor, 1878–1918* (Columbus: Ohio State University Press, 1982); Sergei Kan, *Memory Eternal: Tlingit Culture and Russian Orthodox Christianity Through Two Centuries* (Seattle: University of Washington Press, 1999); B. D. Lain, "The Decline of Russian America's Colonial Society," *Western Historical Quarterly* 7, no. 2 (1976): 143–53; and Michael Oleksa, *Orthodox Alaska: A Theology of Mission* (Crestwood, NY: St. Vladimir's Seminary Press, 1992) and *Alaska Missionary Spirituality* (Mahwah, NJ: Paulist, 1987).

6. For an insightful analysis of this process, see Nicholas Ferencz, *American Orthodoxy and Parish Congregationalism* (Piscataway: Gorgias, 2006).

7. Ferencz, 167–86. Both Slavs and Greeks alike formed lay societies.

8. For a more detailed presentation than what is given here, see my *Turning to Tradition: Converts and the Making of an American Orthodox Church* (New York: Oxford University Press, 2013).

9. This encounter has been recounted numerous times. See, for example, Keith S. Russin, "Father Alexis G. Toth and the Wilkes-Barre Litigations," *St. Vladimir's Theological Quarterly* 16, no. 3 (1972): 132–33; Constance J. Tarasar and John H. Ericksoneds, *Orthodox America: 1794–1976* (Syosset, NY: Orthodox Church in America Department of History and Archives, 1975): 50–51; James Jorgenson, "Father Alexis Toth and the Transition of the Greek Catholic Community in Minneapolis to the Russian Orthodox Church," *St. Vladimir's Theological Quarterly* 32, no. 2 (1988): 127–28; Mark Stokoe, in collaboration with Leonid Kishkovsky, *Orthodox Christians in North America,*

1794–1994 (Syosset: Orthodox Christian Publications Center, 1995), 26–27;
Peter G. Kochanik, *Rus' i pravoslavie v sievernoi Amerikie; k XXV lietiiu Russkago
pravoslavnago obshchestva vzaimopomoshchi, 1895–1920* (Wilkes-Barre: Russian
Orthodox Catholic Mutual Aid Society, 1920), 20–21; "Primiernoe i
muzhestvennoe vysuplenie otsa Aleksiya Tovta na zashchitu pravoclavnych 'i
russko narodnych idealov,'" *Svit* 62, nos. 18–19 (May 1959). Konstantin Simon
notes that one will not find any reference to this encounter in Ireland's
correspondence. See Konstantin Simon, "Alexis Toth and the Beginnings of the
Orthodox Movement among the Ruthenians in America (1891)," *Orientalia
Christiana Periodica* 54, no. 2 (1988): 391.

10. Documents relating to the canonization, including liturgical service
materials, may be found in Alexis Toth, *The Orthodox Church in America and
Other Writings by Saint Alexis, Confessor and Defender of Orthodoxy in America*,
trans. George Soldatow (Minneapolis: AARDM, 1996). See also John
Kowalczyk, "The Canonization of Fr. Alexis Toth by the Orthodox Church in
America," *St. Vladimir's Theological Quarterly* 38, no. 4 (1994): 424–31.

11. For Morgan's story, see my *Turning to Tradition*, 61–84.

12. My summary and analysis are based on my "American Restorationism,
the Public Sphere, and Anglican-Orthodox Relations: The Case of Ingram
Washington Nathaniel Irvine (1849–1921)," *Anglican and Episcopal History* 83,
no. 1 (March 2014): 42–66.

13. He did have an indirect effect in that he helped inspire McGuire's
African Orthodox Church, most of whose African contingency would later
enter into the Greek Orthodox Church.

14. For a more complete analysis, see my "A Lesson to Be Learned: Fr. Boris
Burden's Failed Attempts to Foster Orthodox Jurisdictional Unity in America,"
St. Vladimir's Seminary Quarterly 55, no. 3 (2012): 317–34.

15. An analysis of the Federated Orthodox Greek Catholic Primary
Jurisdictions may be found in my recent book chapter, "Redressing Religious
Freedom: Anti-Communism and the Rejection of Orthodox Christianity as the
'Fourth Major Faith,'" in *North American Community and the Cold War*, edited
by Paul Mojzes (Grand Rapids, MI: Eerdmans, 2018), 361–71.

16. In the case of Carl McIntire, the classical, historical theological
definitions of fundamentalism would apply, as he sided with Machen in the
modernist-fundamentalist debates at the time and described himself as a
fundamentalist.

17. My analysis is based on my *Turning to Tradition*, 85–145.

18. Peter Gillquist, *Becoming Orthodox: A Journey to the Ancient Christian
Faith* (Ben Lomond: Conciliar, 1989).

19. Examples of each of these may be found in chapters 4 and 5 of my
Turning to Tradition. The EOC's use of spiritual manipulation and

authoritarianism belied a group that saw itself as separate from the culture around it. Shunning, for example, was a standard practice. Members' entire lives focused on their EOC parishes (schedules and minute life decisions, such as whether to remodel a house or get a new car, all had to be leadership approved). With such a strong in-group and out-group mentality, being shunned meant losing all of one's close friends at church and a serious disruption to one's life. At one point, the Gary, Indiana, parish was the subject of a series of news articles by Robin Fornoff, because of abuses. Fred Rogers (now Fr. Gregory Rogers) endangered a man's life by denying him medication and manipulated the lives of other parishioners as well.

20. Kathryn H. Keller, Debra Mollen, and Lisa H. Rosen, "Spiritual Maturity as a Moderator Between Christian Fundamentalism and Shame," *Journal of Psychology and Theology* 43, no. 1 (2015): 34–46. The point here isn't that religious fundamentalism automatically and everywhere causes shame. Rather, this study demonstrated that the more spiritually mature a religious fundamentalist was the less likely they were to be handicapped by shame.

21. See Leonardo Carluoci, Marco Tomassi, and Michela Balsamo, "Religious Fundamentalism and Psychological Well-Being: An Italian Study," *Journal of Pscyhology and Theology* 43, no. 1 (2015): 23–33; as well as Louis Ernesto Mora, Panayiotis Stavrinides, and Wilson McDermut, "Religious Fundamentalism and Religious Orientation Among the Greek Orthodox," *Journal of Religious Health* 53, no. 5 (2014): 1498–513.

22. Rachel Wämser, Brian Vandenberg, and Rachel Hibberd, "Religious Fundamentalism, Religious Coping, and Preference for Psychological and Religious Treatment," *International Journal for the Psychology of Religion* 21 (2011): 228–36.

23. Theta Gribbins and Brian Vandenberg, "Religious Fundamentalism, the Need for Cognitive Closure, and Helping," *International Journal for the Psychology of Religion* 21 (2011): 106–14.

24. John D. Hathcoat and Laura L. B. Barnes, "Explaining the Relationship Among Fundamentalism and Authoritarianism: An Epistemic Connection," *International Journal for the Psychology of Religion* 20 (2010): 73–84.

25. See Keller, Mollen, and Rosen, "Spiritual Maturity."

Fundamentalists, Rigorists, and Traditionalists: An Unorthodox Trinity

R. Scott Appleby

K arl Rahner, SJ, one of the most influential Roman Catholic theologians in the decade leading to the Second Vatican Council, observed that the Christian tradition refuses to grant any concept or way of
knowing final authority in comprehending the Divine. Rather, Rahner explained, God—Creator, Word and Spirit—is encountered as *Absolute Mystery*. Never do we comprehend God—not even in that state of bliss known
as the Beatific Vision. Rather, God is the Mystery who comprehends *us*.

This reminder is particularly relevant in any discussion of Christian
sects, movements, or ideologies that try to circumvent the resistance of the
living God to confinement in denotative language and unambiguous definition. Living with paradox and uncertainty is inevitable for those who are
ordered and mastered by the God who is Absolute Mystery. They recognize the inherent inadequacy of doctrinal formulas. Such doctrines become
pernicious, in fact, when believers attempt to manipulate them to autho-
rize and even deify concrete political or social programs. The continuing
struggle for clarity, not a comfortable certainty, is the mark of fidelity to
the tradition.

To "know in fullness" is not the same as possessing "the fullness of
knowledge," writes the Russian Orthodox theologian Vladimir Lossky.
That the canon of the New Testament was formed relatively late, for example, "shows us that the Tradition is in no way automatic: it is the condition of the church having an infallible consciousness, but it is not a
mechanism that will infallibly make known the Truth outside and above

the consciousness of individuals, outside all deliberation and all judgment."
In fact, Lossky continues,

> If Tradition is a faculty of judging in the Light of the Holy Spirit, it
> obliges those who wish to know the Truth in the Tradition to make
> incessant efforts: one does not remain in the Tradition by a certain
> historical inertia, by keeping, as a "tradition received from the Fathers"
> all that which, by force of habit, flatters a certain devout sensibility.
> On the contrary, it is by substituting this sort of "tradition" for the
> Tradition of the Holy Spirit living in the Church that one runs the
> most risk of finding oneself finally outside the Body of Christ. . . .
> The dynamism of Tradition allows of no inertia either in the ha-
> bitual forms of piety or in the dogmatic expressions that are repeated
> mechanically like magic recipes of Truth, guaranteed by the author-
> ity of the Church. To preserve the "dogmatic tradition" does not
> mean to be attached to doctrinal formulas: to be within the Tradi-
> tion is to keep the living Truth in the Light of the Holy Spirit; or
> rather, it is to be kept in the Truth by the vivifying power of Tradi-
> tion. But this power, like all that comes from the Spirit, preserves by
> a ceaseless renewing.[1]

Living without the fullness of knowledge, even while creatively (re)inter-
preting inherited texts, doctrines, practices, and rituals, is a result of living
with and within "the vivifying power of Tradition." This is very different
from what we mean when we employ the term *fundamentalism*.

My thesis is that fundamentalism is *not* a traditional religious way of
being, nor is it an orthodox mode of religiosity—notwithstanding the
claims of those adherents inhabiting the fundamentalist mode of religion,
that they are defenders of the tradition. The antidote to fundamentalism,
as it were, is stubborn, principled, and creative fidelity to the religious tradition in all its mystery, complexity, nuance, fluidity, and richness. This
conceptualization of tradition, it seems to me, would appeal to the young
as well as the old. But the young do not seem to be listening. And fundamentalisms seem to be entrenched even as they evolve and devolve—and
spread globally, even into the tradition-bearing Orthodox Christian
churches. This raises an intriguing question: What does the rise and persistence of fundamentalism—and its close cousins in the Orthodox milieu,
rigorism, and traditionalism—tell us about religious tradition and its perceived shortcomings among modern seekers?

Modern Religion Yielding to Fundamentalism

A good deal of scholarship on fundamentalisms over the past thirty-five years or so, since the appearance of the first monographs published in light of the Iranian Revolution of 1978–79, has produced a large degree of scholarly consensus about religions operating under the conditions of modernity. Four hundred and sixty-eight years into the Westphalian version of secular modernity, we are fairly confident that we know the multigenerational, transnational religions to be *internally plural* (ethnically, culturally, politically) and *internally contested*, as one would expect from traditions that are inescapably interpretive (of, for example, sacred texts, exemplars, and hallowed practices).

Less obvious perhaps is the condition of modern religions as *internally anxious*, to one degree or another, about the turn that the world has taken. Modern religious actors—modern religions—are anxious about their own inevitable secularity, which has always been a condition of their existence-but now looms as an ominous doppelganger striding alongside religion's *otherworldly* orientation. With the ascendance of a globalizing, infecting, and infectious mode of secularism, the religions' *own* worldliness, their *own* secularity, has become an *internal* threat, a potential demon lurking *within*.

The seemingly irresistible allure of this hegemonic mode of neoliberal technocratic secularism became increasingly apparent to the most insightful Jewish, Christian, Muslim, Hindu, and Buddhist sages with the dawning (about midway through this Westphalian era) of their own critical self-awareness as being actors within history, with all of its contingencies. Once securely at home among their own, these vibrant religious cultures came to feel increasingly vulnerable and even "in exile" from the world, as the modern world has constructed its own comprehensive symbol system of meaning that rivals the religions' own once-dominant cosmologies.

Some of these religious cultures have anxiously attempted to reduce themselves to mere enclaves. Their embeddedness within an open-ended, contingent, and often transgressive history is a fate they try to ignore, an epistemological prison they try to escape but cannot. Confronted with— perhaps culpable in *creating*—the Enlightenment Project, their options in the struggle to remain stable and traditional have seemed agonizingly few:

> They can perform an awkward mimesis of the regnant techno-scientific empiricism, that is, they can attempt to "fight fire with fire." Christian creationists in the 1980s and 1990s, for example,

adopted the dubious strategy: "We'll out-science the scientists by carbon-dating fossils in the effort to support the young earth theory." Unfortunately, the effort failed, and the Bible believers had to seek elsewhere for "proof" of scriptural inerrancy.

They can try to withdraw into the enclave, name the infidel and flee into isolation. But this proves well-nigh impossible in an economically interdependent, socially interconnected milieu. The true believers keep coming back to the need for the Internet if they are going to recruit the next generation, and the most radical among them acquire the stinger missile or dirty bomb in order to provoke and then, eventually, silence the infidel. Thus, they are a subset of the self-anointed true believers compelled by the awful logic of violence. Among the things we think we know about modern religions is that the violent extremist movements that erupt within or around the enclave are the dysfunctional expression of the existential insecurity and anxiety sketched above. These violent religious extremisms are the ironic product of the very radical individualism, spiritual rootlessness, religious illiteracy and narrowing of the tradition, which the extremists rail against.

For the frustrated, anxious traditional believers who cannot bring themselves to violence, there is another, far less strenuous path. They can quietly give up, lovingly beat their swords into plowshares and take refuge in a culture-ratifying, nonscandalous version of liberal Protestantism, Unitarianism, Reconstructionist Judaism or nominal Islam. (In polite company, their fundamentalist coreligionists deride this path as abject capitulation; in vast swaths of the Middle East, tragically, they literally decapitate the apostate as well as the infidel.)

And then, finally, there is another option, one that is most intriguing for the inchoate project that is being tested at this conference. Rather than cling desperately and even hysterically to the "Tradition," forge it into a weapon, or reduce its mystery to a formula or blueprint or ideology, the religious can inhabit their traditions more freely than ever before; they can "go deeper" into their historic and still sacred tradition and traditions, bend their surprisingly elastic boundaries, explore their unplumbed and ever shifting depths, learn to live without closure and with ambiguity, and in this self-liberation from Tradition, paradoxically, deepen their own purchase on who they are and what they are called to be.

The first two options I sketched—two versions of fighting fire with fire (awkward mimesis and violence)—would fall into the fundamentalist mode of reacting to modernity's terrors and challenges, so I will turn my focus to them.

Like modernism and traditionalism, fundamentalism is a mode of religious life that has been on offer, among other alternatives, for at least a century. The almost infinite variety of religious communities, social movements, doctrines, practices, and philosophies on display across the world's great multigenerational religious traditions notwithstanding, in the real world of lived religion fundamentalism has a distinct religious logic unlike any other, and this logic is evident only when one views the following characteristics as feeding off one another, existing in a synergy that produces a unique attitude and approach to the modern, secularizing, globalizing world.[2]

The Ideological Traits of Fundamentalism

The movements we call fundamentalist are both reactive and selective, and these two orientations reinforce and condition one another. Fundamentalisms react primarily to the marginalization of religion—that is, to the displacement of "true religion" by nationalist political leaders, scientific and cultural elites (feminists being a particular *bête noir*), modern bureaucracies and institutions, and competing religious or ethnic groups that find public space under the banner of pluralism.

The marginalization of religion, a disease spread by the West and its hubris, produces many symptoms against which militant Islamists, Hindu nationalists, and Christian extremists try to immunize themselves. One is "Westoxication," a phrase coined by an Iranian intellectual to describe the seduction of the devout by the indulgent lifestyle of the West, offered in exchange for one's integrity and soul. Another is "liberation of women" which, fundamentalists claim, turns the natural order on its head and disrupts God's social plan, leading to divorce, sexual depravity, and crime. Other symptoms of irreligion, in addition to hedonism and paganism, are antinomianism, the disregard for God's law, and its close cousin, relativism, the rejection of moral absolutes.

The modern assault upon belief, furthermore, is not a mere accident of history but the intended fruit of a diabolical conspiracy to uproot authentic religion. Insidiously, fundamentalists warn, the disease infects even those previously found within the domain of Islam, the kingdom of Christ, the people of Israel, the Hindu nation: one can no longer trust one's own coreligionist. Thus the Sunni ideologue, Sayyid Qutb, warned darkly of the descent of *jahiliyya* (the era of paganism reminiscent of the time before the Prophet); the Baptist pastor Jerry Falwell accused fellow born-again evangelist Billy Graham of being "the most dangerous man in America," owing to Graham's functional endorsement of US religious pluralism (he appeared on platforms with rabbis, priests, and mainstream Protestants); and the Jewish mystic Rabbi Kook, forefather of Gush Emunim, spread the doctrine that secular Zionists had lost touch with their inner Jewish identity and needed to be awakened to their true destiny.

When fundamentalists react to the marginalization of religion, they do so as quintessentially modern people. They are not the Amish, seeking a cultural return to premodern purity, or restorationists, hoping to rebuild the lost kingdom or return to the golden age. Although their rhetoric might pine for the pristine moment of origin or the apotheosis of the Davidic kingdom or Christendom or Islamic civilization, the fundamentalists are looking ahead, not backward. Educated and formed epistemologically under the banner of techno-scientific modernity, most "middle managers" of fundamentalist movements are trained as engineers, software experts, medical technicians, soldiers, politicians, teachers, and bureaucrats. They are pragmatists of the soul. Few are astrophysicists or speculative philosophers. Stinger missiles, modern media, airliners, and cyberspace are their milieu. They have little patience and no time for the ambiguities of the vast, multivalent religious tradition.

Given their emergence from the heart of secular modernity, these would-be defenders of traditional religion approach the scriptures and traditions as an architect reads a blueprint or an engineer scans his toolbox: they plumb the sacred sources for the instruments appropriate to the task. By this habit they reveal themselves to be modern not traditional. In competition with the "Westoxicated" moderns, the fundamentalists select, mix and match, innovate, create, and build. They grow impatient and angry with moderate co-religionists who insist on disciplining themselves to the tradition as an organic, mysterious, nonlinear, irreducible, life-giving whole. There is no time for such luxuries, such refinements; as the fundamentalists implore: we are at war, our souls as well as lives depend on swift and powerful retaliation: this is urgent!

And so, the mode of reaction to the marginalization of religion is, ironically, fundamentally modern, instrumental, rational—and manipulative of the historic religious tradition. From the religious sensibility they choose the elements most resistant to relativism, pluralism, and other concomitants of secular modernity that work to reduce the autonomy and hegemony of the religious.

This impatience, this anxiety, leads to the ironic and indeed antitraditional outcomes of the mimetic strategy: These anxious true believers who adopt a fundamentalist mode of selective retrieval of traditional norms tear the fabric of tradition apart. They attempt to eliminate ambiguity, bleach out complexity, and make the "Tradition" politically expedient.

Hence fundamentalists embrace absolutism and dualism as tactics of resistance, and as justification for extremism in the service of a sacred cause. They attempt to protect the holy book or hallowed tradition from the depredations of historical, literary, and scientific criticism—that is, from criteria of knowledge production that deny the transcendence of the sacred. Thus, fundamentalist leaders claim inerrancy and infallibility for their religious knowledge. The truth revealed in scriptures and hallowed traditions is neither contingent nor variable but absolute. To underscore the reason-defying nature of absolute truth, each movement selects from its host religion certain scandalous doctrines (i.e., beliefs not easily reconcilable to scientific rationality, such as the imminent return of the Hidden Imam, the literal virgin birth of Christ, the divinity of the Lord Ram, the coming of the Messiah to restore and rule "the Whole Land of Israel." Such "supernatural dicta" they embellish, reify, and politicize.

The confession of literal belief in these hard-to-swallow "fundamentals" sets the self-described true believers apart from the Westoxicated masses. Moreover, it marks them as members of a sacred remnant, an elect tribe commissioned to defend the sacred against an array of reprobate, fallen, and polluted coreligionists—and against the forces of evil that have corrupted the religious community. This dualist or Manichean worldview valorizes the children of light, in stark contrast to the children of darkness, and reinforces the fundamentalists' conviction that they are specially chosen by God to withstand the forces of irreligion.

Yet a reliance on absolutism and dualism is not enough. Fundamentalist leaders may be tempted to employ extra-legal and sometimes violent measures to realize a meaningful victory over their enemies. But they have a recruiting problem, for their pool of potential disciples is drawn not only from the religiously illiterate and untutored or drifting youth but also from conservative and orthodox believers—people who are familiar with their scriptures, embrace the tradition in its complexity, and recognize that it enjoins compassion and mercy toward others and not intolerance, hatred, and violence. To these conservative or orthodox believers, violence and retaliation are not the only strategies for resisting evil. Separatism or passive resistance might suffice to withstand the encroachments of the world. Guerrilla war, terrorism, and the killing of innocents seem to them a breathtakingly severe and indeed unorthodox reaction.

This is why the resort to millennialism—a heightened emphasis on apocalypticism, eschatology, and the end times—completes the religious logic of fundamentalism. My use of the term *millennialism* includes the full array of doctrines, myths, and precepts embedded in the history and religious imagination of the major religious traditions of the world. Certainly Islam, Christianity, and Judaism each anticipate a dramatic moment in time, or beyond time, in which God will bring history to a just (and often bloody) culmination. In certain religious communities, such as Shi'ite Islam or evangelical Protestant Christianity, this expectation is highly pronounced and developed. (Indeed, the term *millennialism* refers to the prophesied one-thousand-year reign of the Christ, following his return in glory to defeat the Anti-Christ.) What is striking, however, is the recent retrieval of millennial (or messianic, apocalyptic, or eschatological) themes, images, and myths by fundamentalists from religious communities with a muted or underdeveloped strain of "end times" thought.[3]

How does this retrieval and embellishment of apocalyptic or millennial themes function within fundamentalist movements that seek recruits from among their orthodox coreligionists? Leaders seeking to form cadres for jihad, crusade, or anti-Muslim (or anti-Jewish) riots must convince the religiously literate fellow believer that violence is justified in religious terms. Luckily for them, most scriptures and traditions contain ambiguities and exceptions—including what might be called "emergency clauses." Thus, the Granth Sahib, the holy book and living guru of the Sikhs, repeatedly enjoins forgiveness, compassion, and love toward enemies. It does, however, also contain an injunction calling believers to arms, if necessary, if the Sikh religion itself is threatened with extinction—a passage put to use by Jarnail Singh Bhindranwale, the Sikh militant who cut a swath of terror through the Punjab in the early 1980s. Such "emergency clauses" can be found in the Qur'an, the Hebrew Bible, and the New Testament as well.

And what better "emergency" than the advent of the predicted "dark age" or reign of evil that precedes the coming of the Messiah, the return of the Mahdi, the vindication of the righteous at God's hands?

The fundamentalist invocation of millennialism, in short, strives to convince believers that they are engaged not merely in a mundane struggle for territory, political power, or financial gain, but in a cosmic war, a battle for the soul and for the future of humanity. In such a context, violence is not only permissible, it is obligatory.

Organizational Traits of Fundamentalisms

Fundamentalisms emerge from the enclave, a community physically, mentally or emotionally set apart from the larger society and concerned with maintaining boundaries to prevent its members from deserting. Moral rigorism is the glue that keeps the enclave together as a social group. Enhancing the effectiveness of moral suasion are ideological claims such as the doctrine that the enclave members are elect, chosen, set apart from the fallen world; and practical rewards such as social or economic benefits (e.g., deferment from the army, for haredi Jews in Israel; employment of women as teachers by the Baptist church; or the granting of loans by Islamic banks). Relations within the enclave tend to be egalitarian despite functional differentiation.

As the fundamentalist movement grows, however, the enclave may become a movement, or a network of enclaves; and, eventually, it may establish permanent institutional presence in the larger society (i.e., through the founding of schools, libraries, health care clinics, or political parties). As the movement grows from enclave to network to institutional presence, the reactive and exclusivist oppositional stance of "pure" fundamentalism becomes more difficult to sustain; that is, the enclave's boundaries become porous, the organization more complex, the internal pluralism of the movement more difficult to manage without making the compromises that are at the heart of politics. In this sense fundamentalism becomes less stable as a religious mode as it becomes more successful in winning recruits and making alliances.[4]

Unlike relations among the rank and file, leadership of the fundamentalist movement or organization is hierarchical. It is also charismatic, authoritarian, and patriarchal. The founder is usually possessed of charisma and spiritual or religious virtuosity, and succession at his death often precipitates a crisis in authority. In any case, leaders atop the pyramid are authoritarian, an organizational tendency that is reinforced by the opposition to relativism and critical attitudes toward religious truth (i.e., absolutism).

The evolution of the enclave into a network (and perhaps a regional or transnational network) requires a more complex organizational structure (e.g., separate wings or divisions for finance, recruiting, ideology, and arms) and multiple leaders. Some instincts of the enclave survive the transition to more complicated organizational structures, however, including the emphasis on differentiating the members of the movement from outsiders, including coreligionists.

Accordingly, fundamentalism as a religious mode entails the requirement of distinctive behavioral codes such as special dress and dietary and sexual restrictions and obligations. In itself, this means of differentiating believers from nonbelievers is not a departure from traditional, time-honored religious practice. But in keeping with their reactive and militant attitude toward even their own coreligionists, the self-anointed true believers practice an exaggerated and chauvinistic form of the host religion (e.g., larger than average kippahs for Gush extremists or supervised dating for Christian students at Bob Jones University).

In other words, because the fundamentalists believe themselves to be engaged in a cosmic war against evil, only a double dose of "strong religion" will suffice. As the religious logic outlined here indicates, they are modern warriors and they are happy to select and retrieve organizational features from modern ideological movements that they admire (e.g., fascism), but which failed because these predecessors were insufficiently religious.

Is Fundamentalism a Feature of Orthodox Christianity?

That fundamentalism is only selectively traditional—and quintessentially modern—is a conclusion based on the multidisciplinary study of nearly every multigenerational religious tradition on the planet save Orthodoxy and Roman Catholicism. These tradition-bound traditions have been, until recently, exempt from inclusion in the fundamentalist "family." By virtue of their backward-looking orientation—that is, their respective affinities for the tradition of the hallowed past rather than the allure of the present and the promise of a new, modernized future—the two major premodern Christian communities of East and West have been largely immune to the appeal of fundamentalism.

Fundamentalists—for all their rhetoric about restoring the rule of the ancient gods, the paths of the pious ancestors, or the practices of the apostles and founders—are, in practice, religious engineers and architects and not restorationists. They may model their new religiopolitical edifices on a classical form—but it is no more than a model; the actual building is a work of synthesis, a hybrid of past and present, but with a design dynamism weighted decisively to the future.

By contrast, Roman Catholicism—its roots in premodern Western Christianity—only reluctantly turned its gaze away from the founding medieval era in an attempt to update medieval and Tridentine forms of Catholicism. But Catholics did so by seeking renewal from the (even earlier) apostolic era. Even the most earnest agents of the Second Vatican Council's project of ecclesial updating (*aggiornamento*), however, saw the apostolic past as merely a resource (as in *ressourcement*), not as a charter. Catholicism engaged modernity directly, with the consequences still unfolding. Eastern Orthodox Christianity, the quintessential traditional Christian Church, seemed even more immune to fundamentalism, for it was significantly more resistant to modernity itself.

Can we conclude, then, that Orthodoxy does not belong in a discussion of fundamentalism? No, we cannot. Orthodox Christianity has indeed produced its own variant of what is called fundamentalism in Western Christian, Islamic, and Jewish contexts. Vasilios N. Makrides provides a comprehensive survey of the Orthodox version(s) of militant reactivity against modernism and, arguably, against the pluralist, relativist, and critical-scientific trajectory of modernity itself. Professor Makrides employs the term *rigorism* rather than fundamentalism for the phenomenon, which finds expression in a thin but wide and disproportionately influential stratum of Orthodox organizations, networks, and movements (e.g., Old Believers, Old Calendarists, and "Kantiotists") and a minority of well-placed monks, metropolitans, and bishops.

The distinction between what is signified by the two terms is not always clear. Indeed, the traits Makrides ascribes to rigorism—"eschatological, apocalyptic, Manichaean," "puritanical ethics and patriarchal family values," "enemy syndrome, conspiracy theories, and, last but not least, the use of violence"[5]—could be lifted directly from the ideological and social or organizational logic of fundamentalism sketched here, as could the general characteristics of modern societies against which the rigorists are reacting (e.g., "the present global syncretistic environment with its ideals of pluralism,

secularism, multiculturalism, tolerance and liberalism"[6]). Yet Professor
Makrides gives the reader an important clue to discovering the defining
distinction between fundamentalists and those he calls rigorists. It is not,
as he suggests, that the latter are anti-Western, for many fundamentalists,
while living in the geographical and cultural West, are also vehemently
anti-Western in many respects. Rather, it is that the so-called rigorists are
truly and actively resistant to modernity in virtually *all* its forms. In
this, they are far closer to the buggy-driving, Internet-abhorring Amish of
the United States than to the Southern Baptist media titans, computer software engineers, and political operatives. Indeed, Makrides observes that
the Old Believers, for example, cannot rightly be called fundamentalists
because their aggressive hostility to various forms of change antedates
modernity itself.[7]

The groups and individuals clustered by Makrides under the somewhat
ambiguous term *rigorist* might be more accurately and illuminatingly called
traditionalists, by which I mean those who profess to adhere to a historic
and historical religious tradition, which they present and enforce as timeless, unaltered over the centuries and indeed unalterable. Orthodox Christianity contains within itself this tendency to an extreme and distorted
form of tradition, but mainstream Orthodoxy has by and large resisted allowing itself to be overwhelmed by this distortion and thus has resisted
being reduced to it. As Fr. Georges Florovsky has written: "Tradition is
not a principle striving to restore the past, using the past as a criterion for
the present. Such a conception of tradition is rejected by history itself and
by the consciousness of the Orthodox Church. . . . Tradition is the constant abiding of the Spirit and not only the memory of words. Tradition is
a charismatic, not a historical event."[8] For the Orthodox, therefore, Tradition is typically conceived *not* as a static set of dogmatic precepts, or the
uniform practices of the liturgical ritual of the church. Rather, the "rule
of faith" becomes every day the "rule of worship."

The key intellectual error in Orthodox fundamentalism (or rigorism)
"lies in the presupposition that the church fathers agreed on all theological and ethical matters," notes George Demacopoulos in the preface to the
conference program. "That miscalculation, no doubt, is related to another
equally flawed assumption that Orthodox theology has never changed—
clearly it has or else there would have been no need for the Fathers to build
consensus at successive ecumenical councils. . . . The irony, as identified by
recent scholarship on fundamentalism, is that while fundamentalists claim

to protect the Orthodox Christian faith from the corruption of modernity, their vision of Orthodox Christianity is, itself, a very modern phenomenon. In other words, Orthodoxy never was what fundamentalists claim it to be."

Conclusion: A Secularized Religion?

For the Western or Western-shaped fundamentalist religious movements, the interaction and mutual construction of the religious and the secular is virtually unavoidable. Indeed, the fundamentalist mode of religiosity in the twenty-first century is critically engaged with secularism. Even as they strive to transform certain attitudes and values associated with secular humanism, while rejecting others, the fundamentalists are inscribed within the discourse of worldliness. Within fluid, evolving, and transnational movements and organizations—such as the Islamic State (ISIS), Hezbollah, Hizbut Tahrir, or the Hindutva movement in India—one is challenged to keep track of the ongoing internal debates (e.g., over the use of violence, the relationship between political and military wings, or the timing and targets of propaganda campaigns or public demonstrations); the diversity of interpretations of texts and traditions (e.g., concerning the religious status of the nation or homeland or the theoretical as well as functional place of end-times or eschatological expectation in the movement worldview); disagreements regarding practical issues as well as principles of operation (e.g., how to obtain political goals, what alliances to form and when, or how recruiting is to be conducted); and actual changing behaviors (e.g., the development of new religious NGOs affiliated with or supported by the group, the evolution of political parties and their positions on questions such as participatory self-governance, and the building of seemingly unlikely coalitions).

Like everyone, religious actors face a globalizing milieu characterized by an array of competing forces, each possessed of their own value systems, each vying for public space, and some for hegemony, through the amassing of resources and political capital. Familiar boundaries and "givens"— geographical, religious, cultural, or economic—seem to be eroding or reconfiguring more rapidly than at any time in history. Within this global context, in which homogenization and flattening of values can be seen as concomitant with secularism in a form virulently hostile to religion, how are people committed to transcendence, to the priority of the spiritual and religiously moral, to ensure continuity with the traditional religious past? How best to contest the meanings of core concepts of cosmopolitan discourse, such as freedom, development, or human rights?

These, to me, seem to be the questions faced by fundamentalists, rigorists, and traditionalists alike. All such groups increasingly engage the cosmopolitan project from within. As mentioned, the core members of fundamentalist movements include medical technicians, software designers, biologists, chemists, career politicians, and other mid-level technobureaucrats at home in the domain of applied science and, more recently, cyberspace. Sharpening the profile of fundamentalists as the so-called person next door, your professional colleague, belies the stereotype that recruits into extremist movements hail from premodern or educationally impoverished backgrounds. More widely available are descriptions of relatively deprived or socially alienated engineers, computer software experts, medical technicians, and mid-level bureaucrats. This more nuanced composite profile underscores the fact that the contest, in the minds of the so-called fundamentalists, is not between the religious and the secular, but between different formulas for their interdependence and coexistence in a rapidly modernizing world. In this, of course, they are like other Western or Westernized believers, including especially Western Christians.

As many religious actors have realized, the fundamentalists' attempt to co-opt the secularists, is fraught with risk. The strategy raises anxiety even among its practitioners, who may or may not openly acknowledge their fear that the result will be the dilution of the religious imagination itself. Hence, we see the ratcheting-up of aggressive, triumphal God-talk among some of the movements and groups deeply engaged in negotiating with the secular other.

Furiously religious as a matter of choice, the fundamentalists embrace a disciplined commitment to staying religious as they confront the commanding question of the age: How can religious actors preserve their fidelity to the religious tradition without fleeing the world? Unfortunately, zeal for fidelity to tradition does not relieve fundamentalists from the burden of navigating not only the hazards but also the undeniable advantages of secular modernity.

Is Orthodox Christianity capable of producing fundamentalists as well as traditionalists, that is, of producing aggressive, self-consciously militant believers who seek to fight secular modernity with the tools of secular modernity? Are militant Orthodox traditionalists willing to become fully modern Christian warriors?

The answers to these questions may largely depend on the direction taken by the host religion itself. Thus, the question becomes: Will Orthodox Christianity deepen its fidelity to tradition as an evolving, fluid but coherent set of practices, beliefs, and discernments and be committed to holding the rigorists and traditionalists in check? Or will it set its face against the admittedly challenging encroachments of pluralism and secular cosmopolitanism, thereby giving into the temptation to imitate and adopt the patterns of sectarian exclusion and self-righteousness that provide a seedbed for fundamentalism?

Notes

1. Vladimir Lossky, "Tradition and Traditions," in *In the Image and Likeness of God* (Crestwood, NY: St. Vladimir's Seminary Press, 1974), 159–60.

2. The following discussion of the ideological and organizational traits of fundamentalism is adapted from Gabriel Almond, R. Scott Appleby, and Emmanuel Sivan, *Strong Religion: The Rise of Fundamentalisms Around the World* (Chicago: University of Chicago Press, 2003), 90–120.

3. Barbara Freyer Stowasser, "A Time to Reap," *Middle East Studies Association Bulletin*, 34, no. 1 (Summer 2000): 1–13.

4. Emmanuel Sivan, "The Enclave Culture," in Almond, Appleby and Sivan, *Strong Religion*, 1–89.

5. Vasilios N. Makrides, "Orthodox Christian Rigorism: Attempting to Delineate a Multifaceted Phenomenon," *Interdisciplinary Journal for Religion and Transformation in Contemporary Society* 2, no. 2 (2016): 232.

6. Makrides, 233.

7. Makrides, 219. In an unconvincing conclusion to his otherwise compelling essay, Makrides notes that no individual or group can fully escape the influence of modernity in the twentieth and twenty-first centuries. This is true enough, but the observation is not convincing, given the evidence presented elsewhere in the article, that the Orthodox rigorists have adamantly refused to come out of their tortoise shells into the light of technoscientific, rationalist modernity to a degree unthinkable to the fundamentalists, who are modern scientists, engineers, or bureaucrats. See Makrides, 237.

8. Fr. Georges Florovsky, "The Catholicity of the Church," in *Bible, Church, Tradition: An Eastern Orthodox View* (Belmont, MA: Nordland Publishing Company, 1972), 47.

"Orthodoxy or Death": Religious Fundamentalism during the Twentieth and Twenty-First Centuries

Nikolaos Asproulis

In 1972, Esfigmenou,[1] one of the twenty monasteries of Mount Athos,[2] ceased all ecclesiastical and administrative communion with the Ecumenical Patriarchate (Istanbul) and the other autocephalous Orthodox churches (such as the Church of Greece). This revolutionary reaction was triggered, in part, by the ongoing ecumenical dialogue and historic contact between the then Ecumenical Patriarch Athenagoras and Pope Paul VI.[3] Since then, a group of zealot monks have ignored the official declarations or decisions issued by the Ecumenical Patriarchate (to which the monastery administratively belongs) and the Greek state. Instead, they adopted "Orthodoxy or death" as their slogan because, in their view, the heresy of ecumenism (just like secularization and modernity) threatens the purity of Orthodoxy.[4]

In this essay, I will first contextualize the question of the relationship between the religious and secular aspects of contemporary Greece that must be considered in any discussion of its fundamentalism. Next, I will provide a brief overview of the main aspects of religious fundamentalism in contemporary Greece. And then, I will describe the basic contours of an Orthodox secular theology that offers a response to the current state of this Orthodox fundamentalism.

The Religious and the Secular in Contemporary Greece

In order to understand the reality and the character of religious fundamentalism in Greece, one must understand the relationship between the religious and the secular.

In the words of a liberal Greek historian:

Modern Greeks are a deeply religious people . . . in an obvious and all-encompassing way, in public and in their private lives, in good times and in bad times, in times of turmoil and in times of calm. The vast majority baptize their children, choose to be married in the church, and bury their loved ones with a funeral service. They attribute a religious dimension to the most secular holidays, to national anniversaries, and to their political and military activities. They bless the Parliament, the courts, the schools. . . .

Modern Greek religiosity has a strongly national character. It is something that concerns almost all Greeks, but no one else. Modern Greeks ascribe national significance to religious holidays and celebrate their national holidays inside the church. They are not interested in missionary work . . . and they become angry when they detect encroachment onto Greek soil, Mount Athos, or even the Greek diaspora, by other confessions, including even the Russian Orthodox. The presence of non-Orthodox Christians and people of other religions in Greek territory is an ongoing affront to them; . . .

When Patriarch Athenagoras met with Pope Paul VI, he faced forceful protest not only from the Archbishop of Athens at the time, Chrysostomos, but also from the people. Archbishop Christodoulos also had difficulty speaking with Pope John Paul II, even though nothing important was discussed at that meeting. . . .

In modern Greek society, the church is often in conflict with the state, claiming certain privileges and rights. But primarily it reproaches the state when it believes that the state is not equating the Greek citizen with the Greek Christian (as occurred recently with the issue of the identity cards) or when the state fails to carry out its national agenda with perfect consistency (as is happening now with the Macedonian issue).[5]

This illuminating passage provides a full account of the state of secularization in Greece and the role of religion both in the establishment of the Greek state and in the formation of a Greek identity in the context of modernity or late modernity and globalization. In the context of secularization theory, this should be understood, first and foremost, as a sociopolitical theory.

Taking into consideration the debate on secularization theory in both Europe and the United States,[6] as well as the degrees of secularization in various contexts, one may want to apply contextual hermeneutics to avoid misrepresenting the Greek context by projecting general sociopolitical theories.[7] Although Greece has been part of the European Union as well as the United Nations and NATO for several decades, and despite the strong claims by more than one contemporary politician (including Konstantinos Karamanlis [1907–1998]) that Greece has always been part of the West, many Greek citizens and officials feel ambivalent about the role of Greece in East-West relationships (a reality that reemerged during the last years because of the economic crisis and the emergence of a radical-left government). This ambivalence renders impossible any undifferentiated (one-dimensional) approach that would lead to various misconceptions.[8]

Contemporary sociologists of religion agree that secularization is a more nuanced and complex reality that is context dependent. Some have rightly argued that the religious and the secular are "inextricably bound and mutually conditioned,"[9] which means that one is obliged to talk about multiple secularizations or patterns of secularization, just as we account for "multiple modernities."[10] Nevertheless, sociologists and political theorists have identified three features that describe this phenomenon: structural differentiation of the secular sphere, the decline of religious belief, and the privatization of religion.[11]

In context, Greek society indeed looks quite different from other Western societies. Despite the apparent changes in their everyday lives and their institutions and because of the current economic crisis,[12] the Greek people—whether Orthodox, indifferent, or pagan—remain deeply religious, even though church attendance is not what it used to be. According to a 2015 survey, 74.2 percent of Greeks believe in God.[13] Therefore, despite the efforts of socialist governments to redefine the state-church relationship along more secular lines (see, for example, the government of Costas Simitis or the identity cards crisis in 2001),[14] one can hardly argue that Greek society as a whole has been secularized.

Although religion in Greece has less direct influence on the various institutional spheres (what might be described as an "inter-institutional secularization"[15]), the Orthodox Church's influence remains strong because of its connection to national ideology and its undisputed role in charitable activity and political advocacy.[16] The Orthodox Church in Greece remains visibly present in the public square despite the current radical left government. Thus, any attempt to approach the distinctiveness of the Greek experience through the lens of "Christian nominalism,"[17] "vicarious religion,"[18] "top-down secularization theories,"[19] or a more inclusive European secularization (rather than a more limited American one[20]) fails to grasp the core character of Greek religiosity.

In Greece, the challenge for religion is not to *re*-enter into the public domain, an important premise of modernity, but of *remaining* in the public domain,[21] to preserve its important political role (i.e., the constant politicization of the religious discourse) and privileges in society and to continue to influence it in terms of safeguarding the national identity, visibility, and validity of its moral principles.

Indeed, the strong bond between Orthodoxy and the Greek nation prohibits, to a great extent, the progression of secularization in the country. This means that any attempt to raise an American-like "wall of separation" between the religious and the secular becomes counterproductive,[22] because it would most likely further strengthen the tie between Orthodoxy and state instead of weakening it.

Aspects of Religious Fundamentalism in Orthodox Greece

Although Martin Marty and Scott Appleby's groundbreaking Fundamentalism Project did not engage Orthodox Christianity,[23] some recent studies have traced possible characteristics of and trends in fundamentalism within Eastern Orthodoxy.[24] The overall definition of the causes, characteristics, or species of the general phenomenon of fundamentalism studied by Marty and Appleby could also apply to the Orthodox context, despite the unique ways in which secularization operates in (mainly traditional) Orthodox societies. This section applies the typologies of the Fundamentalism Project to the various figures, characteristics, and possible trends of Orthodox fundamentalism in Greece.

For example, the case of Greek fundamentalism fits both Abrahamic and syncretic modes,[25] wherein the former refers primarily to the mainly religious character of fundamentalism and the latter designates a mixture of religious and ethnocultural elements.

However, before describing instances of religious fundamentalism in Greece, a brief explanation of the interlinked ideological and organizational criteria for this label is in order.[26]

As has been argued, the most basic characteristic that lies at the heart of any fundamentalist movement is the latent reactivity to any attempt of marginalization or erosion of religion from the public sphere. Even though secularization and modernity have a long way to go in traditional Orthodox countries, and especially Greece, fundamentalists feel the duty to react against any real and seeming changes (such as conspiracy theories against the present and the future of the Orthodox faith and nation) they believe threaten the central—historically achieved—role of Orthodoxy. Further characteristics may also include: selectivity of particular aspects of tradition (e.g., the golden age of the church fathers or the Byzantine system of *symphonia* of the church-state relationship); modernity (e.g., the Internet, blogs, or European funds); moral Manicheanism (i.e., the secular world lies in the dark in contrast to the pure mainly monastic and spiritual communities); absolutism and inerrancy (referring to the church fathers but also to contemporary spiritual elders of Mount Athos and other monastic centers); and a sense of apocalyptism. All these evidently constitute the ideological backbone of the Greek religious fundamentalism.

Most of the so-called organizational characteristics apply also to the religious fundamentalism in Greece. In most cases a spiritual father or elder (primarily from the monastic and charismatic communities and not from the body of bishops or the church) plays the role of an elect that more or less has the final word in terms of new membership. The boundaries between the saved and the sinful—that is, the wall that separates morally liberal, atheist, heterodox, irreligious people and foreigners from the charismatic community that follows the right path of God—can also be found in different aspects of religious fundamentalism (especially in brotherhoods, monastic communities, and political parties). A strong emphasis on behavioral requirements—which, because of moral connotations, is considered as a basic feature of orthopraxy (correct conduct)—can be linked to all forms of fundamentalist movements of both types (e.g., the moral values of the Helleno-Christian culture). Not surprisingly, religious brotherhoods or monastic circles have more or less strict rules regarding drinking and gender-based dress codes, for example. With the ideological and organizational characteristics of fundamentalism in mind, I will proceed with

my critical overview of the phenomenon of fundamentalism in contemporary Greece.

Abrahamic or Theological Fundamentalism

Abrahamic fundamentalism, for me, involves groups, associations, and religious fellowships and brotherhoods as well as individuals, bishops, professors, theologians, or spiritual elders (*gerontes*) that seek the transformation
of civil society or the creation of a new world based primarily, if not solely,
on their "evangelical" premises or under the auspices of God.[27] Some
characteristics of this so-called Abrahamic fundamentalism in Greece
include:

> An essentialist understanding of ecclesiastical tradition that must
> remain unchangeable and fixed during the time,[28] providing ready-
> made answers to all the modern problems. This "radical traditional-
> ism" is exemplified by the so-called traditional Orthodox or Old
> Calendarists movements, and theological brotherhoods such as Zoe,[29]
> Soter, and Stavros, as well as by the monastic community of Mount
> Athos, which has considered itself the guardian of the genuine
> Orthodox tradition since the tenth century.[30]
>
> A superficial understanding of the normative, patristic character
> of Orthodox theology to the extent that the Fathers—or rather a
> specific ahistorical, almost literal understanding of the patristic
> corpus—becomes the ultimate criterion of doing Orthodox theology
> and practice.[31] This criterion measures all the seemingly heretical her-
> meneutical efforts of contextualizing and bringing to the fore the
> existential importance of the patristic ethos. In that case, the defend-
> ers of this type of patristic fundamentalism argue for what seems
> like an infallibility of the church fathers as a diachronic *magisterium*
> that provides all the necessary responses to the various challenges,
> even though profoundly not all anthropological or ethical perspec-
> tives of the patristic tradition could apply to our era. This patristic
> fundamentalism is quite similar to the fundamentalism of the Bible
> in various Protestant traditions.
>
> Representatives of this theological fundamentalism often seek to
> preserve the seeming Christian and moral character of their society
> either by using an apocalyptic language (e.g., the late Metropolitan

Kantiotis who interpreted the 1983 earthquake in Northern Greece as God's punishment for the immoral behavior of its people[32]) through which they hope to keep alive the Orthodox consciousness of believers,[33] or by applying a moral Manicheanism,[34] dividing the people between the purified and already deified members of the church (especially the clerics, monks, and elders) against the immoral, ordinary people and the world inside and outside the boundaries of the church, which is then understood as a sanatorium for the salvation of the soul.

The phenomenon of gerontism,[35] namely, the privileged position enjoyed by the spiritual Fathers in Mount Athos and other monasteries as leaders of the life of obedient individuals—ordinary people, religious teachers, and marginal politicians, among others—that are often manipulated toward various ends.

Hierarchs of the Church of Greece who boldly criticize and often condemn a Synod for its openness to the other Christian churches and traditions and the modern world (as was the case with the Holy and Great Council in Crete in 2016). They even argue in the name of synodality of the Orthodox Church that such a synod would never be approved by the consciousness of the faithful because of its anti-traditional pursuits.[36] This reaction dates back to the "Confession of Faith against Ecumenism,"[37] which came out of a meeting of clerics and monks in 2009 and has since been signed by more than twenty-four thousand people. That goal of the document has been to form a strong group within the Church of Greece that would push the Archbishop of Athens and the Holy Synod to withdraw from the ongoing official ecumenical dialogue.

Each of these examples of fundamentalist reaction was triggered by a series of overlapping causes, including:[38]

1. The involvement of the Orthodox Church in the official ecumenical and inter-Christian dialogues.

2. The belief that Western Christianity (especially the figure of the Pope) and its theology are considered to be deviating from the undivided church.

3. The idea promoted by some influential thinkers (such as Christos Yannaras[39]) that Western Christianity represents a constant threat to the truth of Orthodoxy.

4. The efforts by certain politicians and liberal activists to secularize Greek society and diminish the influence of the church in
modern culture.[40]

5. The increased presence of secular intellectual conceptions,
such as the language of human rights,[41] which gives rise to the
modern subject and individual, a reality still not evident in Greek
society because it remains more communitarian, based on traditional agrarian and authoritarian values.

For the most part, the dimensions of Abrahamic fundamentalism in Greek
society avoids strictly aggressive practices, limiting itself to an overall theoretical accusation and condemnation of its opponents (including hierarchs,
theologians, intellectuals, and liberal politicians). This type of fundamentalism is applied in a wide spectrum of cases, from a reactionary attitude
against the official dialogue of the Church of Greece with other Christian
churches and traditions, against any imaginary or real antireligious initia-
tive by the state, against any serious academic work or use of modern scientific methods of interpreting the Fathers, against any change in the
hard-core denominational character of the religious subject in all levels of
the compulsory state education, and against any openness toward any
religious, gender, racial, or ethnic otherness.

Syncretic or Ethnoreligious Fundamentalism

Syncretic fundamentalism refers to a wide spectrum of groups, radical or
marginal political parties, ethnic and cultural associations, and individuals
(including university professors, theologians, and monks) that all share a
peculiar amalgam of ethnic, cultural, and religious views. If the core of
Abrahamic or theological fundamentalism is a more or less religious goal,
namely, the transformation of the world, then the concerns of the syncretic
or ethnoreligious fundamentalists lie in using theological rigidity to serve
an ethnic and cultural scope. In other words, the history of salvation and
the divine economy as it is narrated and recorded in the Gospels and in the
Christian tradition has been subsumed into the history of the Greek nationality.[42] What is at the core of this species of fundamentalism is not the
church as the body of Christ but the church as the ark of the nation that
uses religion and faith for purposes alien to the church's mission, for purposes that have to do with the ethnic, cultural continuity, and purity of the

nation at the expense of the flourishing of the body of Christ. Here, too, one can see multiple overlapping causes for a syncretic fundamentalism:

1. The migration crisis that Greece has experienced in recent years, as well as the cultural and religious pluralism following this migration influx in traditional Orthodox societies, tests the very coherence of the Greek society to an extent that a considerable number of people, otherwise faithful Christians, do not hesitate to join various racist or nationalist and anti-immigrant movements. This reality is seemingly at odds with the supposed traditional solidarity of the Greek people.

2. The collapse of the Greek economy, followed by an often radical neoliberal economic policy, has provoked a harsh, although naïve and populist, reaction against foreign creditors. Even certain church officials, priests, and theologians have aligned with various protestors against those who are accused as being ready to compromise the nation's independence for a fistful of euros.[43]

3. Bearing in mind the deep tie between religion and nation in Greek history, it is not surprising that we find expressions of ethno-nationalist fundamentalism in some prominent hierarchs of the church, including the late archbishop of Athens, Christodoulos (1998–2008), who is partially responsible for the politicization and nationalization of the church discourse in recent years,[44] and the late metropolitan of Florina, Augoustinos Kantiotis (1907–2010), who advocated for the liberation of Northern Epirus from the alien occupation,[45] as well as various metropolitans who appeal to religious identity in their criticism of Turkish colonial policy against Greece.

4. A variety of ethnoreligious political associations, such as the "Greek Orthodox Salvation Movement-Free Greeks" (ELKIS),[46] play a significant role in agitating for the spiritual rebirth of the Greek nation on the basis of the moral values of the Greek Orthodox culture. More radical-right political parties, such as "Popular Orthodox Alert" Laos,[47] employ Orthodox symbols and references to express views reminiscent of the "Great Idea" of a new Hellenic Empire formed in 1922 after the "Catastrophe of Smyrna."[48]

5. A peculiar and quite dangerous case is that of the Golden Dawn neo-Nazi party,[49] which, since the Greek double elections of 2012, has gained a strong position in the Greek parliament,

representing more than one half of one million people who one way or another feel quite familiar with this aggressive and militant form of religious and nationalist fundamentalism. Although Golden Dawn, by its own admission, is anti-Christian,[50] it tries to conceal its inherent possible antireligious and profoundly pagan views to draw the support of certain nativist metropolitans in the Church of Greece, who supported their goal of a homogenous, pure Greek-Orthodox nation.[51] This recent alliance between official church leaders with neo-Nazi ideology has a precedent in the alliance between the Church of Greece and the dictatorship in the late 1960s and early 1970s, a fraught collaboration from which the church has yet to fully emerge.[52]

6. Furthermore, the bold nationalistic tendency expressed by all of these groups lies in contradistinction to the official foreign policy of the government. It is precisely for this reason that these groups employ various conspiracy theories (e.g., Zionism is the ultimate evil[53]) in order to misguide the Greek population and embolden them to fight against an imaginary enemy (e.g., Germany, the IMF, or Turkey) that is offered as the main cause for all of their problems.

This syncretic or ethnoreligious fundamentalism relies on a targeted selectivity and oversimplification of the cultural past in order to advance an ideology that is wholly inconsistent with the core elements of Orthodox Christian teaching (e.g., the love of the stranger or humility).[54] By expanding on ideas found in widely read Greek intellectuals of the twentieth century (such as Christos Yannaras and John Romanides), the advocates of this ethnoreligious fundamentalism are able to present their radical ideas as mainstream.

A key component of their strategy is to promote themselves as the guardians of the so-called Christian and homogenous character of the Greek society. And, here too, they rely on precedents set by other twentieth-century movements such as the well-known religious brotherhoods—Zoe, Soter, and Stavros—which developed as a countermeasure against the rise of communism and the threat it posed to Christian faith.[55] The threat of the Soviets may have faded, but for the ethnofundamentalist the danger posed by secularist modernity offers an existential threat to the Orthodox character of the nation.

Although one could list more individual or group fundamentalist trends in Greece during this and the previous century, this brief glimpse describes more or less the basic framework within which any fundamentalist figure or movement could be included. This (schematic) dichotomization, however—between theological and ethnoreligious fundamentalism or, in the terms of the Fundamentalist Project, between Abrahamic and syncretic fundamentalism—should not be regarded in absolute terms since a close interrelation between the two categories is evident.[56] This bond can be further defined by virtue of the deep historical tie between Greek religiosity and ethnicity.

World Dogmatics as an Orthodox Theology of Secularization

Although it is widely recognized that modern Orthodox theology has finally overcome its "Babylonian or scholastic captivity,"[57] it seems to have fallen prey to a new form of captivity, which I call a premodern captivity. By this I mean that the perception of a glorious patristic or Byzantine past (often affirmed triumphalistically) has become an insurmountable obstacle for the Orthodox Church to engage the modern world. This premodern captivity determines both the method, the content, and the character of theological practice and discourse.

The distinction between church dogmatics and church and world dogmatics, proposed by Paul Valliere in his groundbreaking *Modern Russian Theology*,[58] offers a constructive methodological point of view for escaping the snare of fundamentalism.

In my view,[59] the concept of church dogmatics is primarily related to a theology proper, that is, to a theology *ad intra* in terms of classic dogmatics, whereas church and world dogmatics are intended to express an open-ended theological reflection on secular issues, that is, a kind of systematic theology in the current sense of the term. The way that Orthodox theology is related to the world as people experience it in their everyday lives is closely related to the second methodological way of doing theology—that of church and world dogmatics—which, without putting aside the doctrinal or biblical theology (theology proper), attempts by virtue of a deep interpretation or *re*-lecture of tradition to find what the latter would have said in addressing the challenges posed by the current modern reality.[60] In the context of this discussion, one could recommend a third type, that of a world dogmatics. In this case, without minimizing the centrality of theology, one is searching for a common ground (for instance, the concepts of being, experience, or divine-human communion) in order to bring into closer contact and mutual inclusiveness both the church and the world, but this time from the perspective of the latter. This sort of understanding makes clear the necessarily complementary character of the three perspectives, even though one could start with the second or third without taking explicitly into account the first and vice versa. In this light, the following are the basic prospects of a world dogmatics theology that takes seriously both church and church and world dogmatics:

1. *The self-revelation of God in history and the world in the person of Christ*:[61] Revelation is the very starting point of doing Christian theology. Despite the variety of understandings in the context of the diverse Christian traditions, it is commonly accepted that the way by which God is made known through His self-revelation in Christ in the realm of history and creation *determines* the way of theological discourse. In this perspective, the church and its theology have as their basic task first to grasp and then clearly to express and articulate the yet underdeveloped and hidden aspects of this revelation as deposited in the church tradition, so as to be able subsequently to address modern challenges by interpreting it in a modern tongue. If this is the case, modern Orthodox theology should confirm the very *sophianity* of creation,[62] its *graced* character, as the place where God chooses to meet humanity in Christ by being joined in a constant relationship through His body, the church, finally overcoming any sort of Manichean dichotomy between the sacred and the secular. Since "in its original theological meaning, to secularize meant to 'make worldly,'"—that is, the "saeculum/secular . . . emerged first as a theological category of Western Christendom . . ."[63]—and beyond any dualistic misconception of it, evidently the self-revelation of God in history mainly by His incarnation means exactly this: God became forever an immanent reality, His materiality and humanity will never be withdrawn. The scholastic legacy of the deep distinction between *grace* and *creation* (nature) should be abandoned as far as theology is dealing with the *magnalia Dei* in history and not with some super-historical or ahistorical reality and truth beyond or outside of history and creation. Therefore, a new model of Orthodox theology would be primarily based on the very revelational-historical

context of Christian theology that inevitably highlights the relevance
of the synergetic divine-human communion as well as determines the
basic aspects of this communion. In this sense a theology of secularization accounts for a theology of incarnation, where the church is
secularized so as to assume the whole of Creation.

2. *The importance of eschatology*: Since the beginning of the
twentieth century, eschatology seems to have regained its central
place within the body of Christian theology.[64] Being in the first place
a sort of an "eschatological revolution" within the Protestant world,
this revitalisation of the eschatological outlook soon spread out
over the entire Christian world. Georges Florovsky, Sergius Bulgakov, and John Zizioulas are only some of those who pointed out the
central place of eschatology in contemporary Orthodox theology.[65]
Despite the possible variety of definitions of eschaton by the previously mentioned theologians and others, it is evident that eschatology should have a crucial role to play in this quest of a new model of
doing Orthodox theology in the context of late modernity. To the
extent that this eschatological outlook is determined by the fresh and
always innovative Spirit of God, and is perceived not as a fixed reality but as an expectant hope (as the freedom from every kind of
historical, individual, or communal pathogen, or failure, like nationalism, self-referentiality, egocentricity, ecclesiastical culturalism,
oppression, and, in our case, fundamentalism), it becomes quite
obvious that the *eschata*—the coming Lord—will finally judge our
way of individual and ecclesial being and doing theology. In other
words, Christ's Kingdom is the very criterion that manifests the
truth of every individual (Christian) or communal (church) enterprise, or even of tradition itself. The real dynamism of this eschatological outlook allows the church and its theology to search for new
and necessary syntheses in the realm of the ongoing history of salvation insofar as the church has not yet fully articulated every aspect
of the revealed truth in history. If it is true that according to Maximus the Confessor the whole world will be churchified in the Kingdom (as the other side of the coin as described above), then one is
obliged to ask the following critical and crucial question: will there
be any aspect of human life (e.g., reality outside the church or secular world) that will be excluded from this eschatological perspective?
A negative reply to this question will oblige us to realign our way of

doing theology towards the eschatological coming Lord, who alone will judge and justify our Christian identity. Thus, Orthodox theology needs to be open and ready to proceed to a creative perception and interpretation of tradition according to the apostolic *kerygma* and in the light of the eschaton, without the fear that this would be in opposition to the Gospel. If Jesus Christ is the "same yesterday, today, and forever" (Heb 13:8), then the new challenges posed by modernity and secularization can be only understood as creative opportunities, rather than obstacles, toward the goal of the "divine-human communion."[66]

3. *Searching for the one common truth*:[67] It was commonly accepted in the so-called formative patristic era of Orthodox theology, that truth had not only strictly theological but also cosmological and sociological implications. In other words, the truth concerned not only some aspects of human life or separate parts of the whole creation but the very being of the world in its fullness. Based on this assumption, theology for instance was for a long time considered in a natural close relation with the various disciplines (a normal phenomenon of the early church was that the Fathers had studied in almost all the scientific fields of their time), since they were somehow converged in the one and indivisible truth. Despite the different developments throughout the centuries and the sometimes radical specialization present in modern university curricula,[68] or even an attitude of excluding theology in various seminaries in favor of religious studies, the modern institution of the university is rooted initially in this early perception of the indivisible nature of truth, where all the different disciplines (in other words, the aspects of reality) exist side by side, in close cooperation in view of searching for the one common truth. In contrast to the dominant Manichean position, according to which theology exclusively deals with a spiritual reality while the other especially positive disciplines and technology deal mainly with the material, in the above more *inclusive* and holistic perception of truth, theology (as every individual discipline) does not claim access or look for a special part or aspect of the truth (so to say a spiritual one), but addresses the mystery of being itself, that is the *saeculum*, from its own standpoint, but in close relation and cooperation with all the different worldly perspectives. In such an understanding of the dialogical and deeply relational character of

theology as such, it could be inconceivable for it to be in tension and unaware (as it is still the case in all the traditional Orthodox contexts) about the content, methodology, and the achievements of every other individual discipline to the extent that all of them, theology included, are addressing more or less the same existential needs of humanity. Despite the different method or means utilized by theology and the other disciplines, the object and the main locus of all the disciplines remains the same—namely, the very being of humanity and the whole world. Although theology in its Christian understanding is not merely or primarily a human enterprise but a divine/human one, it is true that its soteriological scope has anthropological and cosmological (or rather secular) implications, a fact that brings it in close cooperation with the surrounding reality to facilitate human life in different ways or to fulfill the truth of its existence.

4. *The existential concern*: In an understanding of the nature and the scope of theology in terms of church and world dogmatics, or rather world dogmatics, one should admit that the common ground between the secular and the religious is their common existential concern. By the latter we mean especially the questions related to life-death issues, a question that is deeply located in the very existence of the human being throughout the centuries. How could a theology, chiefly considered as self-sufficient, self-referential, and closed to a denominational, ahistorical, moral, and premodern understanding of its truth and the surrounding reality, find the most adequate ways of reincarnating the Word of God and of addressing the existential needs of humanity in the midst of secularization? Without taking late modernity and secularization seriously as the current period of the ongoing history of salvation, Orthodoxy will be constantly caged in the trap of fundamentalism that finally denies the very reality.

Conclusion

The most serious problem facing the Orthodox Church in the twenty-first century is fundamentalism. If secularism is considered by the so-called traditional Orthodox as the most serious threat against which Orthodox Christians should constantly fight, fundamentalism should be seen as the most serious heresy in the history of Christianity, since it confuses the very saving truth, that is the person of Jesus Christ, with national or ideological factors that are totally alien to God's will for the salvation of the whole creation. Although the Pan-Orthodox Synod in its official message condemned "the explosions of fundamentalism observed within various religions" and "the extension of military violence, persecutions, the expulsion and murder of members of religious minorities, forced conversions,"[69] supporting at the same time the interreligious dialogue, paradoxically, it did not condemn explicitly or radically the increasing fundamentalist mentality of various individuals, groups, or even local churches, within Orthodoxy itself. In this latter case, that of increasing fundamentalism, the so-called "death of Orthodoxy" instead of "Orthodoxy or death" would more properly express the real meaning of this essay's title.

Notes

1. For more details on the history of Esfigmenou Monastery and the controversy, see the Monastery's official website, accessed August 25, 2016, http://www.esphigmenou.gr/index.php?mid=1&sid=6.

2. For a general overview of Mount Athos, see, for example, Graham Speake, *Mount Athos: Renewal in Paradise* (New Haven, CT: Yale University Press, 2002).

3. On the theological and ecumenical importance of their historical encounter, see John Chryssavgis, ed., *Dialogue of Love: Breaking the Silence of Centuries* (New York: Fordham University Press, 2014).

4. For more information about this slogan, the overall ideology, and information about the reactions of the old brotherhood of Esfigmenou Monastery, see their blog, accessed August 25, 2016, http://esfigmenou.blogspot.gr/.

5. Dimitris Kyrtatas, "Modern Greek Christianity," a paper presented at the workshop *Helleno-Christianity (19th–20th century)*, organized by the School of History, Archaeology, and Social Anthropology of the University of Thessaly in cooperation with the Volos Academy for Theological Studies in Volos, Greece, on March 12, 2008 [in Greek] (courtesy of the author, trans. Fr. Gregory Edwards). See also Pantelis Kalaitzidis, "The Image of the West in Contemporary Greek Theology," in *Orthodox Constructions of the West*, ed. George Demacopoulos and Aristotle Papanikolaou (New York: Fordham University Press, 2013), 142–60.

6. See, for instance, José Casanova, "Rethinking Secularization: A Global Comparative Perspective," *Hedgehog Review* (Spring/Summer 2006): 7–22; and *Public Religions in the Modern World* (Chicago: University of Chicago Press, 1994); Craig Calhoun, Mark Juergensmeyer, and Jonathan VanAntwerpen, eds.,

Rethinking Secularism (Oxford: Oxford University Press, 2011); and Charles Taylor, *The Secular Age* (Cambridge, MA: Belknap Press, 2007), chap. 14.

7. See Aristotle Papanikolaou, "From Sophia to Personhood: The Development of the 20th c. Orthodox theology from S. Bulgakov through V. Lossky and D. Staniloae to Metropolitan John D. Zizioulas," unpublished talk, delivered at a Patristic Seminar, organized on May 14, 2016, by the Volos Academy for Theological Studies (Volos, Greece) with support from the Virginia H. Farah Foundation.

8. On the multilateral situation (sociological, political, economic) in Modern Greece, see, for example, Nicos Mouzelis, *Modern Greece: Facets of Underdevelopment* (London: Macmillan, 1979); Constantinos Tsoukalas, "Between 'East' and 'West,' the Meaning of the Mediterranean in Modern Greece, and Possibly Elsewhere as Well," *Mediterranean Historical Review* 17, no. 2 (2002): 32–46; and Lina Molokotos-Liederman, "The Religious Factor in the Construction of Europe: Greece, Orthodoxy, and the European Union," unpublished research paper, accessed, August 29, 2016, http://www.lse.ac.uk /europeaninstitute/research/hellenicobservatory/pdf/1st_symposium/molokotos .pdf; Stathis Kalyvas, *Modern Greece: What Everyone Needs to Know* (Oxford: Oxford University Press, 2015). See also Christos Yannaras, *Orthodoxy and the West*, trans. P. Chamberas and Norman Russell (Brookline, NY: Holy Cross Orthodox Press, 2006) for the still more or less normative, in most Greek Orthodox theological circles, evaluation of the relationship and the role and presence of Greek Orthodoxy in the Western context; and Vasilios Makrides, "Orthodox Christian Rigorism: Attempting to Delineate a Multifaceted Phenomenon," *Interdisciplinary Journal for Religion and Transformation in Contemporary Society* 3, no. 1 (2016): 216–52, for updated comments and details of this ambivalent relation of Greek (Orthodox) people with Western (mainly European) culture.

9. See Casanova, "Rethinking Secularization," 10 and passim.

10. Casanova, 11. The term *multiple modernities* was initially coined by S. N. Eisenstadt, "Multiple Modernities," *Daedalus* 129, no. 1 (Winter 2000): 1–29.

11. On this perspective, see Casanova, "Rethinking Secularization," 7–9; and his "The Secular, Secularizations, Secularisms," in *Rethinking Secularism*, ed. Craig Calhoun, Mark Juergensmeyer, Jonathan VanAntwerpen, (Oxford: Oxford University Press, 2011), 60–62; Nicos Mouzelis, "Modernity: Religious Trends," Universal Rights in a World of Diversity: The Case of Religious Freedom, Pontifical Academy of Social Sciences, *Acta* 17 (2012): 71–90. See also David Martin, *A General Theory of Secularization* (Oxford: Blackwell, 1978); and also his *On Secularization: Towards a Revised General Theory* (Aldershote: Ashgate, 2005); Rhys H. Williams, "Movement Dynamics and Social Change: Transforming Fundamentalist Ideology and Organizations," in *Accounting for*

Fundamentalisms, ed. Martin E. Marty and R. Scott Appleby, The Fundamentalism Project 4 (Chicago: University of Chicago Press, 1994), 798.

12. For a theological and comprehensive general overview and assessment of the current economic crisis in Greece, see Metropolitan Ignatius of Demetrias, *The Orthodox Church of Greece and the Economic Crisis*, trans. Gregory Edwards (Volos: Volos Academy Publications, 2017), based on a lecture given at the invitation of the Hellenic Observatory of the London School of Economics, London, November 12, 2014.

13. See, for instance, http://ikivotos.gr/post/896/statherh-aksia-h-ekklhsia-alla (accessed August 20, 2016). Even though the amount of the Greek people that claim to believe in God is still the highest in Europe, it is in decline.

14. For the reaction of the Church of Greece regarding the decision of excluding the reference of religion from Greek identity cards by the government of Costas Simitis, see the very balanced approach by Yannis Stavrakakis, "Politics and Religion: On the 'Politicization' of Greek Church Discourse," *Journal of Modern Greek Studies* 21, no. 2 (2003): 153–81, which includes an extensive bibliography on the debate. See also Molokotos-Liedermann, "The Religious Factor."

15. See Casanova, "Rethinking Secularization," 7–20; and his "Secular, Secularizations, Secularisms," 60–65; and Mouzelis, "Modernity: Religious Trends," 71–90.

16. On this perspective, see Daphne Halikiopoulou, *Patterns of Secularization: Church, State and Nation in Greece and the Republic of Ireland* (Farnham, MA: Ashgate, 2011). See also similar observations about the close tie between the Greek Orthodox Church and nationalism in Evangelos Karagiannis, "Secularism in Context: The Relations between the Greek State and the Church of Greece in Crisis," *European Journal of Sociology* 50, no. 1 (April 2009): 133–67. About religion and patriotism in various contexts, see Taylor, *Secular Age*, 506, 514, 529. For a robust theological critical evaluation, see Pantelis Kalaitzidis, "The Temptation of Judas: Church and Nation Identities," *Greek Orthodox Theological Review* 47, nos. 1–4 (2002): 357–79.

17. For the meaning of the term *Christian nominalism*, see Grace Davie, *Religion in Britain since 1945: Believing without Belonging* (Oxford: Blackwell, 1995).

18. For the meaning of the term *vicarious religion*, see Grace Davie, *Europe: The Exceptional Case: Parameters of Faith in the Modern World* (London: Darton, Longman and Todd, 2002), 46.

19. See Taylor, *Secular Age*, 530. See also Mouzelis, "Modernity: Religious Trends," passim.

20. See Casanova, "Rethinking Secularization," 8–11.

21. See Karagiannis, "Secularism in Context," 162.

22. On this view, see Casanova, "Rethinking Secularization," 20.

23. Martin Marty and R. Scott Appleby, eds., *Fundamentalisms Observed*, vol. 1 of The Fundamentalism Project (Chicago: University of Chicago Press, 1991); *Fundamentalisms and Society*, vol. 2 (Chicago: University of Chicago Press, 1993); *Fundamentalisms and the State*, vol. 3 (Chicago: University of Chicago Press, 1993); *Accounting for Fundamentalisms*, vol. 4 (Chicago: University of Chicago Press, 1994); *Fundamentalisms Comprehended*, vol. 5 (Chicago: University of Chicago Press, 1995). Hereafter cited as *FP* and volume number.

24. On these efforts to describe the phenomenon of fundamentalism in Eastern Orthodox contexts or different aspects of it, see Pantelis Kalaitzidis, "Theological, Historical, and Cultural Reasons for Anti-ecumenical Movements in Eastern Orthodoxy," in *Orthodox Handbook for Ecumenism: Resources for Theological Education*, ed. P. Kalaitzidis et al. (Volos: Volos Academy Publications in cooperation with WCC Publications and Regnum Books International, 2014), 134–52; and his "Church and State in the Orthodox World: From the Byzantine 'Symphonia' and Nationalized Orthodoxy, to the Need of Witnessing the Word of God in a Pluralistic Society," in *Religioni, Liberta, Potere*, ed. Emanuela Fogliadini (Milano: Vita e Pensero, 2014), 39–74; George Demacopoulos, "Orthodox Fundamentalism," accessed August 15, 2016, https://blogs.goarch.org/blog/-/blogs/orthodox-fundamentalism; Cyril Hovorun, "Orthodox Fundamentalism: From Religion to Politics," *Wheel* 4 (2016): 54–60; Vasilios Makrides, "L'autre orthodoxie: courants du rigorisme orthodoxe grec," *Social Compass* 51 (2004): 511–21; and his "Fundamentalism, Orthodox," in *Encyclopedia of Greece and the Hellenic Tradition*, vol. 1, ed. Graham Speake (London: Routledge, 2000), 632–33; "Fundamentalismus: Problimata ellinikis apodosis toy oroy," *To Vima Koinonikon Epistimon* 4, no. 14 (1994): 83–103 (in Greek); "Aspects of Greek Orthodox Fundamentalism," *Orthodoxes Forum* 5 (1991): 49–72; and "Orthodox Christian Rigorism"; Vasilios Makrides and Dirk Uffelmann, "Studying Eastern Orthodox Anti-Westernism: The Need for a Comparative Research Agenda," in *Orthodox Christianity and Contemporary Europe*, ed. Jonathan Sutton and Wil Van den Bercken (Leuven: Peeters, 2003), 87–120; and Theodoros Exintaris, "Greek Orthodox Fundamentalism (History, Sociology, Theology)," master's thesis, University of Thessaloniki, 2016.

25. On this useful typology, see Gabriel A. Almond, Emmanuel Sivan, and R. Scott Appleby, "Fundamentalism: Genus and Species," in *FP* 5:399–424; and their *Strong Religion: The Rise of Fundamentalism around the World* (Chicago: University of Chicago Press, 2003), 90–115.

26. For what follows in this paragraph, see Almond, Sivan, and Appleby, *Strong Religion*, 93–98.

27. For this general orientation of the fundamentalist trends as "world conquerors," "world transformers," and "world creators," see Nancy T. Ammerman, "The Dynamics of Christian Fundamentalism: An Introduction," *FP* 4:14–15; Almond, Sivan, and Appleby, *Strong Religion*, 95–96, 146–49; and Almond, Sivan, and Appleby, "Explaining Fundamentalisms," in *FP* 5:428–30.

28. On this view, see similar attitudes of the fundamentalist movements in Nancy T. Ammerman, "Accounting for Christian Fundamentalisms: Social Dynamics and Rhetorical Strategies," in *FP* 4:150–56. See also Martin E. Marty and R. Scott Appleby, "Introduction: A Sacred Cosmos, Scandalous Code, Defiant Society," in *FP* 2:3; Almond, Sivan, and Appleby, "Fundamentalism: Genus and Species," in *FP* 5:402, 406. On the Orthodox case, see Hovorun, "Orthodox Fundamentalism," 56; and Makrides, "Aspects of Greek Orthodox Fundamentalism," 54, 66.

29. For a comprehensive account of the role and the work of this important theological brotherhood, see Angelos Giannakopoulos, *Die Theologen-Bruderschaften in Griechenland: Ihr Wirken und ihre Funktion im Hinblick auf die Modernisierung und Säkularisierung der griechischen Gesellschaft* (Frankfurt am Main: Peter Lang Verlag, 1999); On the "Old Calendarists," see Kallistos Ware, "Old Calendarists," in *Minorities in Greece: Aspects of a Plural Society*, ed. Richard Clogg (London: Kurst and Company, 2002), 1–23; and Constantine Cavarnos, *Orthodox Tradition and Modernism* (Etna: Center for Traditionalist Orthodox Studies, 1992).

30. See Makrides, "Orthodox Christian Rigorism," 220–30; "Aspects of Greek Orthodox Fundamentalism," passim; "Fundamentalismus," passim; and "L'autre orthodoxie," passim.

31. See the quite challenging critique of "patristic fundamentalism" in Pantelis Kalaitzidis, "From the Return to the Fathers' to the Need for a Modern Orthodox Theology," *St. Vladimir's Theological Quarterly* 54, no. 1 (2010): 5–36, as well as the groundbreaking conference on the general theme: "Neo-patristic Synthesis or 'Post-patristic' Theology? Can Orthodox Theology Be Contextual?," organized by the Volos Academy for Theological Studies in cooperation with the Orthodox Christian Studies Center of Fordham University and other Orthodox organizations in Central and Eastern Europe, of which the proceedings are under publication in English and Greek language. See also Demacopoulos, "Orthodox Fundamentalism."

32. See Makrides, "Aspects of Greek Orthodox Fundamentalism," 61.

33. On this aspect of the fundamentalist trends, see Almond, Sivan, and Appleby, *Strong Religion*, 95, 102, 150. On the Orthodox context, see Makrides's contributions mentioned in note 24.

34. For the central role that moral concerns play in the fundamentalist movements in general, see, for example, Nancy T. Ammerman, "The Dynamics

of Christian Fundamentalism: An Introduction," in *FP* 4:154; Almond, Sivan, and Appleby, *Strong Religion*, 95, 98; Helen Hardacre, "The Impact of Fundamentalisms on Women, the Family, and Interpersonal Relations," in *FP* 2:131–39; and John H. Garvey, "Introduction: Fundamentalism and Politics," in *FP* 3:17. On the Orthodox context in particular see, for example, Makrides, "Aspects of Greek Orthodox Fundamentalism," 60–61; and "Orthodox Christian Rigorism," passim.

35. See, for example, Kalaitzidis, "Theological, Historical, and Cultural Reasons," 149–50, Stavros Yangazoglou, "Eucharistic Ecclesiology and Monastic Spirituality: The Issue of Gerontism," in *Turmoil in Post-war Theology: The 'Theology of the 60s'*," ed. P. Kalaitzidis, Th. Papathanasiou, and Th. Abatzidis (Athens: Indiktos, 2009); Hovorun discusses "gerontolatria," elders worship, in "Orthodox Fundamentalism," 57. On the role of the zealot gerontes (elders) of Mount Athos, see also Makrides's articles, cited in note 24.

36. The convocation of the Holy and Great Synod in Crete in June 2016 elicited a number of publications, conferences, and various kinds of reactions when it was announced. See, for example, the reaction of Mount Athos, accessed August 15, 2016, http://aktines.blogspot.gr/2016/05/blog-post_167 .html; or the official letter of Metropolitan Seraphim of Piraeus against the Synod because of its ecumenical commitment, accessed August 15, 2016, http://news.in.gr/greece/article/?aid=1500079168.

37. See the Impantokratoros, accessed August 15, 2016, http://www .impantokratoros.gr/B742476A.el.aspx.

38. See Kalaitzidis, "Theological, Historical, and Cultural Reasons," passim; his "Hellenicity and Anti-Westernism in the 'theology of the 1960s,'" PhD dissertation, University of Thessaloniki, 2008 (in Greek); and "The Discovery of Hellenicity and the Theological Anti-Westernism," in Kalaitzidis, Papathanassiou, and Ambatzidis, *Turmoil in Post-war Theology*, 429–514, and Makrides's articles mentioned in note 24.

39. See, for instance, Christos Yannaras, "Orthodoxy and the West," *Greek Orthodox Theological Review* 17 (1972): 115–31; and *Orthodoxy and the West*. See also John Romanides, *Franks, Romans, Feudalism, and Doctrine: An Interplay between Theology and Society* (Brookline: Holy Cross Orthodox Press, 1981). For a general evaluation of Orthodox theology, see Brandon Gallaher, "'Waiting for the Barbarians': Identity and Polemicism in the Neo-Patristic Synthesis of Georges Florovsky," *Modern Theology* 27 (2011): 659–91.

40. For the various reactions against different state decisions and the difficult relationship between the state and the church, see Molokotos-Liederman, "The Religious Factor,"; Stavrakakis, "Politics and Religion"; Makrides, "L' autre orthodoxie," 516–17; Karagiannis, "Secularism in Context," 145–47.

41. For the crucial importance of the relation between Orthodoxy and modernity in general, see Pantelis Kalaitzidis, *Orthodox Christianity and Modernity: Prolegomena* (Athens: Indiktos, 2007) (in Greek); Aristotle Papanikolaou, *The Mystical as Political: Non-Radical Orthodoxy and Democracy* (South Bend, IN: University of Notre Dame Press, 2012); Vasilios Makrides, "Orthodox Christianity, Modernity and Postmodernity: Overview, Analysis and Assessment," *Religion, State and Society* 40, nos. 3–4 (2012): 248–85; and my "Is a Dialogue between Orthodox Theology and (Post-)Modernity possible? The case of the Russian and Neo-patristic 'Schools,'" *Communio Viatorum* 54, no. 2 (2012): 203–22, and "Östliche Orthodoxie und (Post-)Moderne: Eine unbehagliche Beziehung," *Una Sancta* 74, no. 1 (2019): 13–37.

42. On this perspective, see especially Kalaitzidis, "Temptation of Judas," passim.

43. For a balanced assessment of the current situation, see Metropolitan Ignatius, *Orthodox Church of Greece*; and Th. N. Papathanasiou, *The Clash with the Null: Some Sips of Political Theology* (Athens: Armos, 2015) (in Greek).

44. See Stavrakakis, "Politics and Religion"; Makrides, "Orthodox Christian Rigorism," 225; Halkiopoullou, introduction to *Patterns of Secularization*; and Molokotos-Liederman, "Religious Factor."

45. See the official page of the late metropolitan which lists examples of his activities, accessed August 15, 2016, http://www.augoustinos-kantiotis.gr/?cat=116.

46. For more information about this ethno-religious association, visit its blog, accessed August 14, 2016, https://eleftheroiellines.wordpress.com/category /%CE%B5%CE%BB%CE%BA%CE%B9%CF%83/. See also Makrides, "Aspects of Greek Orthodox Fundamentalism," 57.

47. For a clear idea of the program and activities of this radical right party, see its official website, accessed August 15, 2016, http://www.laos.gr/.

48. The "Great Fire of Smyrna" or the "Catastrophe of Smyrna" refers to the events that took place a few days after the Turkish army regained control of the city, which led to the end of the Greco-Turkish war (1919– 1922). See Giles Milton, *Paradise Lost: Smyrna 1922: The Destruction of Islam's City of Tolerance* (London: Sceptre, Hodder and Stoughton, 2008).

49. For a comprehensive critical overview of the neo-Nazi ideology of this party, see *Neo-Nazi Paganism and the Orthodox Church*, ed. Stavros Zoumboulakis (Athens: Artos Zoes, 2013) (in Greek); and Demetrios Bathrellos, "The Golden Dawn Nightmare: The Orthodox Church and Greece's War against Neo-nazism," accessed August 13, 2016, http://www.abc.net.au/religion/articles/2013 /10/07/3863712.htm.

50. See, for example, the appendix with various extracts of the official texts of "Golden Dawn" and its leaders, *Neo-Nazi Paganism and Orthodox Church*, 99–168.

51. See, for example, Stavros Zoumboulakis, "Welcome Greeting," in *Neo-Nazi Paganism and Orthodox Church*, 15, and the more or less positive official statement by Metropolitan Ambrosius of Calavryta, accessed August 20, 2016, http://www .ethnos.gr/koinonia/arthro/ambrosios_glykia_elpida_h_xrysi_augi-63730220/. See also Monk Anthimos of Mount Athos, "Repetance, Faith, and the Golden Dawn Will Save Us," accessed February 11, 2017, http://www.xryshaygh.com /enimerosi/view/g.-anthimos-oagioreiths- h-metanoia-h-pisth-kai-h-chrush-augh-tha-mas-swsou.

52. On the role played by the official church and the antidictatorship political action of various individual Orthodox Christians and associations, see Andreas Argyropoulos, *Christians and Political Action during the Dictatorship (1967–1974)* (Athens: Psifida Publications); Y. Karagiannis, *Church and State 1833–1977: A Historical Overview of Their Relationship* (Athens: Pontiki Publications, 1997). See also Makrides, "Aspects of Greek Orthodox Fundamentalism," 70; and Karagiannis, "Secularism in Context," 154–55.

53. See, for example, Makrides, "Aspects of Greek Orthodox Fundamentalism," 57.

54. This selectivity of sources characterizes fundamentalist trends in general as shown by Almond, Sivan, and Appleby, *Strong Religion*, 95; and Marty and Appleby, "Introduction: A Sacred Cosmos, Scandalous Code, Defiant Society," in *FP* 2:3.

55. See, for instance, Makrides, "Aspects of Greek Orthodox Fundamentalism," 69.

56. As indicated by Almond, Sivan, and Appleby, *Strong Religion*, 90.

57. This refers to the use of alien, principally Western/scholastic methods of doing theology, which was prevalent in Orthodoxy from the fall of Byzantium until the twentieth century.

58. On this quite fruitful typology, see Paul Valliere, *Modern Russian Theology: Bucharev, Soloviev, Bulgakov; Orthodox Theology in a New Key* (Edinburg: T and T Clark, 2000), 306–9. Specifically, Valliere differentiates between the two dominant theological trends in modern Orthodox theology, that is, "neo-patristic theology" (including Florovsky, Meyendorff, Schmemann, and Zizioulas) and the "Russian Religious Renaissance" (including Soloviev, Bulgakov, and Florenski).

59. For more on this understanding, see my "Is a Dialogue between Orthodox Theology and (Post-)Modernity Possible?"

60. See my "'Church and World Dogmatics' as a new model of theological education: The case of the 'Orthodox Handbook,'" *Scientific Review of the Post-Graduate Program, Studies in Orthodox Theology* 4 (2013): 87–99 (in Greek).

61. See my "The Bible as *Heilsgeschicte*: The Basic Axis and Scope of Georges Florovsky's Neo-patristic Synthesis," in *What Is the Bible? The*

Patristic Doctrine of Scripture, ed. M. Baker and M. Mourachian (Minneapolis: Fortress, 2016), 121–36; and Georges Florovsky, "Revelation and Interpretation," in *Bible, Church, Tradition: An Eastern Orthodox View* (Belmont, MA: Nordland, 1972), 1:17. See also Florovsky, "Revelation, Philosophy, and Theology" in *Creation and Redemption* (Belmont, MA: Nordland, 1976), 3:21–42, and "Révélation, Expérience, Tradition (Fragments théologiques)," in *La tradition: La pensée orthodoxe*, ed. Constantin Andronikof (Paris: Institute St. Serge, 1992), 54–72.

62. On this quite positive perception of the created order, especially by S. Bulgakov, see A. Nichols, *Wisdom from Above: A Primer in the Theology of Father Sergei Bulgakov* (Leominster: Gracewing, 2005).

63. See Casanova, "Secular, Secularizations, Secularisms," 56.

64. For my perception of eschatology, I follow mainly John Zizioulas's account in his "Towards an Eschatological Ontology," unpublished lecture given at King's College, London, 1999; "Eschatologie et Societe," *Irénikon* 73, nos. 3–4 (2000): 278–97; "Deplacement de la perspective eschatologique," in *La Chrétienté en débat*, ed. G. Alberigo et al. (Paris: Les Editions du Cerf, 1984), 89–100, rep. Metropolite Jean (Zizioulas) de Pergame, *L'Eglise et ses Institutions* (Paris: Les Editions du Cerf, 2011), 459–73; and "Eschatology and History," in *Cultures in Dialogue: Documents from a Symposium in Honor of Philip A. Potter*, ed. T. Wieser (Geneva: WCC, 1985), 62–71, 72–73.

65. For an overview of the reception of eschatology in contemporary Orthodox theology, see Marios Begzos, "L'eschatologie dans l' orthodoxie du XXe siècle," in *Temps et Eschatologie: Données biblique et problematiques contemporaines*, ed. J.-L. Leuba (Paris: Les Editions du Cerf, 1994), 311–28; and G. Vlantis, "In Erwartung des Künftigen Äons: Aspekte orthodoxer Eschatologie," *Ökumenische Rundschau* 56, no. 2 (2007): 170–82.

66. On the meaning and importance of this concept, see Aristotle Papanikolaou, *Being with God: Trinity, Apophaticism, and Divine-Human Communion* (South Bend, IN: University of Notre Dame Press, 2006).

67. See especially John D. Zizioulas, "The Ecumenical Dimensions of Orthodox Theological Education," in *Orthodox Theological Education for the Life and Witness of the Church* (Geneva: WCC, 1978), 33–40, rep. in *Orthodox Handbook for Ecumenism: Resources for Theological Education*, ed. P. Kalaitzidis et al. (Volos: Volos Academy Publications, 2014), 929–34. See also John Meyendorff, "Theological Education in the Patristic and Byzantine Eras and Its Lessons for Today," *St. Vladimir's Theological Quarterly* 31, no. 3 (1987): 204.

68. In this regard, see E. Farley, *Theologia: The Fragmentation and Unity of Theological Education* (Augsburg: Fortress, 1994).

69. The official message of the Pan-Orthodox Synod is available on the Holy Council website, accessed August 26, 2016, https://www.holycouncil.org/-/message.

CONFESSION AND THE SACRAMENT OF PENANCE AFTER COMMUNISM

Nadieszda Kizenko

he essays in this book ask under what circumstances and in what form fundamentalism may emerge in response to the secular. In post-communist Russia, a tendency to fundamentalism appears especially in the practice of confession. In imperial Russia, confession served the goals of the state as well as those of the church. The supplement to the Spiritual Regulation of Peter the Great and Bishop Feofan (Prokopovich) explicitly enjoined Russian Orthodox Christians not to put their trust in icons, relics, or visits to monasteries, but in confession followed by communion. After 1917, with the abdication of Nicholas II, however, confession was no longer a legal requirement, and the administrative structures that had fostered it fell apart.

The fall of communism marked another turning point. For the first time in nearly four centuries, state pressure no longer appeared to be either encouraging or discouraging confession, and the Russian Orthodox Church could decide for itself how to approach the sacrament of penance. The choices the church made with regard to confession from the 1990s onward tell us about contemporary relations between church and state, the usefulness of fundamentalism as a conceptual category, and the sacrament of penance as such.[1]

This connection between confession and political fortune is not surprising. In both Russian Orthodoxy and in Roman Catholicism, confession is the sacramental rite most closely tied to modernity. Michel Foucault described the centrality of confession in the Western tradition with particular force:

> The confession became one of the West's most highly valued techniques for producing truth. We have singularly become a confessing

society. The confession has spread its effects far and wide. It plays a part in justice, medicine, education, family relationships, and love relationships, in the most ordinary affairs of everyday life, and in the most solemn rites; one confesses one's crimes, one's sins, one's thoughts and desires, one's illnesses and troubles; one goes about telling, with the greatest precision, whatever is most difficult to tell. One confesses in public and in private, to one's parents, one's educators, one's doctor, to those one loves; one admits to oneself in pleasure and in pain, things it would be impossible to tell to anyone else, the things people write books about. . . . Western man has become a confessing animal.[2]

Perhaps more than any other sacrament, penance is closely tied to changes in the Russian Orthodox Church and in society. Confession reflects how people imagine their lives, how they assess their lives, and how they tell the story of their lives to someone who is signaling the presence of God. Unlike baptism or a funeral, confession has the potential to be repeated over and over again, a steady potential companion as one takes stock in life's ups and downs. For Russian Orthodox Christians, first confession, not first communion, is the sacrament that signals that one has reached the age of discernment. And, as for Catholics, confession and communion are ideally the last sacraments one takes part in before one passes from life to death.

Penance in Russian Orthodox Practice before 1917

Between the seventeenth and early twentieth centuries, unlike most other Orthodox nations, the Russian empire was a sovereign state. This allowed the Russian Orthodox Church and the Russian state to enforce confession in ways that resembled the Roman Catholic world more than they did other Orthodox nations. Indeed, from the seventeenth century onward, confession in the Russian empire intimately connected the individual to the rest of society and indeed to the Russian state.[3]

Tsar Aleksei Mikhailovich (1629–1676), the father of Peter the Great, appears to have been the first Russian tsar to realize that trying to get his subjects to show up for anything—confession first and foremost—was a way of making them better subjects as well as better Christians. His son Peter went even further in linking confession and political utility, requiring priests to report anything treasonous they might hear at confession.[4] From their reigns through the abdication of Nicholas II in 1917, sacramental confession was a legal requirement for Orthodox Christians in imperial Russia. It was enforced by the agents and agencies of the secular government (most notably, the Department of Police) as well as those of the Orthodox Church (most notably, the Orthodox priests who were required to maintain detailed records of the dates of parishioners' confessions and to submit those records annually to their Religious Consistory). In the mid-nineteenth century, if people skipped confession for several years, they could expect a visit from the local police, who acted as a combination of summons delivery service, investigators, and escorts.[5]

One might think that such attempts to enforce participation and to undermine the confessional seal might make confession suspect in the eyes of prerevolutionary penitents. But this was not the case in imperial Russia any more than it was in seventeenth-century Bavaria, Salzburg, or Spain.[6] When pressed to go more frequently than before, Orthodox believers in imperial Russia, like Roman Catholics after the Council of Trent, found ways of making confession tolerable, even meaningful.[7] Through the beginning of the twentieth century, *govienie*, the week-long process of preparation for confession and communion during Great Lent, was an important marker in people's religious lives. Before 1917, most Russian Orthodox believers followed the practices of preparing for annual confession and communion together, scheduling their *govienie* for the first or last weeks of Great Lent. Thus, although confession was a private conversation between penitent and priest, the ritualized timing and performance of this action also made this sacrament a communal action, which most Orthodox Christians in the Russian empire undertook at the same time. Participation in confession was both private and a sign of collective belonging to the Russian Orthodox Church and loyalty to the Russian state.[8]

Choices and Consequences in an Age of Revolution

When the imperial machine collapsed, organized confession might have been expected to fall with it. Secularization in the USSR was not something imagined; it was real, occasionally brutal, and almost immediately imposed on a largely still-observant population in the first quarter of the twentieth century by an atheistic communist government.[9] Secularization in the USSR was a central element to socialist modernity and the communist state. The Soviet state deliberately tried to purge the public sphere of religious practice and to shrink the institutional infrastructure of the Russian Orthodox Church in particular, attacking first monasteries and then the parish. It broke with the old religious ways of marking time. Magazines and newspapers with names such as *The Godless*, published by the League of Militant Atheists, ridiculed both religious practices and those who continued to practice them.[10] The martyrdom of thousands of clerics and monastics took secularization to the most extreme form.[11]

In many respects, these aims succeeded. Such standard indicators as falling church attendance were lower in 1966 than they had been in 1916.[12] Confession, however, did not vanish, but changed in several crucial ways. Instead of classic auricular confession, where the individual Christian confessed her sins in secret conversation to a priest—the norm in prerevolutionary Russia—most Orthodox Christians in the Soviet period grew more accustomed to general confession. That meant simply that, before communion, the priest gave a homily about confession and sometimes listed the various kinds of sin, while most of the flock listened to the list and repented privately.[13] People approached the priest for a subsequent individual confession only if they had something else to say. So even those Russians who went to Orthodox services—and by the 1980s most Russians did not—could go for most of their lives without having gone to auricular confession. They could go to communion without having gone to auricular confession.

Some dedicated Orthodox, however, could and did pursue the opposite approach. Because other, more public, forms of religious practice—such as cross-processions and large-scale pilgrimage—had become harder to pursue, confession and disclosure of thoughts to a spiritual father-confessor became more central to a religious life than they had before the revolution.[14] As Aleksei Beglov argues, for a small group of Orthodox "virtuosi," lay practice came to approach that of nuns and monks.[15] Another phenomenon that arose in the Soviet period was that of the confessional family, like those of seventeenth-century Orthodox and Old Believers. In confessional "families," people who shared the same father-confessor maintained contact in other aspects of their everyday lives.[16] In short, during the Soviet period, individual sacramental confession went from something shared by even nominal Orthodox Christians to something limited to a small group—but more important to that small group than it had been in the Russian empire.[17]

After Communism

With the fall of communism in 1991, the Russian Orthodox Church was in a unique position. It could in theory look over its historical experience over the previous four centuries and make choices. For example: Orthodox Russians might have asked whether it was a good idea to continue to link confession and communion, and to again make auricular confession a prerequisite for communion, or whether the two acts might be decoupled. They might have asked whether it was a good idea to encourage more frequent communion, even if it meant separating communion from the sacrament of penance. There was also the issue of deciding what to do about some practices that had emerged specifically in the Soviet period, such as general confession as opposed to individual (auricular) confession.[18]

But to answer these and other questions, the Russian Orthodox Church did not have to look only at its own experience. It could also in theory look at the experience of other Orthodox churches in Europe—the very different experience of, say, Greeks, Bulgarians, Romanians, or Serbs.[19] The Russian Orthodox Church could also look at the experience of the Orthodox in historically non-Orthodox countries—France, Australia, Latin America, the United States—who had been exposed to other trends and made other choices. Father Alexander Schmemann (whose sermons had been broadcast in the Soviet Union on Radio Liberty), for example, successfully argued that Orthodox Christians ought to commune at every liturgy, and should not regard confession as a necessary "admission ticket."[20] The Russian Orthodox Church could also look to the experience of the Roman Catholic Church after Vatican II and after the 1973 Rite of Penance.

What the Russian Orthodox Church actually did with the sacrament of penance after the fall of communism offers an interesting perspective on fundamentalism and modernity. When the Russian Orthodox Church sought to re-church its flock after the fall of communism, they faced a situation very different from the one eighty years before. In 1991, confession was no longer something familiar to the vast majority of society. Before 1917, individual auricular confession had been something institutionalized, routine. Most Orthodox inhabitants of the Russian empire had gone to confession for the first time at the age of seven and continued to do so annually during Great Lent. Confession may have been a formality—but, paradoxically, that was one of its institutional strengths. Almost every Orthodox Christian in the Russian empire in 1911 knew what confession was, knew how one was supposed to do it, and knew when one was supposed to do it. This was not the case in 1991. Most of the population in the former Soviet Union had never gone to confession as adults. So, as far as confession, most of the potential Orthodox Christians in the Russian Federation in 1991 were a blank slate. Unlike 1941, when German invasion allowed churches in occupied areas to reopen and religious practice to resume, in 1991 people could not just go back to what they had been doing all along—because they had not been doing it all along. They could when churches reopened during World War II after more than a decade of intense persecution, in 1941: memories and practices of confession then were still alive for enough of the population, even if they had not been in a church for ten years.[21] In 1991, they were not. After communism, most people in Russia had no idea of how auricular confession worked.

The millennium of Christianity in Rus' in 1988, which made the Orthodox Church in the Soviet Union more emboldened and more visible, and the fall of communism in 1991, sharply changed the attitude of the Russian Orthodox hierarchy to confession. Most Soviet-era changes to confessional practice were largely abandoned. General confession, for example, vanished rather quickly. Dismissed as a forced, unfavorable concession to temporary unfavorable circumstances, general confession had frustrated the Orthodox hierarchy.[22] Now, with more churches, more priests, and no restrictions on when church doors could be opened (under communism, that had meant only twenty minutes before and twenty minutes after a church service), general confession could be, and was, dropped, replaced by individual confession. The confessional family largely vanished as well.[23]

Given Orthodox practice outside post-Soviet Russia, Ukraine, and Belarus, given that Fr. Alexander Schmemann had broadcast his sermons in the USSR on Radio Liberty for thirty years, and given Roman Catholic practice after Vatican II, what strikes observers from outside Russia is what did *not* happen in the 1990s. There was no discussion about decoupling confession and communion. This, however, may not be as surprising as it seems. After all, confession before communion had been the norm in the Russian empire, as indeed it had been in the Roman Catholic Church and Greek Catholic Church before Vatican II. Also, the large influx of utterly "unchurched" people meant that clerics and hierarchs, who had been unhappy with general confession to begin with, were even more loath to admit to communion people they barely knew.[24] But this was more than an automatic reproduction of what had been the norm nearly a century ago. Rather, this was a conscious desire cast off those things—like general confession—that had been imposed on the Russian Orthodox Church in hostile circumstances, and to do things "as they always had been."

Here this book's overarching theme of fundamentalism becomes especially relevant. According to Bob Altemeyer and Bruce Hunsberger, "fundamentalism has come to apply to a tendency among certain groups that is characterized by a markedly strict literalism, and a strong sense of the importance of maintaining ingroup and outgroup distinctions, *leading to an emphasis on purity and the desire to return to a previous ideal from which advocates believe members have strayed*. Rejection of diversity of opinion as applied to these established 'fundamentals' and their accepted interpretation within the group is often the result of this tendency."[25] The italicized phrase sheds light on the choices that the Russian Orthodox Church has made about confession after the fall of communism. The desire to return to a previous ideal and going back to the sources meant a specific category of sources: what had been published before 1917. In the 1990s, the amount of reprinted prerevolutionary church publications was extraordinary. Of them, one of the most widely distributed genres was that of preparing for confession. Prerevolutionary guides to confession, some reproduced directly in the old orthography, and translations of patristic texts like those of St. Ephraim the Syrian, became the basis of new, postcommunist practice.[26]

These were quickly followed by guides to confession by priests, bishops, and monks from the Soviet period.[27] Indeed, it is very telling that, while in the 1990s there were proportionately more guides to confession from the prerevolutionary period in Russian Orthodox Church bookstores, from about 2000 onward there were proportionately more guides written by clerics and hierarchs from the Soviet period.[28] This confirms Sergei Chapnin's suggestion that, as with the embrace of the victory in World War II and Stalin's legacy in the secular political sphere, so the Russian Orthodox Church is moving to embrace the specifically religious legacy of the Soviet period. Soviet experiences, Chapnin argues, are closer to where Russians are in 2017 than anything that happened before 1917. Contemporary Russians are children of the Soviet period and the Patriarchate—not of the Synodal period or the tsars.[29]

The question then arises: was this initial embrace of the specifically tsar-ist, and then Soviet-era, guides to auricular confession, fundamentalist? If by fundamentalism one means a return to a previous ideal, as opposed to preserving *existing* practice in, say, 1990, then it was. If one means a con-cern for purity, especially the purity of the Chalice and the purity of the believers approaching the Chalice and maintaining ingroup versus out-group distinctions—that could be construed as "fundamentalist" as well.

Some new aspects of postcommunist approaches to confession and com-munion, however, might seem to undermine the fundamentalist argu-ment. One is the practice of the written confession, or an examination of conscience in writing as a preparation for a traditional auricular confes-sion. In itself, this is neither specifically Russian nor particularly new. Upper-class Russians had turned to written examinations of conscience at the start of the nineteenth century, and people of many different class back-grounds, including peasants, had written their confessions to St. John of Kronstadt at the start of the twentieth century.[30] Written examinations of conscience and aides-memoires for confession figure in Roman Catholic and Anglican practice as well. (One crucial plot twist in Dorothy Sayers's *Unnatural Death* has Lord Peter Wimsey solve a murder with a scrap of paper he has found outside a confessional booth.) What is new, however, is how widespread written confession, or written examination of conscience, quickly became in Russia after the fall of communism. Almost every dis-cussion of sacramental confession acknowledges that written preparation for confession is a useful preparation or even a substitute for the standard auricular confession. Almost every guide to confession published since 1988 includes a section for writing down one's sins every day, the idea being that one will bring these notebooks or lists and use them to jog one's memory. Such monasteries as the Raifa, outside Kazan, *require* penitents to bring written confessions when they come for the sacrament, although the con-fession itself still takes the form of a conversation.

If this practice does not strike one as fundamentalist, it is worth asking why. Perhaps because it is new, or perhaps it is because it is not a restoration, and allows for some latitude, for maintaining some individual voice. Or perhaps it is because there was one new postcommunist practice that did not allow for either much latitude or much voice. It struck many observers, including Alexis II, Patriarch of Moscow, as misguided. This was the em-brace of spiritual direction of laypeople by a spiritual elder to a much greater extent than in the Russian empire. As embraced in late twentieth-century

Russia, spiritual eldership was not going back to an earlier ideal. It was creating a new ideal on the very loose basis of earlier models.[31]

The abuses associated with eldership in 1990s Russia were something new as well. To people living outside of Russia, the tradition of spiritual elders was linked to such historically positive examples of sympathetic clairvoyancy and training in the mystical life as Dostoyevsky's Father Zosima, or the holy Optina elders, or St. John of Kronstadt. But after the fall of communism the practice mutated into something quite different from what it had been at the beginning of the twentieth century. Maia Kucherskaia's satires show with devastating detail what happened when women's dependence on priests' counsels led them astray.[32] Dmytro Rybakov suggested that the problem lay in the old Soviet hypertrophied cult of personality and a correspondingly atrophied sense of individuality. In the free-market atmosphere of free-for-all, he claimed, Russians newly embracing Orthodox Christianity were looking for a leader (*vozhd'*), and a spiritual elder appeared to be the best available such guide.[33] Priests roundly insisted that it was primarily their flocks themselves, and especially women, who sought such relationships of spiritual dependency.[34] But church structures seemed as eager as the postcommunist neophytes to reinforce such dependence. Church kiosks from Solovki to Yakutia were filled with booklets titled "How to find a spiritual father *dukhovnik* according to the counsels of elders and holy fathers of the Church." They contain the message that regular confession is necessary and good, but having a true spiritual director—a *dukhovnik*—is even better. Citing abundantly from classic works of Orthodox mystical theology and asceticism, they sought to recreate the discipline of monastic obedience in the lay world.[35]

Even such apparently neutral titles as "The Sacrament of Repentance" had questions about sins, or lists of sins, so detailed that they boggle the mind. One list had people repent of 296 kinds of sin.[36] At least one over-earnest elder confessed his spiritual children straight from the old Mount Athos ordo, which included the query of whether they had had improper relations with a chicken.[37]

These illustrations might seem simply anecdotal. More serious, and of particular concern to the church hierarchy, were those cases where the *dukhovnik* extends his sphere above and beyond the call of duty. Women seemed to be particularly vulnerable, both in the sense of actively seeking out spiritual subordination and in the sense of falling victim to over-eager elders. As a result, in 1998, the Moscow Patriarchate officially forbade father-confessors to compel their spiritual children to enter the monastic life, carry out any sort of church obedience, make any kind of donations, get married, divorce or refuse to marry, except in such cases where there were canonical impediments, refuse their spouses normal marital relations, refuse to serve in the military, refuse to take part in elections or other civic responsibilities, refuse to seek medical help, refuse an education, or to change jobs or homes.[38]

But the very fact that these limits had to be spelled out, and the fact that the Synod recognized that it was addressing explicit and numerous complaints, suggests that the problem had reached significant proportions. In this respect post-Soviet space illustrated what can happen when living traditions are not preserved and people seek to recreate an ideal Orthodox reality "by the book." But the backlash against spiritual eldership, and more recently a general anticlerical tendency, suggests that both excessive dominance and excessive submission were characteristic of a transitional period, and that now Russian penitents are asking less both of themselves and their confessors, as was the case in Russia before 1917 and as is the case in Orthodox communities outside Russia. In this sense fundamentalism might not seem to be a useful label for confession in post-Soviet Russia.

A newer development offers another angle from which to test the limits of the term *fundamentalist* as regards sacramental confession. In 2012, the Russian Orthodox Church decided to do something interesting. As they worked for a new guide for how Russian Orthodox Christians should prepare for communion, they turned to social media to get as much feedback as possible. The blog and portal of the Interconciliar Presence of the Russian Orthodox Church, the portal Bogoslov.ru, and other forums, offered people the possibility of commenting. On the basis of this feedback, the Interconciliar Presence prepared a document that since 2013 remains the official guide to confession and communion in the church.

It is worth noting what is *not* in the document. A 2006 roundtable on the topic at the Danilov monastery sparked a lively discussion in the church press about the connection between confession and communion. The publications of Archpriests Pavel Velikanov, Aleksii Uminskii, and Priest Georgii Kochetkov querying the connection, are only among the best known.[39] Based on the final document produced in 2013 and in force today, however, one would hardly know that the discussion had ever happened. As per its latest official statements, however, the Russian Orthodox Church continues to regard sacramental confession as a prerequisite for each partaking of the Eucharist. Although there may be exceptions—Bright Week after Pascha, certain devout parishioners with special blessings from their spiritual fathers—still, "confession is an inextricable part of preparation for communion."[40] The other components of preparation for communion—fasting, church attendance, a special preparatory prayer rule—remain (at least in theory) in force as well.[41]

Most Russian clerics and hierarchs appear to support these requirements. To bolster their argument, they cite the canons making priests responsible for those they allow to commune unworthily. Archpriest Fedor Borodin, for example, opined that if after the fall of communism Russians had had a situation "like that in Greece, where confession was when-you-wish and communion was whenever-you-want, it would have been terrible." He continues, "Yes, every priest spent thousands of hours in confession discussions, but it had to be that way. That was the grace of God to our Church, it was the only way of bringing the souls of thousands and thousands of people to something approaching Church consciousness." The only people really worthy of partaking of communion without a preliminary confession every time, he thought, were those so steeped in church thinking "they would not dream of it" without being persuaded to do so by the priest. But everyone else needed a personal confession before communion—even a brief one.[42]

Is this justification and embrace of prerevolutionary Russian practice, the concern to protect the sanctity of the Chalice, and the explicit dismissal of contemporary Orthodox practice elsewhere, fundamentalist? One might more appropriately call it conservative. After all, the sacrament of penance before communion was a requirement for centuries in both the Orthodox and Roman Catholic Churches, and the dread of communing "unworthily" was very real.[43] And not every local church with roots in the Russian tradition developed a liturgical consciousness akin to that of post-Vatican II Rome or Greece (as did, for example, the Orthodox Church of America and the London parish of Metropolitan Antony of Sourozh). But is it appropriate to label *fundamentalist* other strands of the Russian tradition simply because they preserved the linkage between confession and communion required in both prerevolutionary Russia and the Roman Catholic Church before Vatican II? It is worth pondering on whether the experience of the diaspora Russian Orthodox Church Outside of Russia (ROCOR), which came under the omophorion of the Moscow Patriarchate in 2007, and the Russian Orthodox Church, were both fundamentalist, whether neither is fundamentalist, or whether each supplemented each other's tendency to fundamentalism in a different way. The ROCOR reproduced nearly intact the prerevolutionary practice of *govienie* (confession, fasting, sexual abstinence, and church attendance—all usually during Lenten periods or such special occasions as one's namesday—before partaking of the Eucharist). The church in the Soviet Union continued to preserve the confessioncommunion linkage in form, even when the general confession temporarily replaced the auricular. Although the ROCOR's legacy of conservation hardly played a key role in Moscow's approach to confession and communion after the fall of communism, one wonders if one conservative tendency reinforced the other, with both sides rejecting the liberalism of the Orthodox Church of America and the Exarchate.

Still, it is important to note that there are Russian clerics and hierarchs who criticize the Interconciliar document's requiring confession before every communion in terms that echo those of Father Alexander Schmemann. Archpriest Andrei Kordochkin develops his argument with particular detail. The Interconciliar document, Kordochkin notes, says nothing about what the Eucharist means for the nature of the church. It says nothing about the liturgy as the common work of the church community. It speaks of communion only as an individual act carried out by the individual Christian. It says nothing about anticipating and preparing for the Eucharist as the entire foundation of church life. Kordochkin criticizes the document for suggesting that in some cases people may be "freed" from the obligation to confess before communion: people cannot be freed or exempted from confession any more than they can be compelled to confess. He notes that although the document is concerned with safeguarding the purity of the Chalice, it does not seem concerned with the sins people may fall into without regular partaking of the Eucharist. He asks why, if confession is mandatory for the lay Orthodox Christian, is it not mandatory for the priest? He singles out the phrase that confession testifies to the absence of canonical obstacles to communion as a perversion, where the priest acts as a sergeant and not a pastor. He notes the words of Father Alexander Schmemann about how Russian practice distorts church tradition as regards confession as a mandatory preparation for communion. When confession is a formal requirement for communion, then it runs the risk of replacing true inner repentance. After a three-minute confession and the absolution, people can feel themselves entitled to approach the Chalice—that is, the opposite of the humility and compunction they ought to feel.[44] Archimandrite Petr Meshcherinov, a scholar of Johann Arndt, takes a similar approach.[45]

Some bishops go further than these and other priests. Bishop Pankratii, chair of the Synodal commission on canonization, for example, declared that Russia now should not be directed by either the Soviet period or the prerevolutionary one. Because people who go to church now tend to go to communion more often than they ever did before, he resisted setting out any firm guidelines. He reminded people that penance was something that the Christian ought to feel all the time, and that going to communion at every liturgy one attended ought to be the norm.[46] Priest Georgii Kochetkov is perhaps closest to Father Alexander Schmemann's position.[47] Thus, there is a diversity of views in the Russian Orthodox Church, even though the official line appears to be uniformly conservative.

Conclusion

As regards the sacrament of penance in Russia, then, there are both quasi-fundamentalist tendencies and those offering the potential to move away from fundamentalism. On the one hand, one sees strict literalism, an emphasis on purity, and the desire to return to a previous ideal from which advocates believe members have strayed. On the other hand, it is important to note that the postcommunist Russian attempts to return to or revive authentic confession were mediated by the very context in which the "recovery" occurred. Recovery, in other words, is never only recovery. Russian "fundamentalism" as regards confession and communion was not only fundamentalism. It was also the reconfiguration of the original meaning, or at least what was imagined to have been the original meaning, of the Russian practice of confession, now identified as the source of confessional authenticity. But diversity of opinion on the connection between confession and communion has not been altogether rejected. And other confessional practices, in particular written confession, signal that new forms altogether might arise. In short, although the Russian Orthodox Church after the fall of communism approached confession in a way that might seem to be fundamentalist, the presence of diverse opinions and practices suggests that the potential for moving away from fundamentalism is there as well—should people wish it.

Notes

1. In many Orthodox traditions, the sacrament of penance is neither synonomous with confession nor reducible to it; see Constantine N. Tsirnpanlis, *Introduction to Eastern Patristic Thought and Orthodox Theology* (Collegeville, MN: Liturgical, 1991), 140–41; John Karmiris, *A Synopsis of the Dogmatic Theology of the Orthodox Catholic Church* (Scranton, PA: Christian Orthodox Edition, 1973), 107. In imperial Russia, penance was understood as a week-long process called *govienie*, consisting of fasting, week-long church attendance, and finally confession to an ordained priest; see S. V. Bulgakov, *Nastol'naia kniga dlia sviashchenno-tserkovno-sluzhitelei*, vol. 2 (St. Petersburg, 1913, repr. Moscow: izd. otdel Moskovskogo Patriarkhata, 1993), 1047–128.

2. Michel Foucault, *The History of Sexuality*, vol. 1, *An Introduction* (New York: Vintage Books, 1978), 58–59.

3. Protopresbyter Georgii Shavel'skii, for example, wrote his guide to confession because after emigrating to Bulgaria he was unfavorably struck by the lack of confession among Bulgarian Orthodox. See his discussion in Protopresbyter Georgii Shavel'skii, *Pravoslavnoe pastyrstvo* (St. Petersburg: Izd. Russkogo khristianskogo gumanitarnogo instituta, 1996), 597–602.

4. See "Supplement to the Spiritual Regulation of Peter the Great," in *The Spiritual Regulation of Peter the Great*, trans. and ed. Alexander V. Muller (Seattle: University of Washington Press, 1972), 60–63.

5. These policies applied throughout the Russian empire. For examples from the Kiev Consistory, see TsDIAK (Ukraine Central State Historical Archives), f. 127, op. 28 (1825), d. 88 (on collecting a fine from the peasant F. Kuplenko for not going to confession); from St. Petersburg, see TsGIA SPb (Central State Historical Archive of St. Petersburg), f. 19, op. 32, d. 142 (on assigning Timofei Vorobiev a penance for not going to confession and holy communion in 1837 (1840–1847); from Moscow, see TsIAM (Central Historical Archive of Moscow), f. 203, op. 341 (1869–1879), d. 9 (on assigning penances to peasants A. Kharlamov and A. Sukov for not having gone to confession).

6. See W. David Meyers, *"Poor, Sinning Folk": Confession and Conscience in Counter-Reformation Germany* (Ithaca, NY: Cornell University Press, 1996); and Sara T. Nalle, "Self-Correction and Social Change in the Spanish Counter-Reformation," in *Religion and the Early Modern State: Views from China, Russia, and the West*, ed. James D. Tracy and Marguerite Ragnow (Cambridge: Cambridge University Press, 2004), 302–23.

7. Waldemar Kowalski, "Change in Continuity: Post-Tridentine Rural and Township Parish Life in the Cracow Diocese," *Sixteenth Century Journal* 35, no. 3 (Fall 2004): 700–10.

8. Viktor Zhivov argues that state compulsion made confession in Russia inherently flawed and less "genuine" than its Roman Catholic counterpart. See Viktor Zhivov, "Pokaiannaia distsiplina i individual'noe blagochestiie," in *Druzhba: ee formy, ispytaniia i dary: Uspenskie chteniia* (Dukh i litera): 303–43.

9. See, for example, the exhumation of relics discussed in Robert H. Greene, *Bodies Like Bright Stars: Saints and Relics in Orthodox Russia* (DeKalb: Northern Illinois University Press, 2009), 103–212.

10. See Daniel Peris, *Storming the Heavens: The Soviet League of the Militant Godless* (Ithaca, NY: Cornell University Press, 1998), 75–76.

11. See Helmut Altrichter, "Insoluble Conflicts: Village Life Between Revolution and Collectivization," in *Russia in the Era of NEP: Explorations in Soviet Society and Culture*, ed. Sheila Fitzpatrick, Alexander Rabinowitch, and Richard Stites (Bloomington: Indiana University Press, 1991), 192–209; and Richard Stites, "Bolshevik Ritual Building in the 1920s," in *Russia in the Era of NEP*, 295–309; Glennys Young, *Power and the Sacred in Revolutionary Russia: Religious Activists in the Village* (University Park: Pennsylvania State University Press, 1997); and Dimitry Pospielovsky, *The Russian Church Under the Soviet Regime, 1917–1982* (Crestwood, NY: St. Vladimir's Seminary Press, 1984).

12. For a theoretical and historiographical survey, see the discussion in the introduction to *State Secularism and Lived Religion in Soviet Russia and Ukraine*, ed. Catherine Wanner (New York: Oxford University Press, 2012), 1–26. For signs of shifts in practice on the eve of the Great War, see Gregory L. Freeze, "A Pious Folk? Religious Observance in Vladimir Diocese, 1900–1914" in *Jahrbücher für Geschichte Osteuropas*, Bd. 52, H. 3, Themenschwerpunkt: Religion und Gesellschaft in Rußland vor der Revolution von 1917 (2004), 323–40.

13. See the homilies of Prot. Nikolai Golubtsov, *Besedy pered ispoved'iu* (Moscow: Izd. Moskovskogo Podvor'ia Sviato-Troitskoi Sergievoi Lavry, 2009).

14. For Soviet-era pilgrimage practices, see Stella Rock, "'They Burned the Pine, but the Place Remains All the Same': Pilgrimage in the Changing Landscape of Soviet Russia," in *State Secularism and Lived Religion*, 159–89.

15. Monakhinia Ignatiia, *Starchestvo v gody gonenii: Prepodobnomuchenik Ignatii (Lebedev) i ego dukhovnaia sem'ia* (Moscow: Izd. Moskovskogo podvor'ia Sviato-Troitskoi Sergievoi Lavry, 2001).

16. For seventeenth-century confessional families, see P. S. Stefanovich, *Prikhod i prikhodskoe dukhovenstvo v Rossii v XVI–XVII vekakh* (Moscow: "Indrik," 2002). For the confessional families of Priests Vsevolod Shpiller, Dimitry Dudko, and others in the 1970s and 1980s, see Dimitrii Dudko, *O nashem upovanii* (Paris: YMCA, 1975); Prot. Nikolai Krechetov, *Starets Protoierei Tikhon Pelikh: zhizneopisanie, propovedi, dnevniki* (Moscow: Sviato-Troitskaia

Sergieva Lavra, 2009); and Arkhim. Ioann Krest'iankin, *Opyt postroeniia ispovedi* (Sviato-Uspenskii Pskovo-Pecherskii monastyr', 1993).

17. Nadieszda Kizenko, "Sacramental Confession in Russia and Ukraine," in *State Secularism and Lived Religion*, 190–217.

18. Some hierarchs continued to resist general confession, seeing it as a deviation. See Metropolitan Grigorii Chukov, "Address, November 8, 1944," in *Selected Speeches, Talks, and Articles* (Moscow, 1954), accessed April 15, 2019, https://ispowed-prichastie.ru/tainstvo-pokayaniya-i-obshhaya-ispoved/, and GARF (State Archive of the Russian Federation), f. 6991, op. 2, d. 34a, l. 57.

19. For Russian influence on Serbian practice, see Vladislav Puzovich, "Utitsaj Dukhovnog Regulamenta (1721) na *Sveshtenichka* i *Monashka Pravila* Mitropolita Beogradsko-Karlovachkog Vikentiia (Jovanovicha)," *Matica Srpska: Otdelene za drushtvene nauke* (Novy Sad: Matica Srpska, 2014), 37–54; and Vladimir Vukashinovich, *Srpsko Barokno Bogoslovl'e: Biblijsko i svetotajinsko bogoslovl'e u Karlovachkoj Mitropoliji XVIII veka* (Beograd, 2008), 94–105. For Shavel'skii's criticism of twentieth-century Bulgarian practice, see Protopresbyter Georgii Shavel'skii, *Pravoslavnoe pastyrstvo*, 5, 541–45.

20. Father Alexander Schmemann, "Some Reflections on Confession," *St. Vladimir's Seminary Quarterly* 5, no. 3 (Fall 1961): 38–44, accessed April 15, 2019, http://schmemann.org/byhim/reflectionsonconfession.html.

21. Interview with Borys Petrovich Okopnyi (grandson of two priests in Melitopol'), Jackson, NJ, February 15, 2010. See also the work of Hieromonk Serafim (Vladimir L. Amel'chenkov) on the Smolensk region, including *Russkaia pravoslavnaia tserkov' i obshchestvo v period Velikoi Otechestvennoi voiny 1941–1945 godov (na materialykh Smolenskoi oblasti)* (Smolensk: Svitok, 2012).

22. See, for example, the comments against general confession by Metropolitan Grigorii Chukov on November 8, 1944, in *Izbrannye rechi, slova, i stat'i* (Moscow, 1954), accessed April 15, 2019, https://ispowed-prichastie.ru /tainstvo-pokayaniya-i-obshhaya-ispoved/; and prot. Aleksei Uminskii, "Taina primireniia," March 15, 2013, accessed April 15, 2019, https://www.pravmir.ru /tajna-primireniya/.

23. In some communities the confessional family does persist. The active parish surrounding the Karpovka convent founded by St. John of Kronstadt, and which calls itself "The Large Ioann Family," is one such example. But this is now connected to a concrete parish more than to a charismatic individual father-confessor. For the Family website, see http://pravprihod.ru. For an account of Family activity, see "The Lives and Afterlives of St. John of Kronstadt," *Wheel*, no. 7 (Fall 2016): 9–16.

24. *Unchurched* here refers to people who were baptized, but who grew up with little or no church consciousness. For a discussion of churched, enchurched,

and unchurched in the Russian context, see Sergei Chapnin, "A Church of Empire," *First Things*, November 2015, accessed April 15, 2019, https://www .firstthings.com/article/2015/11/a-church-of-empire.

25. Bob Altemeyer and Bruce Hunsberger, "Authoritarianism, Religious Fundamentalism, Quest, and Prejudice," *International Journal for the Psychology of Religion* 2, no. 2 (1992): 113–33.

26. See, for example: Sviatitel' Dimitrii Rostovskii, *O neraskaiannykh greshnikakh* (Rostov-na-Donu: izd. Rostovskoi-na-Donu eparkhii, 2007), Arkhim. Spiridon (Kisliakov), *Iz vidennogo i perezhitogo. Vospominaniia propovednika-missionera* (Moscow: Novospasskii monastyr', 2008); Sviatitel' Ignarii (Brianchianinov), *V pomoshch kaiushchimsia* (Moscow: Artos-Media, 2005); *V pomoshch kaiushchimsia: posobie k ispovedi (dlia sviashchennosluzhitelei i ispoveduiushchikhsia)* (Kiev: informatsionno-izdatel'skii tsentr UPTs, 2000); Leonid Denisov, ed., *Dushespasitel'nyia besiedy o pokaianii iz tvorenii Sv. Efrema Syrina*, repr. of 3rd (prerevolutionary) ed. (Moscow: izd. A. D. Stupina, repr. Minsk: "Svitok," 1992). In old orthography: *Podvizhnik viery i blagochestiia: protoierei Valentin Amfiteatrov* (Moscow: pravoslavnyi sviato-Tikhonovskii Bogoslovskii institut, 1995).

27. Ioann (Krestiankin), *Opyt postroeniia ispovedi: pastyrskie besedy o pokaianii vo dni Velikogo Posta* ([Pechory]: Izd. Sviato-Uspenskogo Pskovo-Pecherskogo monastyr, 1993). A later version is available at http://azbyka.ru /otechnik/Ioann_Krestjankin/opyt-postroenija-ispovedi/ (accessed April 15, 2019).

28. Sviashchennik Mikhail Shpolianskii, *Kak prigotovitsia k ispovedi i prichastiiu: prakticheskoe posobie dlia pravoslavnago khristianina* (Moscow: izd. "Otchii dom," 2008); G. A. Pyl'neva, comp., *"Daite nam ot eleia vashego . . ." Sovety opytnykh dukhovnikov* (Saratov: izd. Saratovskoi eparkhii, 2009); Ierom. Iov (Gumerov), *Tainstvo pokaianiia* (Moscow: izd. Sretenskogo monastyria, 2011); Prot. Andrei Tkachev, *Mysli o pokaianii*, 2nd ed. (Moscow: izd. Sretenskogo monastyria, 2011); Sviashchennoispovednik Sergii Pravdoliubov, *O postakh, ispovedi i priobshchenii sviatykh Khristovykh tain: zaveshchanie solovetskogo uznika*, 2nd ed. (Moscow: Pravoslavnyi Sviato-Tikhonovskii gumanitarnyi universitet, 2010), accessed April 15, 2019, http://www.pravmir.ru /eshhyo-ob-ispovedi/.

29. Sergei Chapnin, "They Never Met: Church and Civil Society in Present-Day Russia," *Wheel*, no. 1 (Spring 2015): 13–21; and Chapnin, *Tserkov' v postsovetskoi Rossii: vozrozhdenie, kachestvo very, dialog s obshchestvom* [The Church in Post-Soviet Russia: Rebirth, Quality of Faith, Dialogue with Society] (Moscow: Arefa, 2009).

30. For confessions of aristocrats in the first half of the nineteenth century, see E. E. Liamina and N. V. Samover, *Bednyi Zhozef. Zhizn' i smert' Iosifa*

Viel'gorskogo: opyt biografii cheloveka 1830kh godov (Moscow: Iazyki russkoi kul'tury, 1999), 284–88; and Nadieszda Kizenko, "Written Confession and Religious Thought in Early Nineteenth-Century Russia," in *Thinking Orthodox in Modern Russia: Culture, History, Context*, ed. Patrick Lally Michelson and Judith Deutsch Kornblatt (Madison: University of Wisconsin Press, 2014), 177–95. For late nineteenth- and early twentieth-century peasant confessions, see Kizenko, "Written Confessions, 1898–1908," in *Orthodox Christianity in Imperial Russia: A Sourcebook on Lived Religion*, ed. Heather J. Coleman (Bloomington: Indiana University Press, 2014), 152–71.

31. This would then be a variant of the now-class "invented tradition" model made popular by Eric Hobsbawm and Terence Ranger, ed., *The Invention of Tradition* (Cambridge: Cambridge University Press, 1983).

32. Maia Kucherskaia, *Sovremennyi paterik: chtenie dlia vpavshikh v unynie* (Moscow: Vremia, 2005), translated into English by Alexei Bayer as *Faith and Humor: Notes from Muscovy* (New York: Russian Life, 2011).

33. Personal communication, February 2008.

34. Prot. Maksim Kozlov, *Klir i mir: kniga o zhizni sovremennogo prikhoda* (Moscow: Khram Sviatoi Muchenitsy Tatiany pri MGU, 2008), 211–18.

35. *Kak naiti dukhovnika po sovetam startsev i sviatykh otsov Tserkvi* (Moscow: "Kovcheg," 2004).

36. See prot. Aleksii Moroz, *Ispovedaiu grekh, Batiushka* (St. Petersburg: "Smirenie," 2005); *Lekarstvo ot grekha* (Moscow: Blagovest, 1999).

37. Mitrokhin *Russkaia pravoslavnaia tserkov'*, 107.

38. *Podlinnyi starets*, 17.

39. See the following websites, accessed April 15, 2019: http://www.pravmir.ru/tajna-primireniya/; http://www.pravmir.ru/protoierey-aleksiy-uminskiy-esli-molitva-stala-formalnostyu/; http://www.pravmir.ru/ispoved-i-sindrom-nedoveriya-k-bogu/; and http://iliya-monastery.livejournal.com/476737.html. See also Georgii Kochetkov, *Pered ispoved'iu i prichastiem: v pomoshch novotserkovlennym*, 4th ed. (Moscow: Sviato-Filaretovskii pravoslavno-khristianskii institut, 2011).

40. See http://www.pravmir.ru/proekt-dokumenta-o-podgotovke-ko-svyatomu-prichashheniyu/ (accessed April 15, 2019).

41. See http://www.pravmir.ru/proekt-dokumenta-o-podgotovke-ko-svyatomu-prichashheniyu/ (accessed April 15, 2019).

42. See http://www.pravmir.ru/protoierej-feodor-borodin-dokument-o-podgotovke-ko-prichashheniyu-daet-sushhestvennuyu-stepen-svobody-duxovniku-i-prixozhaninu/ (accessed April 15, 2019).

43. For the development of penitential discipline leading to confession before communion, see Joseph M. Bryant, "The Sect-Church Dynamic and Christian Expansion in the Roman Empire: Persecution, Penitential Discipline,

and Schism in Sociological Perspective," *British Journal of Sociology* 44, no. 2 (June 1993): 303–39.

44. See http://www.pravmir.ru/prot-andrej-kordochkin-kommentarij-k -proektu-dokumenta-mezhsobornogo-prisutstviya-o-podgotovke-ko-svyatomu -prichashheniyu/ (accessed April 15, 2019).

45. See http://www.pravmir.ru/eshhyo-ob-ispovedi/ (accessed April 15, 2019).

46. See http://www.pravmir.ru/episkop-troickij-pankratij-nado-pomnit-chto -pokayanie-proisxodit-ne-tolko-v-moment-ispovedi/ (accessed April 15, 2019).

47. See https://psmb.ru/a/ispoved-i-pokayanie-v-drevnosti-i-segodnya.html (accessed April 15, 2019).

Conscience and Catholic Identity

Darlene Fozard Weaver

George Demacopoulos has posed this animating question, "How does a faith community that values tradition operate in a secularized world without lapsing into fundamentalism?"[1] This question bears on issues that predate the emergence of secularization and the rise of contemporary religious fundamentalism. Indeed, religious communities grapple with standing challenges such as: How should we delineate orthodoxy and heterodoxy? How should we respond to internal expressions of dissent, infractions, and moral failure? How do we position ourselves in relation to other faith traditions and secular communities? How do we respond to moral disagreements with those outside our community? Both the integrity of a faith community and its own prospects for social reproduction are at play in these standing questions. Demacopoulos's overarching query helpfully intimates that secularism can be perceived as a threat—not that it must be so perceived or that secularism inherently is a threat—and that fundamentalism represents a temptation, a more or less chosen way of inhabiting, interpreting, and handing on a tradition. At stake in a faith community's encounter with secularism is nothing less than the community's own integrity and the viability of its social reproduction or long-term viability.

These standing challenges find distinctive contemporary expression amidst several paradoxical features of the current American context. The United States is both a secular and a peculiarly religious culture. On the one hand, religious traditions confront the erosion of many religious subcultures, diminishing religious literacy, and increasing disaffection for formal

religious affiliation.[2] Demographic shifts in religious affiliation and practice influence perceptions of the value of tradition, the stability and long-
term viability of religious identity, and the degree to which secularism is
benign or hostile. On the other hand, religious belief and practice continues to enjoy substantial protections and wield significant influence.[3] The
contemporary American context is marked by forms of diversity, including religious, moral, ethnic, and cultural diversity. It is polarized, and too
often fractious. Nonetheless, there is considerable uniformity under
economic and political systems that give the illusion of more choice and
individualism than is often the case. Finally, the contemporary American
context is marked by forms of moral agnosticism (the conviction that there
is no shared understanding of the good to order our common life) as well
as palpable forms of dogmatism (for example, American exceptionalism and
political correctness). In short, the current American context is neither
wholly hospitable nor inhospitable to religious traditions. This ambiguity
makes this topic all the richer. It underscores the insight that the temptation of fundamentalism includes a hermeneutic dimension.

A premise of this essay is that religious fundamentalism includes moral
fundamentalism. Religious fundamentalism is, among other things, exclusive, separatist, oppositional, absolutist, opposed to development, opposed
to relativism and hermeneutics, and teleological.[4] Taken separately, a rejection of relativism or a teleological understanding of creation do not
amount to fundamentalism. According to R. Scott Appleby and Martin
Marty, fundamentalism is not simply conservatism or traditionalism but
a reaction against modernity. My premise is that the reactive, oppositional,
hermetic character of religious fundamentalism extends to a faith community's moral convictions and commitments. These characteristics dispose
or even commit religiously fundamentalist communities to moral fundamentalism. By moral fundamentalism I mean a variety of religious ethics
that, like religious fundamentalism, is opposed to relativism and hermeneutics, and is absolute, separatist, and oppositional. Moral fundamentalism resists or rejects evolution in moral teaching and emphasizes standards
of rigor and purity. It posits the sufficiency of its own ethics, so confident
about its grasp of moral reality, so certain that its moral commitments are
adequately understood, articulated, and applied that there is nothing to
learn from other moral traditions or perspectives. Indeed, these alternative moralities appear as rival positions that require not only correction but
active resistance. We might therefore rephrase Demacopoulos's question

as follows: How does a faith community that understands morality as objective and universally valid operate in a secularized world without lapsing into moral fundamentalism?

This essay considers Catholic responses to secularism and modernity. It does not argue that certain sectors of the Catholic population in America or worldwide are religious fundamentalists, as Appleby and Marty understand that term, or suggest that Catholicism possesses distinctive safeguards against religious fundamentalism. Nor does it mount an argument about the precise meaning of secularism or fundamentalism. Rather, this essay explores the phenomenon of conscience and Catholic teaching about it in order to think about its import for temptations to moral fundamentalism. Catholic debates about conscience illustrate internal struggles over the moral presuppositions of modernity and secularism and their import. Conscience, however, is more than an illustrative example. It is closely bound with personal and communal moral identity. Conscience lies at the heart of Catholic responses to secularism and modernity. Catholic responses to secularism and modernity involve morally freighted choices about what to emphasize, defend, and adapt, who to include, empower, or marginalize, and how to interpret internal plurality, external influences, and alternative modes of thought. Indeed, Catholic responses to fundamentalism, secularism, and modernity *enact* conscience, as individuals and communities decide what sort of ecclesial community the church will be.

The Temptation of Moral Fundamentalism in Context

In the current American context, demographic changes in Catholic affiliation, Catholic institutions, and Catholic belief and practice all impact debates about conscience and responses to secularism and modernity. The picture for Catholicism in America is not rosy. The robust Catholic subcultures once found in parts of the United States have faded. Vocations to clerical and religious life have declined. Catholic parishes and schools are consolidating or closing. According to the Pew Research Center the number of US Catholics is declining, both as an absolute number and as a share of the population. The Catholic population is also aging. The median age of American Catholics is forty-nine. Only 17 percent of Catholic adults are under the age of thirty, whereas 35 percent of the "nones" (the religiously unaffiliated) are under thirty, and 44 percent of Muslims.[5] "Nearly one-third of American adults (31.7%) say they were raised Catholic. Among that group, fully 41% no longer identify with Catholicism. This means that 12.9% of American adults are former Catholics."[6] Put differently, one out of every ten Americans is a lapsed Catholic.[7] "Just 2% of U.S. adults have converted to Catholicism from another religious tradition. No other religious group in Pew's 2014 Religious Landscape Study has such a lopsided ratio of losses to gains."[8]

Unsurprisingly, some former Catholics attribute their defection to the sex abuse scandals, disagreement with church teaching, and unhappiness with church leadership or with one's parish community.[9] Traditionalist Catholics are more likely to argue that the church is losing members because the Second Vatican Council has watered down Catholic tradition. They point to examples such as liturgical reforms, softer requirements regarding fasting and religious dress, and the inclusion of girls as altar servers. More strenuously, they argue that Vatican II permitted modernizing and secularizing forces to infect and distort the tradition.[10] My concern is not to weigh in on the causes of so many defections. Surely, they must be many. For our purposes two points are noteworthy. First and more generally, the overall decline in formal religious affiliation and rates of Catholic disaffiliation make questions of social reproduction, stewardship of tradition, and response to secularization all the more urgent. Second, and more particularly, disagreement with Catholic moral teaching and dissatisfaction with Catholic moral leadership are among the most notable findings in recent research on American Catholics.[11] According to a 2015 Public Religion Research Institute report on the effect of Pope Francis's papacy, Francis enjoys higher approval numbers than the Catholic Church does. According to the study, 67 percent of Americans hold a favorable view of Pope Francis, compared to 56 percent of Americans who view the Catholic Church favorably. The difference is more striking among young adults (age 18 to 29). In this group, 65 percent view the pope favorably while only 48 percent view the church favorably. In open-ended responses about the church "Americans are more than twice as likely to offer negative than positive associations with the Catholic Church. . . . About one-quarter of Americans have a negative association with the Catholic Church, saying it is judgmental or dogmatic (7%), hypocritical (8%), overly concerned with money (4%), or offering a less specific negative comment (6%)."[12] Fewer than half of all Catholics agree with Pope Francis's beliefs on abortion (38 percent), same-sex marriage (48 percent), and climate change (47 percent).[13] Half agree with his beliefs on immigration, and slightly more (52 percent) agree regarding the role of government in reducing the gap between the rich and the poor.[14] When asked whether the Catholic Church should focus more on issues of social justice and helping the poor or issues such as abortion, 57 percent of Catholics said the former.[15] Indeed, Catholics in general virtually mirror the moral positions of the American public on issues including abortion, same-sex marriage, immigration, and government responses to climate change and economic disparity.[16] With regard to immigration, climate change, and economic disparity most American Catholics appear to hold positions consonant with Catholic moral teaching. With regard to abortion and same-sex marriage, a majority of American Catholics hold positions that depart from Catholic moral teaching.

Secularism and Modernity in Catholic Tradition

The demographic picture of American Catholicism reflects Catholic tradition's ambivalence over secularism and modernity. In Catholic theology and ecclesial practice, the church displays engagement, appropriation, critique, and denunciation. Catholic intellectual tradition has long borrowed from secular thinkers. The theology of St. Augustine and St. Thomas Aquinas, for example, and the development of natural law tradition are all indebted to secular interlocutors. Episcopal commentary and lobbying on select social issues (both against and for aspects of the Affordable Care Act, for example) show engagement with secular governing bodies.[17] Catholic tradition affirms the complementarity of faith and reason, the unity of truth, and the possibility of acquiring moral knowledge apart from explicit Christian faith. The tradition holds that persons of good will can in principle discern moral insight and recognize virtue in secular traditions and ways of life. Finally, Pope Benedict XVI, no fan of secularization, nonetheless recognized the value of "healthy secularism," which includes a separation of church and state and a public neutrality regarding matters of faith.[18] A healthy secularism benefits the church by reinforcing the necessity of free and personal commitment to the practice of faith.

That said, the Catholic Church has also spoken against secularism. Secularism becomes unhealthy when its neutrality toward religion becomes hostility. Recent examples of hostility toward religions may be found in the development of the "new atheism" as expounded by Richard Dawkins and Christopher Hitchens.[19] The question whether American secularism is unhealthy is more complicated. Anti-Catholic discrimination in US history is well documented.[20] US Catholic bishops argue that religious liberty is currently endangered. They point, for example, to mechanisms in health care legislation surrounding access to contraception, the effect antidiscrimination laws have had on Catholic-sponsored adoption agencies, and instances in which business owners and Protestant churches or ministers faced legal charges because they would not provide services to same-sex couples.[21] Each of these issues centers on how the Catholic-affiliated organizations and individual Catholics may be faithful to their consciences while living among others who have differing moral beliefs and while respecting their civil liberties and human rights. Long-standing aspects of Catholic moral tradition are assumed in episcopal arguments about religious freedom, regarding cooperation with evil and the avoidance of scandalizing others but not explicated at length or in detail. These examples not only involve normative disagreements between (some) Catholics and others in a context of moral pluralism, they also instantiate normative choices regarding how to interpret and frame the disagreements, what it means to live out fidelity to one's moral convictions, the relationship between church and government, and the very meaning basic human interactions and exchanges (for instance, that providing a service to a same-sex couple equals moral endorsement of their marriage). These cases comprise an opportunity for faith communities to think more fully about what fidelity to their moral commitments requires in the context of secularism and moral pluralism.[22]

The role of such normative judgments (which are essentially judgments of conscience) is also worth pondering in relation to demographic shifts in American Catholicism. Tom Beaudoin coins the phrase "secular Catholics" to describe "those with a Catholic heritage, however nominal, who cannot find Catholicism central to the everyday project of their lives, and are in varying degrees of distance from what they take to be normative or prescribed Catholicism."[23] In doing so he challenges practices of describing such Catholics as "non-practicing," "lapsed," or "recovering," thereby "aggregating people under moralistic categories which do not themselves reflexively call normative Catholic identity and praxis into question."[24] In other words, Beaudoin recognizes the normative assumptions built into narratives regarding Catholic disaffiliation. Beaudoin suggests that "secular Catholicism is a negotiation with the religious tradition and the American context, and not simply a capitulation to the U.S. culture or a widespread 'loss of faith.'"[25] Without denying that some interpretations of these demographic trends are more sound than others—and therefore more correct or true—we can acknowledge that they are unavoidably hermeneutic decisions and normative judgments. Conscience is at work as the Catholic community interprets and responds to contemporary manifestations of Catholicism.

Just as Catholic attitudes toward secularism are mixed so too are Catholic attitudes toward modernity. As Peter Berger puts it, the church did initially respond to modernity "with militant and then defiant rejection."[26] Nearly a century later, however, the church sought to engage with modernity. Vatican II represents a rapprochement between the church and the modern world. John O'Malley argues that Pope John XXIII's opening address to the council signaled his intention that the council "should look forward; it should not be afraid to make changes in the church wherever appropriate; it should not feel constrained to stay within the old methods and forms, as if hermetically sealed off from modern thought; it should look to human unity, which suggested an approach that emphasized commonalities rather than differences; it should encourage cooperation with others; it should see its task as pastoral."[27]

Bearing in mind that the council concluded a scant fifty years ago, a short time when it comes to the process of receiving a council, it is fair to say that Catholic tradition has imbibed some aspects of modernity (consider Catholic support for freedom of religion and the embrace of much of secular human rights discourse) while critically resisting others (consider Catholic critiques of freedom understood as autonomy).[28] Importantly, Vatican II calls for and inaugurates engagement with the modern world not in the form of accommodation but in an evangelical and pastoral mode of dialogue.[29] Through this dialogue, the church undertakes her mission to be a sacrament of salvation to the world. Catholic tradition, then, includes important resources for critical appreciation of modernity and secularism, although this requires openness to possibilities that moral tradition can develop by learning from and collaborating with them. In this regard, debates between traditionalists and revisionists serve the church's task, although they would do so more efficaciously if they were conducted in a more irenic spirit. Ecclesial processes of responding to modernity, secularism, and even the internal pluralism of the church are moral expressions of Catholic commitments. They are nothing short of enactments of a communal conscience.

Conscience in Catholic Tradition

We can now look more closely at Catholic treatment of conscience. Doing so will give us greater purchase on the church's struggle to respond to modernity and secularism while faithfully stewarding her tradition. Conscience provides more than a microcosm of these larger dynamics. The phenomenon of conscience is at the heart of the church's discerning dialogue with the modern world.

Conscience is not monolithic in Catholic thought. The language of conscience provides a particular though by no means exclusive conceptual resource for naming a complex human phenomenon. Accounts of conscience privilege different aspects of this phenomenon and serve different and sometimes conflicting ends. Nonetheless, we may say that conscience has both objective and subjective dimensions.[30] Objectively, conscience names capacities to know right from wrong, to apprehend goods, understand and apply norms, reason about moral cases by analogy, and consider morally relevant circumstances. In these ways, conscience refers to a moral reality "outside" the person, an experience of moral obligation and accountability. Someone or something confronts our freedom, convicts us by its authority, and constrains our choices. Accordingly, conscience is sometimes spoken of as a call or summons, or in a more juridical manner, as a tribunal. Subjectively, conscience names the person's apprehension of moral reality as a question about one's own identity and integrity. Whether our experience of moral obligation is framed primarily in terms of law, the inviolability of goods, or the non-contingent worth of creatures, conscience captures the deeply personal and individual character of this experience. Descriptions of conscience in terms of the "heart" or as a "sanctuary" speak to the subjective dimension of conscience. Vatican II captures the interrelation of conscience's objective and subjective dimensions by calling conscience a dialogue between God and the person.[31]

Conscience is multidimensional in its operation. It is a capacity for knowledge of right and wrong. As such conscience can be a healthy appetite for the good, a sensitive, diligent, and curious appetite, and is related to virtues of intellectual humility, prudence, and justice. Conscience also names the process by which we make moral decisions and the judgments or convictions that we endorse. Ethicists sometimes speak of conscience as *antecedent*, as the process of considering choices, weighing relevant norms, and formulating a judgment about what is to be done. Conscience here is the activity of moral deliberation or reasoning, which includes reflection on specific cases or decisions, but is also arguably active across moral reasoning as it operates, for example, in study, seeking counsel, or prayerful discernment. Ethicists also speak of conscience as *consequent*. The consequent conscience appears in a retrospective verdict that confirms we acted well or in the pangs of guilt and remorse that arise when we know that we did not.

Conscience, Human Freedom, and Objective Morality

Internal Catholic debates about conscience have centered on the freedom or authority of individual conscience vis-à-vis ecclesial authority. A little more than a century before Vatican II Pope Gregory XVI had denounced freedom of conscience in his encyclical *Mirari Vos*. But Vatican II affirmed that individuals have a responsibility to form and exercise their conscience, and then are obliged to obey it. Moreover, this obligation is linked to human freedom. As *Gaudium et spes* declares: "Man's dignity demands that he act according to a knowing and free choice that is personally motivated and prompted from within, not under blind internal impulse, nor by mere external pressure. Man achieves such dignity when, emancipating himself from all captivity to passion, he pursues his goal in a spontaneous choice of what is good, and procures for himself through effective and skillful action, apt helps to that end."[32] Freedom of conscience does not mean that persons are morally permitted to do as they like, to decide *what* is good. The dignity of conscience consists in the free choice of what *is* good. Put differently, a person enjoys freedom when her choices are ordered both to her human and the common good, when an interior conformity of her will to the objective moral order issues in rightly executed outward actions. Freedom of conscience, then, does not amount to an intuition or vague feeling of right and wrong but a judgment of right reason. Conscience in Catholic tradition presupposes a commitment to moral realism, the position that moral claims can be true or false, and moral claims are not only matters of opinion—their validity lies in their correspondence with a moral reality we do not invent but discover. That said, both our discovery of the moral order and our application of this knowledge in moral claims, arguments, decisions, and actions is a mess, subjective to sin, and always involves a hermeneutical process.

In his 1993 encyclical *Veritatis splendor*, Pope John Paul II argued that much moral theology since Vatican II is marked by false understandings of human freedom and conscience, consequentialism and moral subjectivism, and the denial of intrinsically evil acts and absolute moral norms. The pope criticizes "some theologians," by which he seems to mean certain moral theologians working in the academy, for tendencies that appear to run away with the spirit of Vatican II. Specifically, he criticizes what he calls a "creative" understanding of conscience. A "creative" understanding of conscience undermines conviction in an objective moral order because, according to the pope, it attenuates the relations between conscience and law, freedom and truth. The revisionist theologians criticized in *Veritatis splendor*, for example, are said to believe that moral norms are not objectively binding on conscience but simply specifications of a moral perspective that orients the person's moral deliberation. Specific norms have this more provisional character out of necessity, since they are inevitably insufficient given the complexity of moral life. Moral norms cannot account for unique circumstances, personal histories, and as yet unknown developments in human history, knowledge, and technology. What truly and unconditionally obliges persons morally lies at some existential level that may or may not cohere with the particular doctrinal requirement proposed by the church. John Paul II criticizes these ways of qualifying moral norms by saying, "a separation, or even an opposition, is thus established in some cases between the teaching of the precept, which is valid in general, and the norm of the individual conscience, which would in fact make the final decision about what is good and what is evil (VS 56)." For John Paul II, a creative conscience implies that human freedom is not dependent upon the truth. The pope charges that the moral theologians he criticizes enlist a creative understanding of conscience to justify "pastoral" exemptions to moral rules and excuse moral actions that are contrary to the teaching of the magisterium.

For John Paul II, revisionist theologians exemplify some ill effects from the church's encounter with modern secularism. Catholic teaching about conscience brings a great insight to bear in considering the moral presuppositions and import of modernization and secularism. Varieties of both can imply or outright champion a vision of creation. John Paul II worried that varieties of secularization and modernization entail a vision of creation (which includes human nature) as shorn of any significance except that which we choose to invent for it. By contrast, Catholic moral tradition regards the given world and our given humanity seriously. Catholic confidence in an objective moral order that is discernible at least in part via reflection on features of human existence and interpreted in light of revelation is a strength of the tradition. Nevertheless, the risk of moral fundamentalism arises when Catholics, for example, deny development in their moral tradition and minimize the extent to which our understanding of our humanity and our world are culturally constructed. And yet, Catholic confidence can give way to overconfidence, becoming forgetful of development in moral tradition and minimizing the degree and significance social location makes for understanding what it means to be human and to nurture the human and common good. To clarify my concern, it is fruitful to consider two recent public responses to the 2016 mass shooting at a gay nightclub in Orlando, Florida.

Conscience, Catholic Tradition, and Moral Fundamentalism after Orlando

In the early morning hours of June 12, 2016, Omar Mateen entered the gay night club Pulse in Orlando, Florida, where he killed forty-nine people and wounded fifty-three others. That evening was Latin Night at the club. Most of the victims were Latino. The shooting claimed more lives than any other instance of LGBTQ violence in the United States to date. Following the attack many public figures and private citizens offered expressions of grief and support at the site of the attack, in social media, and in other public venues. One such response came from Fr. James Martin, SJ, the well-known Jesuit priest and editor-at-large of *America* magazine. In a video he posted on Facebook, Fr. Martin pointed out that, up until the video was posted, he was aware of only one American Catholic bishop who had addressed the shooting in a manner that explicitly mentioned that the gunman targeted a LGBTQ population.[33] According to Fr. Martin, by expressing sympathy for the families of the victims and solidarity with the people of Orlando, but remaining silent about the fact that the shooter seems to have been motivated partly by homophobia, bishops contributed to a long-standing Catholic practice of making LGBTQ persons invisible or treating them as other. In the video, Fr. Martin does not reject Catholic teaching about same-sex relations or even challenge binary concepts of gender or sexual complementarity. He simply reminds viewers that in Christ there is no other or them, only us. It is worth noting that since the video aired, Fr.

Martin recognized several other bishops who had explicitly acknowledged the victims as LGBTQ or criticized homophobia.

Fr. Martin's video was widely seen. As of this writing, it has been viewed more than 1.6 million times and has been "liked" almost 20,000 times. A commentary on the video appeared in the magazine *First Things*. Deputy editor Elliot Milco wrote the editorial.[34] Milco says that Fr. Martin is not complaining about a lack of sympathy on the part of bishops but about the language with which they identify the suffering, for example, generic phrases such as "the people of Orlando." Milco contends, first, that the designation LGBTQ refers to a "highly developed political and anthropological ideology, which makes hard claims about human nature and desire, morality, the structure of the family, and the proper use of bodies." Milco affirms that LGBTQ persons deserve love, sympathy, and solidarity in the quest for truth, justice, and eternal happiness, "but what we share with our brethren on account of our common humanity does not nullify what divides us in terms of our choices and beliefs *about* happiness, justice, and the truth." Put simply, "The Catholic Church and the LGBTQ Community have divergent understandings of human nature, personal identity, the proper use of bodies, and the requirements for happiness," and this ideology is "fundamentally inimical to the primary end of man." Finally, Milco argues that Martin is asking bishops "to recognize and tacitly endorse the sexual identities promoted by the LGBTQ community—identities bound up fundamentally with the gender ideology promoted by the Community." Doing so would be an "evangelical failure, and a failure of charity."

Attitudinally, Milco's response is at odds with Catholic convictions about human dignity and respect for human life, and with Catholic moral commitments to solidarity and a preferential option for vulnerable populations. He elides the particular circumstances of the Orlando victims, their structural vulnerability to violence, their histories of pain and isolation and joy and community. By eliding their particularity, he compounds the harm done to LGBTQ persons. Milco also ignores Catholic complicity in this harm. I am not suggesting that Catholicism directly influenced the gunman, only that it has been a contributing factor in discrimination against and violence toward LGBTQ persons.

Moreover, Milco elects a hermeneutic of defensive self-definition. In charity, we might surmise that Milco worries that he could tacitly endorse gender ideology because of some concern that he would scandalize other Catholics or confuse people regarding Catholic teaching. But in my reading,

his worry comes across as reactive and therefore more anxious about securing his own identity—and that of his community—over against outsiders who threaten it. Milco is correct in one respect—between Catholic
teaching and gay rights advocates there are substantive disagreements about
hard claims. But it does not follow that the hard claims underlying acceptance of gay rights amounts to a rival ideology that is so utterly discon-
tinuous with insights from Catholic moral tradition that the two are
incommensurable, or that use of the LGBTQ label signals tacit endorsement
of those claims. I hesitate to describe Milco's commentary as an instance
of moral fundamentalism. We would need to hear more from him regarding what he takes this ideology to be. Does he realize that arguments in
support of LGBTQ persons are not monolithic and that references to gender ideology eclipse important differences? Would he present arguments
made by LGBTQ persons in terms that they would recognize as fair, or
does he distort them by requiring them to be folded into the terms of his
own moral tradition? Is he willing to acknowledge that Catholic tradition
exhibits development in moral teaching? Would he grant that the moral
anthropology of Catholic tradition can find fruitful corrections in work
done by liberation theologies, such as feminist or black theology? Whatever the case, Milco clearly elects a hermeneutic of culture wars that privileges disagreements over unity. In doing so, the charity he professes for
LGBTQ persons devolves into an abstraction rather than attentive, textured
concern for them in a time of grief and fear.

Finally, Milco risks conflating recognition with tacit endorsement. He
does, of course, recognize that persons with same-sex attractions exist. He
acknowledges that we all share a common humanity. His refusal to use
the acronym LGBTQ (like the Catholic bishops' use of quotation marks
around every reference to same-sex couples, weddings, or marriage in
their document on religious freedom) is a refusal to recognize the self-
understanding of LGBTQ persons, the civil status of their weddings and
marriages, and the reality of their lived experience, which includes their
differential, discriminatory, and violent treatment at the hands of others.
It is a refusal to acknowledge Catholic complicity in that treatment. It appears that for Milco, LGBTQ persons can only be named or described
through a moral vocabulary that persistently encodes their moral deficiency
from the perspective of Catholic teaching. Insisting on such rhetorical
moves makes professions of love and respect for LGBTQ persons into abstractions and undercuts the acceptance of LGBTQ persons the Catholic

community ought to show.[35] Indeed, Milco's response to Fr. Martin's video punts on the question of how really to welcome, accompany, and include LGBTQ persons in the Catholic church. In the context of a mass shooting sparked by hatred toward a particular community, the claim that Catholics in good conscience love LGBTQ persons by making it clear that their self-understanding is "fundamentally inimical to the good of man" is not only offensive, it shirks the work of neighbor love. Milco's position, not Fr. Martin's, represents an evangelical failure and a failure of charity.

Conscience, Catholic Identity, and Moral Pluralism

Milco's failure is instructive for our consideration of conscience and Catholic identity as a key to Catholic negotiation of secularism and modernity. Religious traditions, like any traditions, are complex and never homogeneous. While there are distinguishing features and normative boundaries, traditions admit of rival interpretations and histories that are inevitably more diverse than some guardians of orthodoxy want to admit. Responses to secularism and modernity are choices to privilege certain interpretations and aspects of tradition over others. One person or community might privilege cultic purity, and another might seek to inhabit the same tradition in practices that prioritize hospitality or mercy.[36] This pluralism is found both within and beyond Catholicism.

Like Milco, I affirm key Catholic claims that there is an objective moral order. Unlike Milco, I am less confident that the hard claims through which Catholic tradition has articulated that order are as settled and nonnegotiable as he takes them to be. The moral pluralism we encounter in secularized society is an opportunity to consider anew our normative judgments about Catholic identity and practice and to marshal aspects of Catholic tradition that prepare and sustain us to engage the world in a manner that testifies to and partakes in God's reconciling love.[37] Because we are social, linguistic, self-interpreting agents, conscience is an act or process of interpretation and appraisal that is informed and guided by the conceptual frameworks that mediate our understanding of ourselves and the world.[38] Conscience is a second-order reflection on what we care about and a critical appraisal of the ways our actions and relations fail to respect and enhance human and nonhuman life as good in itself. Conscience is thus an expression of our moral freedom but one in which freedom encounters claims or constraints that arise in the recognition that others demand our care.[39] Conscience entails conformity to moral claims originating beyond the self. At the same time conscience is a creative act of self-determination and self-expression.[40] The creativity of conscience is linked to my contention that responsible agents must determine in given contexts how to prioritize particular aspects of their identity, and pursue, neglect, or sacrifice particular goods and values in morally ambiguous or even tragic situations. Conscience also designates the human capacity for self-determination before God, a self-determination that unfolds for individuals and, in an admittedly complex way, for communities. This self-determination, however, is not an act of self-creation so much as it is the appropriation of an identity graciously received as we endeavor to live a life faithful to the call of discipleship. As Kathryn Lilla Cox puts it in her study of conscience: "Questions about whether an action is right or wrong retain validity. Yet, other questions more explicitly concerned with relationality and moral formation become more relevant when considering discipleship."[41] Love for God and neighbor, not the self's aspiration for perfection of self or community, is the basic dynamic of the moral life.

Conclusion

The moral diversity of modernity and secularism represents a challenge for Catholics. Temptations to moral fundamentalism may be endemic to the tradition, given Catholic convictions that there is an objective moral order, and Catholic confidence in our capacity to know it, and in the magisterium's ability to interpret it authentically. Nevertheless, the tradition offers resources for resisting temptations for moral fundamentalism. Those resources include Catholic teaching about conscience.

Notes

1. Ancient Faith Radio, featuring Bobby Maddex interviewing George Demacopoulos and Aristotle Papanikolaou. The interview took place on May 20, 2016 and is available in the Fordham University online media library, accessed April 9, 2019, http://www.fordham.edu/info/23001/orthodox _christian_studies_center/4486/media_library.

2. Cary Funk and Greg Smith, "'Nones' On the Rise: One-in-Five Adults Have No Religious Affiliation," Pew Research Center (2012), accessed April 9, 2019, https://www.pewforum.org/2012/10/09/nones-on-the-rise/.

3. Consider the Religious Freedom Restoration Act of 1993, Pub. L. No. 103–141, 107 Stat. 1488 (November 16, 1993), codified at 42 U.S.C. paras. 2000bb–4.

4. Martin E. Marty and R. Scott Appleby, eds., *Fundamentalisms Observed* (Chicago: University of Chicago Press, 1991), 835.

5. Michael Lipka, "A Closer Look at Catholic America," Pew Research Center, September 14, 2015, accessed April 9, 2019, http://www.pewresearch.org /fact-tank/2015/09/14/a-closer-look-at-catholic-america/.

6. Pew Research Center, "America's Changing Religious Landscape," May 12, 2015, accessed April 9, 2019, http://www.pewforum.org/2015/05/12 /americas-changing-religious-landscape/.

7. Pew Research Center, "Faith in Flux," April 2009, rev. February 2011, accessed April 9, 2019, http://www.pewforum.org/2009/04/27/faith-in-flux/.

8. Pew Research Center, "America's Changing Religious Landscape."

9. Pew Research Center, "Faith in Flux."

10. Massimo Faggioli, *Vatican II: The Battle for Meaning* (Mahwah, NJ: Paulist, 2012).

11. Betsy Cooper, Daniel Cox, Rachel Lienesch, and Robert P. Jones, *Exodus: Why Americans Are Leaving Religion—And Why They're Unlikely to Come Back*, PRRI, 2016, accessed April 9, 2019, http://www.prri.org/research/prri-rns-poll -nones-atheist-leaving-religion/; Robert P. Jones and Daniel Cox, "The Francis Effect? U.S. Catholic Attitudes on Pope Francis, the Catholic Church, and American Politics," PRRI, 2015, accessed April 9, 2019, http://www.prri.org/wp -content/uploads/2015/08/PRRI-RNS-2015-Survey.pdf.

12. Jones and Cox, "The Francis Effect?"

13. Jones and Cox. The report documents confusion among American Catholics over Pope Francis's position on same-sex marriage.

14. Jones and Cox.

15. Jones and Cox. This support diverges along partisan lines (68 percent of Catholic Democrats hold this position compared to 39 percent of Republican Catholics).

16. Jones and Cox.

17. See *Zubik v. Burwell* 578 U.S. 14–1418 (2016); for the letter submitted by the United States Conference of Catholic Bishops Committee on Domestic Justice and Human Development to the United States Senate on January 18, 2017, encouraging the Senate to preserve certain provisions in the Affordable Care Act, see the press release on the USCCB website, accessed April 9, 2019, http://www.usccb.org/news/2017/17-013.cfm.

18. John Allen, Jr., "Benedict Makes a Case for Healthy Secularism," *National Catholic Reporter*, September 12, 2008, accessed April 9, 2019, https://www .ncronline.org/news/benedict-makes-case-healthy-secularism.

19. See Richard Dawkins, *The God Delusion* (Boston, MA: Houghton Mifflin, 2008); and Christopher Hitchens, *God Is Not Great: How Religion Poisons Everything* (Toronto: McClelland and Stewart, 2008).

20. See, for example, John Corrigan and Lynn S. Neal, *Religious Intolerance in America: A Documentary History* (Chapel Hill: University of North Carolina Press, 2010), chap. 2. See also Philip Jenkins, *The New Anti-Catholicism: The Last Acceptable Prejudice* (Oxford: Oxford University Press, 2003).

21. See "Redefining Marriage and the Threat to Religious Liberty," accessed April 9, 2019, http://www.usccb.org/issues-and-action/religious-liberty/religious -freedom-and-marriage.cfm.

22. Brakkton Booker, "Kentucky Clerk Again Accused of Interfering with County Marriage Licenses," National Public Radio, September 22, 2015, accessed April 9, 2019, http://www.npr.org/sections/thetwo-way/2015/09/22 /440860617/kentucky-clerk-again-accused-of-interfering-with-county -marriage-licenses. See also Julie Hanlon Rubio, "Cooperation with Evil Reconsidered: The Moral Duty of Resistance," *Theological Studies* 78, no. 1 (2017): 96–120.

23. Tom Beaudoin, "Secular Catholicism and Practical Theology," *International Journal of Practical Theology* 15, no. 1 (2011): 25.

24. Beaudoin, 25.

25. Beaudoin, 33.

26. Peter L. Berger, *The Desecularization of the World: A Global Overview* (Grand Rapids, MI: Eerdmans), 4.

27. John W. O'Malley, *What Happened at Vatican II?* (Cambridge, MA: Harvard University Press, 2010), 310.

28. "Dignitatis Humanae" in *Vatican Council II: The Conciliar and Postconciliar Documents*, ed. Austin Flannery (Collegeville, MN: Liturgical Press, 1996) and Pope John XXIII, "Pacem in Terris," in *Catholic Social Thought: Encyclicals and Documents from Pope Leo XIII to Pope Francis*, 3rd rev. ed., ed. David J. O'Brien and Thomas A. Shannon (Maryknoll, NY: Orbis Books, 2016).

29. *Gaudium et Spes*, in Flannery, *Vatican Council II*, no. 40.

30. See James T. Bretzke, SJ, *A Morally Complex World: Engaging Con- temporary Moral Theology* (Collegeville, MN: Liturgical Press, 2004), 127–31.

31. *Gaudium et Spes*, no. 16.

32. *Gaudium et Spes*, no. 17.

33. The video was posted on Fr. James Martin's personal Facebook page, June 13, 2016, accessed April 9, 2019, https://www.facebook.com /FrJamesMartin/.

34. Elliot Milco, "A Response to Fr. James Martin on the Orlando Massacre," *First Things*, June 15, 2016, accessed April 9, 2019, https://www

.firstthings.com/blogs/firstthoughts/2016/06/a-response-to-fr-james-martin-on
-the-orlando-massacre.

35. United States Conference of Catholic Bishops Committee on Marriage
and Family, *Always Our Children: A Pastoral Message to Parents of Homosexual
Children and Suggestions for Pastoral Ministers* (Washington, DC: United States
Catholic Conference, 1997).

36. See William Schweiker on the cosmopolitan conscience in David E.
Klemm and William Schweiker, *Religion and the Human Future: An Essay on
Theological Humanism* (Malden, MA: Wiley-Blackwell, 2008).

37. Kathryn Lilla Cox, *Water Shaping Stone: Faith, Relationships, and
Conscience Formation* (Collegeville, MN: Liturgical Press, 2015), 160.

38. William Schweiker, *Responsibility and Christian Ethics* (Cambridge:
Cambridge University Press, 1998), 176.

39. Schweiker, 177.

40. Linda Hogan, *Confronting the Truth: Conscience in the Catholic Tradition*
(Mahwah, NJ: Paulist, 2000).

41. Cox, *Water Shaping Stone*, 158.

FUNDAMENTALISM AS A PRECONSCIOUS RESPONSE TO A PERCEIVED THREAT

Wendy Mayer

In this essay, I explore one aspect of why fundamentalist movements tend to emerge or strengthen when tradition—a core value of Roman Catholic and Orthodox Christianity—is perceived to be under threat. I approach the topic through the lenses of religious sectarianism and radicalization, in which contexts tradition and, consequently, fundamentalism become redefined in distinctly negative and reductionist ways: tradition is reduced to something that existed in the past when the religion was pure; fundamentalism becomes the negative pole in the oppositional binary fundamentalism-tolerance.[1] My discussion is not concerned explicitly with Catholicism or Orthodox Christianity but rather with religion per se; although it does use Catholicism as one example. Many of my observations are nothing new; other disciplines have looked at this phenomenon through their own theoretical perspectives. What I want to show here is how recent research in the fields of cognitive science and neuroscience, particularly in the area of moral psychology, not only validates but also nuances many of those earlier observations. With this essay, I seek to offer explanatory models that add another layer to our understanding of how tradition and fundamentalism become co-opted when secularization is posited as a threat to religion.

As my starting point, I take the nine characteristics of religious fundamentalism that Martin Marty and Scott Appleby identified in their Fundamentalism Project. Marty and Appleby divided these characteristics into two categories: ideological and organizational.[2] For the purposes of my argument, the ideological characteristics are the most significant—although the organizational ones also deserve some attention. Attention is paid to this first category rather than the second because the theoretical approaches that I introduce have as their focus social-functional morality. Morality is in essence ideological. Social-functional morality, specifically, is concerned with how operational moral values facilitate the cohesion of social groups (intragroup cooperation) but can also result in intergroup conflict.[3] Of specific interest are four of the five ideological characteristics posited by the Fundamentalism Project:[4]

> Reactivity to the marginalization of religion: Modernization and secularization are perceived as eroding and displacing "true" religion. Fundamentalist movements form in reaction to and as a defense against this perceived threat.[5]
>
> Selectivity: Fundamentalism selects and reshapes aspects of the tradition that distinguish it from the mainstream. It selects some aspects of modernity to affirm and embrace. It selects others and singles them out, usually to oppose them. The three processes of selection are interrelated and result in variability in what is selected in each of the three domains.[6]
>
> Moral Manichaeism: The world is divided into good and evil. The outside world is contaminated. This worldview can be absolute or graded.[7]
>
> Absolutism and inerrancy: Sacred texts and traditions are held to be absolute and inerrant in character. This gives rise to distinctive strategies of interpretation.[8]

All four of the organizational characteristics—elect, chosen membership; sharp boundaries; authoritarian organization; and behavioral requirements[9]—are germane to the four ideological characteristics. Because the psychological mechanisms I discuss here are concerned with social groups and their cohesion, also relevant are the findings published in volume 3 of Marty and Appleby's Fundamentalism Project that concern the fundamentalist view of the family as a powerful symbol of the idealized moral order and microcosm of society.[10]

Sacred Values and Moral Actors

A key premise of the Fundamentalism Project that continues to permeate discussions of the concept is that fundamentalism is a modern phenomenon that has arisen as a reaction to the twin threats of modernization and secularization.[11] Others might argue, however, that the phenomenon can already be traced in the medieval world.[12] Recent research in the field of late antiquity—the period that encompasses both state recognition of Christianity as a religion and the rise of Islam—suggests that many of the same ideological and organizational characteristics of fundamentalism can be found in the third to eighth centuries CE, if not earlier, as well as in non-Abrahamic religions.[13] This suggests that fundamentalist movements are not just a modern phenomenon and that they arise in response to a perceived threat to a religion per se, rather than to the threat of modernization or secularization in particular. In this regard, Jesse Graham and Jonathan Haidt's work on sacred values and Scott Atran's related work on devoted actors provide an insightful explanatory model.[14]

In order to appreciate their contributions, which suggests that fundamentalisms owe less to the nature of religion than to a set of moral intuitions that sit beneath religion,[15] it is important to gain an understanding of the nature of moral cognition and its function in the brain, the agency of moral intuitions in moral judgments, and the role of social-functional moral intuitions in how groups cohere. Although this research can help explain macro trends in groups (explaining, for example, processes of radicalization and the development of fundamentalist movements),[16] it is likely to prove less useful for eliciting the details of how these trends instantiate in a particular case or individual example. That is because a more complex set of factors may be involved when assessing the radicalization and motivation of individual fundamentalists. Also, although I talk about cognitive science *and* religion, I am not appealing to the cognitive science *of* religion. That discipline—which is concerned with how human minds represent, acquire, and act on religious ideas[17]—does engage with the question of morality,[18] but the science of moral cognition to which I appeal here is an area of research in its own right that does not locate religion as its primary subject of investigation. Furthermore, in order to bring together moral cognition and religion in this particular way, the following suppositions apply:

1. A religious movement, denomination, or sect is a social group. A fundamentalist movement satisfies the same requirement.

2. Religious groups are not special. Individuals bind together to form religious groups and religious groups split into sects or come

into conflict with other religious groups on the basis of the same mechanisms that cause all social groups to bind, split, or generate conflict.

3. It is not religion per se but morality that is the primary force that binds social groups.[19] Morality lies beneath and shapes politics, economics, and religion.[20] A religion can be strongly moral but morality can exist without religion.[21]

4. Morality in this sense is distinct from ethics or religious values. It is not about what we should or should not do (determining the morally correct approach to a situation or what is ideally good) but about social-functional values, that is, about the unconscious values and moral judgments that inform our everyday actions and behavior.

These suppositions are open to contestation. Taken together, however, they build a strong foundation for understanding why fundamentalist movements respond to perceived threats in the ways that they do, why those behaviors are shared across such a large range of religions, and why for Protestant fundamentalists authority is invested primarily in the Bible, and for Catholic and Orthodox Christians in tradition.

When we look at some of the recent work on terrorist actors and on religious and political conflict emerging from within the disciplines of social and moral psychology, it is no accident that the ideological characteristics of fundamentalisms express in specific common social organizational behaviors. This is the case regardless of how we might define religion because, as these studies argue, the correlation with militant action lies not in religion but in something that lies beneath religion, politics, economics, and law—social-functional moral values. In this respect it matters little that premodern societies might have made a distinction along a spectrum between what was sacred and profane without having a concept of the secular. Far more important for the purpose of my inquiry is that the modern concept of the secular predicates as its opposite the sacred.[22] It is this latter concept that, in one way or another, sits at the heart of the phenomenon described by fundamentalism, and it is Durkheim's and Weber's ideas of community, authority, and sacredness that have provided the impetus for the development of recent explanatory theories concerning the "motives and motivated reasoning of partisans."[23] Working from these ideas, the moral psychologists Haidt and Graham, together with their colleagues, have spent the past decade building a case that groups organize and facilitate mutual cooperation on the basis of a surprisingly small number of moral foundations.[24] These foundations are the functional basis on which social groups overcome individual selfishness and cooperate—hence the label "social-functional"—and are distinct from the aspirational values (the ethics or moral code) that are consciously held up by a particular social group as the set of ideals according to which individuals should live their lives.[25] The degree of emphasis individual groups place on each of the moral foundations helps to explain, these scholars argue, "how and why the moral domain varies across cultures."[26] The point they make, however, is that the foundations themselves are not variable but cross-cultural, and social groups operate on the basis of all of the five foundations regardless of their particular emphasis.[27] Although these scholars are concerned with modern and postmodern societies, the same foundations shape, as I will show, and thus help to explain premodern societies and the social groups operative within them.[28]

We can make this claim in part because moral judgment, according to the current consensus, is cognitive and operates at the level of intuition.[29] Since the processes in evolution are slow and there is most likely little difference between the first- and twenty-first-century human brain,[30] it is reasonable to assume that such basic ways of thinking are not just cross-cultural but also transhistorical. In fact, when it comes to the brain and moral cognition, as Michael Gazzaniga summed up in 2010, there was at that time more or less consensus among experimental cognitive scientists regarding four basic findings: (1) morality is largely universal, that is, cross-cultural; (2) many moral judgments, however, do not fall into a universal category and appear to be influenced by local culture and learning; (3) *all* moral decision processes resulting in behaviors, regardless of category, are carried out *before* conscious awareness of them (they result from a microsecond, intuitive response); and (4) a special device ("the interpreter"), usually located in the brain's left hemisphere, seeks to understand the rationale behind the pattern of behavior in others or oneself.[31] Haidt calls the latter two processes "the emotional dog and its rational tail."[32] That is, we automatically and without exception make moral decisions or judgments at the preconscious level and rationalize them after the fact. The most important entailment of this discovery is that, while the reasons we give for an action may rationalize a gut response, the rationalization and the moral intuition are not logically consequential.[33] Understanding this helps to explain why the behavior of fundamentalist groups can at times appear to be inconsistent with the espoused moral code.

The potential utility of this body of research becomes clearer when we examine the five moral intuitions or foundations that have thus far been discovered.[34] Extracted from the adaptive challenges of social life discussed by evolutionary psychologists, Moral Foundations Theory seeks "to identify the best candidates for . . . the universal cognitive modules upon which cultures construct moral matrices."[35] Although there is some variation in the labeling as the theory has progressed, the five foundations identified are: care/harm; fairness/cheating; loyalty/betrayal; authority/subversion; and sanctity/degradation.[36] Each is associated with a set of original triggers, characteristic emotions, and relevant virtues (see table 1).[37]

What Haidt and his colleagues found in their experiments is that progressives placed strong emphasis on the first two foundations, whereas conservatives placed equal emphasis on all five.[38] This led Haidt to propose "that there are two common ways that cultures suppress and regulate selfishness, two visions of what society is and how it ought to work . . . the *contractual* approach and the *beehive* approach."[39] In the contractual (or progressive) approach the individual is the fundamental unit of value; in the hive (or conservative) approach, it is the group and its territory. This model further led Haidt to describe care/harm and fairness/cheating as individualizing foundations, in that they generate virtues and practices that protect individuals from each other and allow them to live in harmony as autonomous agents who can focus on their own goals; and loyalty/betrayal, authority/subversion, and sanctity/degradation as binding foundations, because the virtues, practices, and institutions they generate function to bind people together into hierarchically organized interdependent social groups that try to regulate the daily lives and personal habits of their members.[40] When we align these insights with the organizational characteristics of fundamentalists described by the Fundamentalism Project—elect, chosen membership; sharp boundaries; authoritarian organization; and behavioral requirements that impose conformity and strict regulation—we can see that fundamentalist movements are uniformly strongly hivist organizations.[41] In fundamentalist ideology we should thus expect a particularly strong emphasis on loyalty, authority, and moral foundations.

A significant finding of this research is that groups that place strong emphasis on either set may work toward the same prosocial goals but, as a result of the different moral foundations that drive the group, disagree

Table 1. Moral Foundations (adapted from Haidt)

	Care/Harm	Fairness/ Cheating	Loyalty/ Betrayal	Authority/ Subversion	Sanctity/ Degradation
Adaptive challenge	Protect and care for children	Reap benefits of two-way partnerships	Form cohesive coalitions	Forge beneficial relationships within hierarchies	Avoid contamination
Original triggers	Suffering, distress, or neediness expressed by one's child	Cheating, cooperation, deception	Threat or challenge to group	Signs of dominance and submission	Waste products, diseased people
Charac- teristic emotions	Compassion	Anger, gratitude, guilt	Group pride, rage at traitors	Respect, fear	Disgust
Relevant virtues	Caring, kindness	Fairness, justice, trustworthiness	Loyalty, patriotism, self-sacrifice	Obedience, deference	Temperance, chastity, piety, cleanliness

strongly on the best way to achieve them. This finding is corroborated by the work of another moral psychologist, Joshua Greene, who uses the analogy of moral tribes to make the case that the same values that favor and foster intragroup cooperation can prove problematic when one group encounters another.[42] Greene labels the intergroup conflict that can result "the tragedy of commonsense morality." To paraphrase his summary of how this works: groups share some core values; each group's philosophy is woven into its daily life; each group has its own version of moral common sense; they fight, not because they are immoral, but because when they come into competition, they view the contested ground from very different moral perspectives.[43] As one reviewer of his book summed it up: "From an evolutionary perspective, morality is built to make groups cohere, not to achieve world peace."[44] What this research collectively suggests is that, when we look at the phenomenon we currently label fundamentalism, we should view the insiders in these movements not as religious actors but as moral actors, driven intuitively by a particular set of values. This approach allows us to view the phenomenon across the *longue durée* of history, since it moves beyond cultural constructs of religion to something that is, from a cognitive point of view, genuinely cross-cultural and a key driver in the shaping of culturally constructed frames or points of view.

On this basis, we could call the militant, mobilized, or defensive reactions of fundamentalists in response to the perceived threat to religion morally informed, but Atran's work on "devoted actors" suggests that sacred action is closer to the mark.[45] Atran is interested in extreme behaviors that, in logical terms, are out of proportion to prospects of success,[46] as well as in why certain political disputes become intractable. He takes the work of the Moral Foundations theorists one step further to talk about certain moral values as "sacred values" that are intimately linked to personal and group identity. As he puts it: "while the term 'sacred values' intuitively denotes religious belief, in what follows, sacred values refer to any preferences regarding objects, beliefs, or practices that people treat as both incompatible or nonfungible with profane issues or economic goods, as when land or law becomes holy or hallowed and as inseparable from people's conception of 'self' and of 'who we are.'"[47] It is this insight that helps us to understand the attachment of fundamentalisms to inerrancy and absolutism, and why for Protestant fundamentalisms, Scripture is so central, whereas for Catholic and Orthodox fundamentalist groups tradition and ritual is at the center. The utility of this explanatory model is further demonstrated by Atran's summary of his findings regarding the entailments of "sincere attachment to sacred values" in multiple cultures and geopolitical hotspots across the contemporary world:

> (1) commitment to a rule-bound logic of moral appropriateness to do what is morally right no matter the likely risks or rewards rather than following a utilitarian calculus of costs and consequences . . . ; (2) immunity to material trade-offs coupled with a "backfire effect" where offers of incentives or disincentives to give up sacred values heighten refusal to compromise or negotiate . . . ; (3) resistance to social influence and exit strategies . . . , which leads to unyielding social solidarity and binds genetic strangers to voluntarily sacrifice for one another; (4) insensitivity to spatial and temporal discounting, where considerations of distant places and people and even far past and future events associated with sacred values significantly outweigh concerns with here and now . . . ; and (5) brain-imaging patterns consistent with processing obligatory rules rather than weighing costs

and benefits and with processing perceived violations of such rules as emotionally agitating and resistant to social influence.[48]

In essence, when sacred values come into play, perception of what is right or wrong trumps utilitarian considerations (cost-benefit analysis); actors become blind to exit strategies and are more willing "to fight and risk serious loss/death rather than compromise"; and material incentives or disincentives are likely to be viewed as insulting/profane and to make the actors more intransigent.[49] The Manichaean dualism of fundamentalisms, their rule-based mindset and strict regulation of individuals, their concern with millenialism yet appeals to an imagined pure tradition associated with the past—they all are automatic responses, Atran's work suggests, to the perceived threats posed to specific sacred values. This also helps to explain the centrality of the family and its strict regulation in fundamentalisms. As a powerful symbol of the idealized moral order and a microcosm of society, the family is elevated to the status of a sacred value.

In developing his theory of devoted actors further, what Atran adds to the insights of the moral psychologists is fusion theory, taken from the field of social psychology. The theory introduces the idea of the fusing of self-identity with a unique collective identity, which is in turn fused with sacred values, providing all group members with "a similar sense of significance."[50] This has as much to say to the emergence of Christianity and its response to persecution—whether the persecution was real or perceived—as to present-day jihadists and the Muslim Brotherhood. As he explains: "In the sweep of cultural evolution, movements that develop psychological mechanisms to promote devoted actors are more likely to succeed because they exploit evolved psychology (e.g., kin selection) in evolutionarily novel ways. The interaction of identity fusion and sacred values seems to be one such case, where the psychology of kin selection combines with bonding rituals (e.g., sacred oaths, *bayat*, to the brotherhood, *ikhwaniyah*, of jihad and its leaders) to inextricably cement individuals to the group via a shared spiritual and moral mission."[51] This insight highlights the importance of the role of ritual, suggesting that for fundamentalisms, worship and other rituals can serve to reinforce bonding into a cross-cultural kinship group. When ritual is fused with values that the fundamentalist group holds sacred, this fostering of group identity can in turn strengthen the group's shared sense of mission.

This branch of research can contribute in yet another way, through the concept of ideological narratives. As part of their work on moral foundations, Graham and Haidt identified a particular ideological narrative founded on the five moral intuitions that is instrumental in producing terrorist acts and intergroup violence.[52] Building on the work of other scholars on sacredness, they argue for the inclusion of a psychology of sacredness in the "evolved psychological mechanisms" that are part of moral systems.[53] Their definition is slightly different from that of Atran. For Graham and Haidt, sacred values are "moral concerns imbued with value far beyond practical utilities or self-interest. . . . [P]eople, things and ideas . . . can become sacralized because they are linked to these sacred values. And just as something is seen as worthy of ultimate protection, there is a vision of what it must be protected from: This is a vision of evil."[54] The ideological narrative that results from this process, they argue, is simple and effective at group binding and encourages militant action:

> When people join together to pursue political projects—from the demand for civil rights to violent revolution to genocide—they must share a common story, one that they accept as true without having authored it. Ideological narratives, then, by their very nature, are always stories about good and evil. They identify heroes and villains, they explain how the villains got the upper hand, and they lay out or justify the means by which—if we can just come together and fight hard enough—we can vanquish the villains and return the world to its balanced or proper state.[55]

This matches in every respect the Manichaean dualism identified as one of fundamentalism's five ideological characteristics. In my own research into religious conflict and violence in the late antique, premodern world, it matches the overarching narrative embedded in an infamous set of anti-Jewish homilies generated by a sectarian group within Orthodox Christianity.[56] If we understand the Jews, not judaizers, as the villain, the narrative in those homilies unfolds as follows: the Christian *politeia* or way of life is sacred; it is constantly being contaminated or attacked by the Jews and their way of life who have seduced away Christians into Judaism; if we could just vanquish the Jews and their way of life, judaizing would cease, and the pure Christian *politeia* would be restored. It is the kind of narrative generated by a religious group that sees true religion as under threat from weak insiders as well as outside forces.[57] And, it is precisely the kind of ideological narrative that, when fused with a strong group identity, Atran argues, generates devoted actors.

The Implications of Moral Cognition Research

Two modern case studies illustrate the utility of cognition research in explaining the intersection between fundamentalism, secularization, and tradition. In the first study, on the topic of secularization and resacralization in the context of Catholic Christianity, Neil Ormerod points to a critical difference in the ecclesial styles of Popes Benedict and Francis. As he asserts:

> A major aspect of the strategy of re-evangelization under John Paul II and Benedict XVI has been the strong assertion of a distinctive Catholic identity, one which re-asserts its liturgical and religious-cultural aspects, such as forms of piety and religious observance, in the face of the desacralizing power of secularity. . . . [A] key strategy of the new evangelization was to attract people to the Church through the beauty of its liturgical celebrations. At the same time, however, there was debate over the notion of the "smaller, purer Church," a more devout, more religiously intense, more loyal band who would carry the Church into the future.[58]

This particular strategy is characteristic of a response to a perceived threat to sacred values. Ritual is elevated, there is a concern with establishing clear boundaries, and there is an anxiety about purity and loyalty. Its characteristic features are hivist. Ormerod's analysis of the strategy of Pope Francis intuits the lack of a threat to sacred values and indicates that, since the perceived threat is one of religious competition rather than to the religion itself, emphasis has shifted to the contractualist moral foundations:

> Outside of first world countries such as Europe and the US, the picture of Catholicism is very different. Numbers are growing and the main "opponent" so to speak, are not secularism or atheism but Pentecostals and Evangelicals siphoning off Catholics into their burgeoning communities. Religion is far from being on the wane in the two-thirds world of the South. The election of a new pope from the global south, Pope Francis, has brought a different vision for the future of the Church, one less tied to European forms and culture,

less constrained liturgically, and more engaged with social issues around poverty and injustice. These issues, deemed peripheral by those opposed to secularisation, are now back into central focus for a new pontificate. Francis is committed to a Church that goes out to the margins, that does not wait for the world to come to it, but reaches out to the world with the Gospel message.[59]

Although Ormerod goes on to offer a quite different analysis from that of the cognitive models I am adducing here, his characterization of both ecclesial models is illustrative of Graham and Haidt's theory. In the one model, fear of loss of the sacred has led to a strong emphasis on recovering the sacred in ritual practice and on group loyalty, purity, and tradition. In the other, without that fear as a driver, emphasis has shifted to social justice (fairness) and to care for the socially vulnerable and disadvantaged.

The second example demonstrates that there is nothing special about Christianity or Abrahamic religions in this respect, and that what lies behind fundamentalist responses to the concept of secularization as a threat is anxiety about the degradation of the pure religion. The Mari Finnic peoples of the nineteenth century were considered ethnic aliens within Russia and were missionized by both Orthodox Christianity and Islam.[60] Among the diverse ways the adherents of this traditional animist, utilitarian religion reacted to the colonization by two transcendental religions was the emergence of a significantly reformed, in essence new, version of the religion, called Kugu Sorta. This version framed its own reform in explicitly moral terms in contradistinction to the complete absence of any ethical component in the premissionized, strictly animist version of the religion. As Paul Werth, writing from the perspective of a social anthropologist, remarks: "they presented it as the true belief of their ancestors in conscious opposition to contemporaneous Mari practices, which they openly derided as a deviation from the true path."[61] He also points out:

> However much was new in the group's teachings and activities, they were motivated by the idea of preserving old beliefs and even construed their practice as a return to an older, pristine, more genuine Mari past. It was for this reason that they deployed a discourse of purity, whiteness, and authenticity, and associated Christianity with "blackness." Thus the reformers declared in an 1892 petition that they, the *chii Mari* (literally "pure" or "genuine Maris"), "will never be

untrue to our Faith and religion and blacken our conscience, as other Cheremis have done."[62]

In its appeal to morality, purity, Manichaean dualism, and to the authority of a traditional past reclaimed and reinvented, this particular response to a perceived threat to the religion, which resulted in an essentially new religious movement, bears many of the ideological hallmarks characteristic of fundamentalism. The perceived threat in this instance was not secularization but the degradation of the true religion through the introduction of a colonizing religion, Orthodox Christianity.

Conclusion

What this body of research in the cognitive sciences suggests is that the reason that fundamentalisms bear a family resemblance lies in the human brain. Many of the features of fundamentalisms can be shown to be cognitive in origin and independent of religion. They are triggered by largely automatic moral intuitions that elicit specific social behaviors. This helps to explain why fundamentalisms are not specific to transcendental religions or in particular to monotheisms but develop across a wide variety of religions. What the individual religion contributes is, for the most part, what specific values it holds sacred. In this respect, if in Catholic and Orthodox Christianity tradition is in itself a sacred value, in fundamentalisms tradition is something that is both appealed to for authority and subjected to reduction, something that is rewritten and co-opted. This research also challenges us to view fundamentalisms as something larger than a purely modern phenomenon. Demonstrating that the reactivity of fundamentalisms is triggered by threats to the sacred rather than secularization itself, I maintain, opens up the way to exploring the phenomenon in the *longue durée* across a significantly larger range of historical periods and cultures.

Notes

1. On the fundamentalism-tolerance binary, see Jacek Widorowicz, "Dangerous Liaisons of Terrorism and Religion in the Perspective of Visual Culture," *Anglojęzyczny Suplement Przeglądu Religioznawczego*, no. 1 (2013): 55.
2. For a full discussion of their findings, see Gabriel A. Almond, Emmanuel Sivan, and R. Scott Appleby, "Fundamentalism: Genus and Species," in *Fundamentalisms Comprehended*, ed. Martin E. Marty and R. Scott Appleby,

The Fundamentalism Project 5 (Chicago: University of Chicago Press, 1995),
399–424. The authors reprise their findings in Gabriel A. Almond, R. Scott
Appleby, and Emmanuel Sivan, *Strong Religion: The Rise of Fundamentalisms
Around the World* (Chicago: University of Chicago Press, 2003), 9–115. The
nine characteristics are set out in Almond, Appleby, and Sivan, 93–98.

3. See as a starting point the popular summation of the experimental work
of two key researchers in this area: Joshua Greene, *Moral Tribes: Emotion,
Reason, and the Gap Between Us and Them* (New York: Penguin, 2013); and
Jonathan Haidt, *The Righteous Mind: Why Good People Are Divided by Politics
and Religion* (New York: Vintage, 2012).

4. For the fifth characteristic, millenialism and messianism, see Almond,
Appleby, and Sivan, *Strong Religion*, 96–97.

5. Almond, Appleby, and Sivan, 93–94.

6. Almond, Appleby, and Sivan, 94–95.

7. Almond, Appleby, and Sivan, 95–96.

8. Almond, Appleby, and Sivan, 96.

9. Almond, Appleby, and Sivan, 97–98.

10. See esp. Helen Hardacre, "The Impact of Fundamentalisms on Women,
the Family, and Interpersonal Relations," in *Fundamentalisms and Society:
Reclaiming the Sciences, the Family, and Education*, ed. Martin E. Marty and R.
Scott Appleby, The Fundamentalism Project 3 (Chicago: University of Chicago
Press, 1993), 129–50.

11. This is the first of the five ideological characteristics defined by the
Fundamentalism Project. See note 6.

12. See, for example, the brief discussion of the work of Mark Juergensmeyer
in Jonathan Fine, *Political Violence in Judaism, Christianity, and Islam: From
Holy War to Holy Terror* (Lanham, MD: Rowman and Littlefield, 2015), 43; and
Mark Tomass, *The Religious Roots of the Syrian Conflict: The Remaking of the
Fertile Crescent* (London: Palgrave Macmillan, 2016), 97–106.

13. This is emerging in discussions of the phenomenon of religious violence.
See the foundational work of Michael Gaddis, *There Is No Crime for Those Who
Have Christ: Religious Violence in the Christian Roman Empire* (Berkeley:
University of California Press, 2005); Thomas Sizgorich, *Violence and Belief in
Late Antiquity: Militant Devotion in Christianity and Islam* (Philadelphia:
University of Philadelphia Press, 2009) and, together with the other chapters in
the same books, the discussions of recent approaches in this field by Jan
Bremmer in *Violence in Ancient Christianity: Victims and Perpetrators*, ed. Albert
Geljon and Riemer Roukema (Leiden: Brill, 2014); and *Reconceiving Religious
Conflict: New Views from the Formative Centuries of Christianity*, ed. Wendy
Mayer and Chris L. de Wet (London: Routledge, 2018).

14. On fundamentalism as a response to a perceived threat to a religion, see Jesse Graham and Jonathan Haidt, "Sacred Values and Evil Adversaries: A Moral Foundations Approach," in *The Social Psychology of Morality: Exploring the Causes of Good and Evil*, ed. Mario Mikulincer and Phillip R. Shaver (Washington, DC: American Psychological Association, 2012), 11–31; and Scott Atran, "The Devoted Actor: Unconditional Commitment and Intractable Conflict across Cultures," *Current Anthropology* 57, supplement 13 (June 2016): 192–203, building on Graham and Haidt, "Sacred Values."

15. Regarding the argument that a concept of the secular is required for religion as a category to exist, and that this is lacking in premodern societies, see the debate with regard to the ancient to late-ancient world, for example, Brent Nongbri, *Before Religion: A History of a Modern Concept* (New Haven, CT: Yale University Press, 2013); and Carlin Barton and Daniel Boyarin, *Imagine No Religion: How Modern Abstractions Hide Ancient Realities* (New York: Fordham University Press, 2016); and the response to the latter by Anders Klostergaard Petersen, *Bryn Mawr Classical Review*, June 14, 2017, accessed March 18, 2018, http://www.bmcreview.org/2017/06/20170614.html: "To be crude, one could argue that the authors are carrying coal to Newcastle. For a scholar in the study of religion it is an old truth that there can be no term 'religion' in the pre-modern world. This is the basic argument of Max Weber in his seminal *Zwischenbetrachtung*, and one may add the central contention of Durkheim as well. A century ago Weber emphasised how the invention of 'religion' presupposed the detraction of the phenomenon from the wider cultural sphere—something dated by Weber to modernity. One could draw a distinction in the ancient world between the sacred and the profane, the latter designating diminishing degrees of sacredness (*pro-fanum*) but never something categorically secular. I find it striking that this central contention of emerging sociology a century ago has neither been taken into consideration by Barton and Boyarin nor by Nongbri. Ultimately, I claim that their argument affirms Weber's and Durkheim's view, but from the perspective of early sociology it is pouring new wine into old wineskins." The work of Graham and Haidt in the area of moral foundations theory that disrupts the sociology of religion paradigm is itself grounded in a Durkheimian framework. See Jonathan Haidt and Jesse Graham. "Planet of the Durkheimians: Where Community, Authority, and Sacredness Are Foundations of Morality," in *Social and Psychological Bases of Ideology and System Justification*, ed. John T. Jost, Aaron C. Kay, and Hulda Thorisdottir (New York: Oxford University Press, 2009), 371–401.

16. As argued in Wendy Mayer, "Australia's Moral Compass and Societal Wellbeing," in *Wellbeing, Personal Wholeness, and the Social Fabric: An*

Interdisciplinary Approach, ed. Doru Costache, Darren Cronshaw and James R. Harrison (Cambridge: Cambridge Scholars, 2017), 110–31.

17. See Aaron C. T. Smith, *Thinking About Religion: Extending the Cognitive Science of Religion*, Palgrave Frontiers in Philosophy of Religion (London: Palgrave Macmillan, 2014), 14; and Istvan Czachesz, *Cognitive Science and the New Testament: A New Approach to Early Christian Research* (Oxford: Oxford University Press, 2017), esp. chap. 1.

18. See Ryan McKay and Harvey Whitehouse, "Religion and Morality," *Psychological Bulletin* 141, no. 2 (2015): 447–73.

19. This is the thesis of both Greene, *Moral Tribes*, and Haidt, *Righteous Mind*.

20. See Spassena P. Koleva, Jesse Graham, Ravi Iyer, Peter H. Ditto, and Jonathan Haidt, "Tracing the Threads: How Five Moral Concerns (Especially Purity) Help Explain Culture War Attitudes," *Journal of Research in Personality* 46, no. 2 (2012): 184–94, https://doi.org/10.1016/j.jrp.2012.01.006.

21. For the argument that religion is a generic, not unique domain, see Smith, *Thinking About Religion*, 10. On the independence of morality from religion, see, for example, Wilhelm Hofmann, Daniel C. Wisneski, Mark J. Brandt, and Linda J. Skitka, "Morality in Everyday Life," *Science* 345, no. 6202 (September 2014): 1340–43.

22. On the origin of the secular and sacred categories and for a discussion of the relationship between the two, see Jaco Beyers, "The Church and the Secular: The Effect of the Post-Secular on Christianity," *HTS Teologiese Studies/ Theological Studies* 70, no. 1 (2014): 2–5, https://dx.doi.org/10.4102/hts.v70i1 .2605, esp. 2–5. See also Jan N. Bremmer, "Secularization: Notes Toward a Genealogy," in *Religion: Beyond a Concept*, ed. Hent de Vries (New York: Fordham University Press, 2008), 432–37.

23. See Haidt and Graham, "Planet of the Durkheimians," 373–74.

24. See Jesse Graham, Jonathan Haidt, Sena Koleva, Matt Motyl, Ravi Iyer, Sean P. Wojcik, and Peter H. Ditto, "Moral Foundations Theory: The Pragmatic Validity of Moral Pluralism," *Advances in Experimental Social Psychology* 47 (2013): 55–130.

25. The label social-functionalist is generally attached to the emotions that accompany the foundations. See, for example, Cendri A. Hutcherson and James J. Gross, "The Moral Emotions: A Social-Functionalist Account of Anger, Disgust, and Contempt," *Journal of Personality and Social Psychology* 100, no. 4 (2011): 719–37.

26. Haidt and Graham, "Planet of the Durkheimians," 373. See also Yitzhaq Feder, "Contamination Appraisals, Pollution Beliefs, and the Role of Cultural Inheritance in Shaping Disease Avoidance Behavior," *Cognitive Science* 40, no. 6 (2016): 1561–85, https://doi.org/10.1111/cogs.12293.

27. Haidt, *Righteous Mind*, 144–45.

28. In making this case, the work of Yitzhaq Feder in Near-Eastern and Hebrew religion is foundational. See Yitzhaq Feder, "Contagion and Cognition: Bodily Experience and the Conceptualization of Pollution (*tum'ah*) in the Hebrew Bible," *Journal of Near Eastern Studies* 72, no. 2 (2013): 151–67; "The Semantics of Purity in the Ancient Near East: Lexical Meaning as a Projection of Embodied Experience," *Journal of Ancient Near Eastern Religions* 14 (2014): 87–113; "Defilement, Disgust and Disease: The Experiential Basis of Hittite and Akkadian Terms for Impurity," *Journal of the American Oriental Society* 136, no. 1 (2016): 99–116; "Contamination Appraisals"; and "Purity and Sancta Desecration in Ritual Law: A Durkheimian Perspective," in *The Oxford Handbook of Biblical Law*, ed. Pamela Barmash (Oxford: Oxford University Press, forthcoming).

29. Regarding the current consensus concerning a dual-processing model of cognition, see Steve Clarke, *The Justification of Religious Violence* (Malden, NY: Wiley-Blackwell, 2014), 75: "On dual processing accounts of cognition . . . our cognitive activities fall into two basic types: effortful, deliberative and conscious ('reason'); and automatic, intuitive and non-conscious ('intuition')." On the priority of intuition over reason in moral decision-making versus other kinds of decision-making, see the summary provided by Francesca Ervas, Elisabetta Gola, and Maria Grazia Rossi, "Metaphors and Emotions as Framing Strategies in Argumentation," in *Proceedings of the EuroAsianPacific Joint Conference on Cognitive Science/4th Conference on Cognitive Science/11th International Conference on Cognitive Science, Torino, Italy, September 25–27, 2015*, CEUR Workshop Proceedings 1419, ed. Gabriella Airenti, Bruno G. Bara, Giulio Sandini, and Marco Cruciani, 2015, 645–46, accessed March 18, 2018, http://ceur-ws.org/Vol-1419/paper0107.pdf.

30. See Czachesz, *Cognitive Science*, 49–61.

31. Michael Gazzaniga, "Not Really," in *Does Moral Action Depend on Reasoning? Thirteen Views on the Question*, A Templeton Conversation, Spring 2010, 4–7, accessed March 26, 2016, https://www.templeton.org/reason (discontinued). Even though no longer online at the Templeton Foundation website, the debate continues to be referenced in moral psychology and philosophy literature. Debate on the basis of neuroscientific experimental findings published since 2010 tends to nuance these claims rather than overturn them. See, for example, Steve Clarke, *The Justification of Religious Violence* (Malden, MA: Wiley-Blackwell, 2014), 75–81; the essays in *Moral Brains: The Neuroscience of Morality*, ed. S. Matthew Liao (Oxford: Oxford University Press, 2016); and Asia Ferrin, "Good Moral Judgment and Decision-Making without Deliberation," *Southern Journal of Philosophy* 55, no. 1 (2017): 68–95.

32. Jonathan Haidt, "The Emotional Dog and Its Rational Tail: A Social Intuitionist Approach to Moral Judgment," *Psychological Review* 108, no. 4 (2001): 814–34. In Haidt, *The Righteous Mind*, 32–60, this becomes "The intuitive dog and its rational tail."

33. Haidt, *Righteous Mind*, 82–83.

34. Haidt, 197–216, posits a sixth foundation (liberty/oppression) that is not universally accepted and so will not be discussed here.

35. Haidt, 146. The key adaptive challenges are defined as: "caring for vulnerable children"; "forming partnerships with non-kin to reap the benefits of reciprocity"; "forming coalitions to compete with other coalitions"; "negotiating status hierarchies"; and "keeping oneself and one's kin free from parasites and pathogens, which spread quickly when people live in close proximity."

36. Variants to the last four are: fairness/reciprocity; ingroup/loyalty; respect for authority/subversion; authority/respect; purity/sanctity. See McKay and Whitehouse, "Religion and Morality," 454–55; and Jonathan Haidt, "Moral Psychology and the Misunderstanding of Religion," *Edge*, September 21, 2007, accessed September 5, 2014, http://edge.org/conversation/moral–psychology–and–the–misunderstanding–of–religion, revised and published under the same title in *The Believing Primate: Scientific, Philosophical, and Theological Reflections on the Origin of Religion*, ed. Jeffrey Schloss and Michael J. Murray (New York: Oxford University Press, 2009), 278–91.

37. Haidt, *Righteous Mind*, 146, fig. 6.2. The characteristic emotions are of particular interest in that they correlate with the automatic, intuitive response that occurs before rationalization. Rationalization then usually occurs within the conceptual framework of the corresponding moral foundation. On this point, see the summation of their work on disgust in Paul Rozin, Jonathan Haidt, and Clark R. McCauley, "Disgust," in *Handbook of Emotions*, 3rd ed., ed. Michael Lewis, Jeanette M. Haviland-Jones, and Lisa Feldman Barrett (New York: Guilford, 2008), 757–76. The characteristic emotions are: compassion (care/harm); anger, gratitude, guilt (fairness/cheating); group pride, rage at traitors (loyalty/betrayal); respect, fear (authority/subversion); disgust (sanctity/degradation).

38. See Haidt and Graham, "Planet of the Durkheimians," esp. fig. 1. The greater the degree of conservatism, however, the greater the emphasis on the last three. The language of "progressives" and "conservatives" derives from modern political theory. I retain it here for convenience.

39. Haidt, "Moral Psychology."

40. Haidt, "Moral Psychology." Haidt begins "Planet of the Durkheimians" (371–72) with a metaphor (Planet Durkheim) that exemplifies a hivist society. When a contractualist movement develops, the hivists and contractualists, with their different emphases, come into conflict. Neither approach to social

cohesion is good or bad in itself. Both have pro- and antisocial entailments. In
The Righteous Mind and "Planet of the Durkheimians," Haidt, himself
originally a contractualist, in fact advocates the hive approach to some degree as
having greater prosocial benefits than cultural progressives allow.

41. Almond et al., *Strong Religion*, 99: "fundamentalist movements . . . are,
by definition, militant, mobilized, defensive reactions to modernity. . . . The
seven remaining properties coalesce in three overlapping clusters—selectivity,
boundaries, and election. Selectivity revolves around the need to pare down the
tradition to its essentials because of the danger that it faces. Boundaries relate
to the challenge of keeping the group's identity in an open and often tempting
society. Election is an answer to the challenge of how to maintain efficient
decision-making in a group." Note that in this last respect, while
fundamentalist hierarchies are deemed to be relatively small, within the
domestic space the family is ordered in a strictly hierarchical way. See note 11.

42. Greene, *Moral Tribes*.

43. See Greene, 4–5. Haidt, *Righteous Mind*, 219–366, describes this as
"morality binds and blinds", concluding: "[Morality] binds us into ideological
teams that fight each other as though the fate of the world depended on our
side winning each battle. It blinds us to the fact that each team is composed of
good people who have something important to say" (366).

44. Chris Mooney, "6 Surprising Scientific Findings About Good and Evil:
Harvard's Joshua Greene on the Evolution of Morality and Why Humanity
May, Objectively, Be Getting Better in the Long Run," December 13, 2013,
accessed July 2, 2016, https://www.motherjones.com/print/240996.

45. Atran, "Devoted Actor." Here it is important to keep in mind that there
is no direct link between fundamentalism and violent action. Fundamentalisms
can result in a range of behaviors, including withdrawal from society.

46. Scott Atran, *Talking to the Enemy: Faith, Brotherhood, and the (Un)
making of Terrorists* (New York: Ecco 2010), xiv.

47. Atran, "Devoted Actor," 194.

48. Atran, 195.

49. Atran, 195–97.

50. Atran, 197.

51. Atran, 198.

52. Graham and Haidt, "Sacred Values."

53. Graham and Haidt, 14.

54. Graham and Haidt, 17.

55. Graham and Haidt, 16.

56. The seven homilies *Adversus Iudaeos* preached in Antioch by the priest
John Chrysostom in 386–87 CE. For a lengthy analysis of the homilies and
their impact, see Wendy Mayer, "Preaching Hatred? John Chrysostom,

Neuroscience, and the Jews," in *Revisioning John Chrysostom: New Approaches, New Perspectives*, ed. Chris L. de Wet and Wendy Mayer (Leiden: Brill, 2019), 58–136.

57. On a tepid or corrupt religious establishment as one of three antagonists identified by fundamentalisms, see Almond et al., *Strong Religion*, 101. The narrative that runs through the homilies was summarized by William LeRoy Mullen, "The Polemical Sermons of John Chrysostom Against the Judaizers: A Dramatic Analysis," PhD diss. (University of Nebraska-Lincoln, 1990), 120–21, as: "The Christian's life is a continuous striving or a struggle. The struggle may be described generally as follows: A struggle exists in which we are continually confronted by hostile forces. The struggle with the hostile forces may produce victims or a negative outcome. Therefore, we must utilize appropriate counter-measures, which will produce a positive outcome against the hostile forces."

58. Neil Ormerod, "Secularisation and Resacralisation: False Alternatives for a Missionary Church," *Australian eJournal of Theology* 23, no. 1 (April 2016): 33, accessed March 18, 2018, http://aejt.com.au/2016/volume_23/vol_23_no_1 _2016.

59. Ormerod, 33.

60. Described in Paul W. Werth, "Big Candles and 'Internal Conversion': The Mari Animist Reformation and its Russian Appropriations," in *Of Religion and Empire: Missions, Conversion, and Tolerance in Tsarist Russia*, ed. Robert P. Geraci and Michael Khodarkovsky (Ithaca, NY: Cornell University Press, 2001), 144–72.

61. Werth, 156.

62. Werth, 155. In regard to the moral Manichaeism characteristic of fundamentalisms, one further aspect of moral cognition research is noteworthy. The emergence and effectiveness in the discourse of the *chii Mari* of light/darkness and boundary metaphors (morality is following a path, immorality is deviating; morality is light, immorality is darkness) is attributable to the universal primacy of moral metaphors in cognition. On the basic moral conceptual metaphors and their significance, see George Lakoff, *The Political Mind: A Cognitive Scientist's Guide to Your Brain and Its Politics* (New York: Penguin, 2009), 96–98.

ACKNOWLEDGMENTS

Fundamentalism or Tradition: Christianity after Secularism is based upon a conference that took place in June 2016. That conference was the fourth installment of the *Patterson Triennial Conference on Orthodox/Catholic Relations* at Fordham University. We would like to thank Solon and Marianna Patterson for their visionary leadership and commitment to the cause of Christian unity. We would like to acknowledge the members of the Advisory Council of the Orthodox Christian Studies Center at Fordham for their guidance and support. And we would especially like to thank Ms. Valerie Longwood, our partner for many years, who helped to make the center what it is today.

CONTRIBUTORS

R. Scott Appleby is the Marilyn Keough Dean of Notre Dame's Keough School of Global Affairs. He also serves as lead editor of the Oxford University Press series "Studies in Strategic Peacebuilding."

Nikolaos Asproulis is deputy director of the Volos Academy for Theological Studies (Volos, Greece) and Lecturer at the Hellenic Open University (Patras, Greece).

Brandon Gallaher is senior lecturer of systematic and comparative theology at the University of Exeter. He is also a deacon of the Ecumenical Patriarchate and served at the Eastern Orthodox Holy and Great Council as a Theological Subject Expert in the Ecumenical Patriarchate Press Office (Crete, 2016).

Paul J. Griffiths was born in England and, since 1983, has held academic positions at various US universities, including the Warren Chair of Catholic Theology at Duke University (2007–18). In 2019 he retired from academe.

Vigen Guroian is professor of religious studies at the University of Virginia and senior fellow of both the Russell Kirk Center for Cultural Renewal in Mecosta, Michigan, and the Center on Law and Religion at Emory University.

Dellas Oliver Herbel is a full-time chaplain for the Air National Guard. He received his PhD in historical theology from Saint Louis University in 2009.

Edith M. Humphrey is William F. Professor of New Testament at Pittsburgh Theological Seminary and executive secretary of the Orthodox Theological Society of America. She is the author of eight books and numerous articles on topics as diverse as Christian Spirituality, apocalyptic writings, and C. S. Lewis and has started to write children's novels.

Slavica Jakelić is associate professor of humanities and social thought at Christ College, the honors college at Valparaiso University. She is the author of *Collectivistic Religions: Religion, Choice, and Identity in Late Modernity* (London: Routledge, 2010).

Nadieszda Kizenko is professor of history and chair of the history department at the State University of New York, Albany. Her first book, *A Prodigal Saint: Father John of Kronstadt and the Russian People* (University Park: Penn State University Press, 2000), won the Heldt Prize from the Association for Women in Slavic Studies.

Wendy Mayer is professor and associate dean for research at the Australian Lutheran College, University of Divinity. She is also a research fellow in Biblical and Ancient Studies at the University of South Africa.

Brenna Moore is an associate professor of theology at Fordham University and the author of *Sacred Dread: Raïssa Maritain, the Allure of Suffering, and the French Catholic Revival (1905–1944)* (Notre Dame, IN: University of Notre Dame Press, 2013).

Graham Ward is Regius Professor of Divinity at the University of Oxford. He is the author of *How the Light Gets In: Ethical Life* (Oxford: Oxford University Press, 2016).

Darlene Fozard Weaver is professor of theology at Duquesne University, where she leads the Center for Catholic Faith and Culture. She is the author of *The Acting Person and Christian Moral Life* (Washington, DC: Georgetown University Press, 2011).

INDEX

abortion, 44, 63, 226–27
Abrahamic kinds, of fundamentalism, 12–13,
 183; characteristics of, 185–86; dimensions
 of, 187; reactions to, 186–87
absolutism: fundamentalism embracing of
 dualism and, 171; inerrancy and, 184, 242
African Americans, 154–58
African Orthodox Church, 155
agency and responsibility, collectivistic
 Christianities relating to, 36–39, 46, 49,
 52, 53
agnosticism, moral, 224
America, 4, 5, 88; Croatian independence
 helped by, 42; diversity in, 224; Orthodox
 Christianity in, 80–81; as religious and
 secular, 223–24; violence in, 103. *See also*
 "The Secular Pilgrimage of Orthodoxy in
 America"
American Orthodoxy, tradition and restorationism in, 161n1; Berry, M., 156–59;
 conclusion to, 158–61; Gillquist, 156–59;
 history of, 152–53; Irvine, 154–55, 163n12;
 Morgan, 154–55, 158–59, 163n13; restorationism and Orthodox (dis)unity, 155–56;
 Toth movement, 153–54
"The American Way of Life," 86–87, 91
anatheism, 115
Anglican Communion, 156, 211
Anić, Jadranka Rebeka, 42–43
antemuralis Christianitatis, 48, 50
anthropology, 2, 25, 31, 66, 72; of gender
 complementarity, 61; Orthodox, 85;
 relational, 64–65
Antichrist, 8, 17n33

antipluralistic collectivistic Catholicisms, 49
antisecularism, Orthodox, 111–13
anxiety, 167–68, 171, 178
apocalypticism, 145
Appleby, Scott R., 7, 12, 145, 183, 224–25,
 241–42
Asproulis, Nikolaos, 12–13
Athanasius (saint), 136–37, 140
atheism, 21–22, 32, 115, 116, 227–28
atheists, 29
Atran, Scott, on actors, 248–51, 259n45
Augustinian axioms, 97–104
authoritarian organizations, 184, 242
authority/subversion, 246
autonomy, 84

Baptists, 139
Barr, James, 141–42, 149n18
Beaudoin, Tom, 228–29
behavioral requirements, 174, 184, 242
Being, 118–19, 120–22
Benedict XVI (pope), 227, 251
Berger, Peter, 87–89, 92, 229
Berry, Moses, 156–59
Berry, Wendell, 89–91
Beyond Fundamentalism (Barr), 141
biblical and patristic foundation, with
 fundamentalism, 193; Athanasius, 136–37,
 140; Florovsky, 136–38, 144, 176, 192; Holy
 Tradition, 135–37, 144, 147; parables, 135;
 Scriptures, 135, 137, 141–42, 144, 145;
 Sermon on the Mount, 135; Sermon on the
 Plain, 135
Bloy, Léon, 68–69

265

Lucian N. Leustean (ed.), *Orthodox Christianity and Nationalism in Nineteenth-Century Southeastern Europe.*

John Chryssavgis (ed.), *Dialogue of Love: Breaking the Silence of Centuries.* Contributions by Brian E. Daley, S.J., and Georges Florovsky.

George E. Demacopoulos and Aristotle Papanikolaou (eds.), *Christianity, Democracy, and the Shadow of Constantine.*

Aristotle Papanikolaou and George E. Demacopoulos (eds.), *Fundamentalism or Tradition: Christianity after Secularism*

Georgia Frank, Susan R. Holman, and Andrew S. Jacobs (eds.), *The Garb of Being: Embodiment and the Pursuit of Holiness in Late Ancient Christianity*

Ecumenical Patriarch Bartholomew, *In the World, Yet Not of the World: Social and Global Initiatives of Ecumenical Patriarch Bartholomew.* Edited by John Chryssavgis. Foreword by Jose Manuel Barroso.

Ecumenical Patriarch Bartholomew, *Speaking the Truth in Love: Theological and Spiritual Exhortations of Ecumenical Patriarch Bartholomew.* Edited by John Chryssavgis. Foreword by Dr. Rowan Williams, Archbishop of Canterbury.

Ecumenical Patriarch Bartholomew, *On Earth as in Heaven: Ecological Vision and Initiatives of Ecumenical Patriarch Bartholomew.* Edited by John Chryssavgis. Foreword by His Royal Highness, the Duke of Edinburgh.